T0213623

Lecture Notes in Computer Science   10223

Commenced Publication in 1973
Founding and Former Series Editors:
Gerhard Goos, Juris Hartmanis, and Jan van Leeuwen

More information about this series at http://www.springer.com/series/7408

Jácome Cunha · João P. Fernandes
Ralf Lämmel · João Saraiva
Vadim Zaytsev (Eds.)

Grand Timely Topics
in Software Engineering

International Summer School GTTSE 2015
Braga, Portugal, August 23–29, 2015
Tutorial Lectures

 Springer

Editors
Jácome Cunha (iD)
Universidade Nova de Lisboa
Caparica
Portugal

João P. Fernandes (iD)
Universidade de Coimbra
Coimbra
Portugal

Ralf Lämmel (iD)
Universität Koblenz-Landau
Koblenz
Germany

João Saraiva (iD)
Universidade do Minho
Braga
Portugal

Vadim Zaytsev (iD)
Universiteit van Amsterdam
Amsterdam
The Netherlands

ISSN 0302-9743   ISSN 1611-3349   (electronic)
Lecture Notes in Computer Science
ISBN 978-3-319-60073-4   ISBN 978-3-319-60074-1   (eBook)
DOI 10.1007/978-3-319-60074-1

Library of Congress Control Number: 2017943037

LNCS Sublibrary: SL2 – Programming and Software Engineering

Printed on acid-free paper

This Springer imprint is published by Springer Nature
The registered company is Springer International Publishing AG
The registered company address is: Gewerbestrasse 11, 6330 Cham, Switzerland

Preface

The fifth instance of the International Summer School GTTSE, GTTSE 2015, was held in Braga, Portugal, August 23–29, 2015. For the first up to the fourth instance of GTTSE, the acronym was expanded to "Generative and Transformational Techniques in Software Engineering." For the fifth instance, we adopted a broader scope also hinting at an adjusted vision; GTTSE now stands for "Grand Timely Topics in Software Engineering." That is, historically, in the first four editions of GTTSE, the school series focused on generative and transformational techniques in software engineering. With the rise of the Software Language Engineering conference, the school series also covered that field. As of the fifth edition, a broader scope is applied to include additional areas of software engineering, e.g., software analysis, empirical research, modularity, and product lines, as reflected by the new expansion of the GTTSE acronym. The notion of *timely topics* is inspired by the ICSE conference, which, in some editions, features technical briefings as "a venue for communicating the current state of a timely topic related to software engineering."

The biannual, week-long GTTSE summer school brings together PhD students, lecturers, as well as researchers and practitioners who are interested in timely topics in software engineering. Given the community behind GTTSE, the program does not cover software engineering in a perfectly balanced manner. Instead, there continues to be a focus on language engineering, programming languages, modeling, and software transformation.

The previous four instances of the school were held in 2005, 2007, 2009, and 2011 and their proceedings appeared as volumes 4143, 5235, 6491, and 7680 in Springer's LNCS series. There was no summer school edition in 2013.

The GTTSE 2015 program offered ten tutorials ("briefings"), three hours of plenary time each, and a special tutorial on how to prepare for an interview in industry, one hour of plenary time. All of these tutorials were given by renowned researchers in the extended GTTSE community.

We adopted the notion of "briefing" in an effort to combine survey, research vision, and tutorial regarding an important subject. GTTSE 2015 covered probabilistic program analysis, ontologies in software engineering, empirical evaluation of programming and programming languages, model synchronization, management of software product families, "people analytics" in software development, DSLs in robotics, structured program-generation techniques, advanced aspects of software refactoring, and name binding in language implementation.

The program of the school also included a participants workshop (or students workshop) to which all students had been invited to submit an extended abstract beforehand. The Organizing Committee reviewed these extended abstracts, and invited 14 students to present their work at the workshop. The quality of this workshop was exceptional, and two awards were granted by a jury of senior researchers that was formed at the school. Three of the participants responded to the call for contributions to the proceedings; two of the submissions were accepted through peer review.

The program of the school and additional resources remain available online.[1]

In this volume, you can find revised and extended lecture notes for eight tutorials or "briefings," in the terminology of GTTSE 2015. Each of these lecture notes was reviewed by three members of the Scientific Committee of GTTSE 2015. You will also find two peer-reviewed participant contributions. Where necessary, two rounds of reviewing were executed.

We are grateful to our sponsors for their support, and to all lecturers and participants of the school for their enthusiasm and hard work in preparing excellent material for the school itself and for these proceedings. Thanks to their efforts the event was a great success, which we trust the reader finds reflected in this volume. Our gratitude is also due to all members of the Scientific Committee, who not only helped with the labor-intensive review process that substantially improved all contributions, but also sent their most suitable PhD students to the school.

March 2017

Jácome Cunha
João P. Fernandes
Ralf Lämmel
João Saraiva
Vadim Zaytsev

---

[1] http://gttse.wikidot.com/2015.

Organization

GTTSE 2015 was hosted by the Departamento de Informática, Universidade do Minho, Portugal.

General Chair

João Saraiva   Universidade do Minho, Portugal

Briefings Chair

Ralf Lämmel   Universität Koblenz-Landau, Germany

Program Chair

João P. Fernandes   Universidade de Coimbra, Portugal

Industry Chair

Joost Visser   Software Improvement Group, The Netherlands

Participants Workshop Chair

Felienne Hermans   Delft University of Technology, The Netherlands

Organization Chair

Jácome Cunha   Universidade Nova de Lisboa, Portugal

Publicity Chair

Vadim Zaytsev   Universiteit van Amsterdam, The Netherlands

Scientific Committee

Bram Adams	École Polytechnique de Montréal, Canada
Benoit Baudry	Inria, France
Xavier Blanc	Bordeaux 1 University, France
Darius Blasband	Raincode, Belgium
Paulo Borba	Federal University of Pernambuco, Brazil
Mark van den Brand	Eindhoven University of Technology, The Netherlands
Martin Bravenboer	LogicBlox Inc., USA
Jordi Cabot	Inria-École des Mines de Nantes, France

Richard Paige	University of York, UK
Alfonso Pierantonio	Università degli Studi dell'Aquila, Italy
Juergen Rilling	Concordia University, Canada
Sibylle Schupp	Hamburg University of Technology, Germany
Bran Selic	Malina Software Corp., Canada
Alexander Serebrenik	Eindhoven University of Technology, The Netherlands
Tony Sloane	Macquarie University, Australia
Simão Melo de Sousa	Universidade da Beira Interior, Portugal
Tijs van der Storm	Centrum Wiskunde & Informatica, The Netherlands
James Terwilliger	Microsoft Corporation, USA
Laurence Tratt	King's College London, UK
Antonio Vallecillo	Universidad de Málaga, Spain
Eric Van Wyk	University of Minnesota, USA
Jurgen Vinju	Centrum Wiskunde & Informatica, The Netherlands
Joost Visser	Radboud University Nijmegen, The Netherlands
Markus Völter	Independent
Tanja E.J. Vos	Universidad Politécnica de Valencia, Spain
Andreas Winter	Carl von Ossietzky University, Germany
Victor Winter	University of Nebraska at Omaha, USA
Andy Zaidman	Delft University of Technology, The Netherlands
Vadim Zaytsev	Universiteit van Amsterdam, The Netherlands

Sponsoring Institutions

Contents

Probabilistic Program Analysis 1
  Matthew B. Dwyer, Antonio Filieri, Jaco Geldenhuys, Mitchell Gerrard,
  Corina S. Păsăreanu, and Willem Visser

How Ontologies Can Help in Software Engineering 26
  Cesar Gonzalez-Perez

Empirical, Human-Centered Evaluation of Programming and Programming
Language Constructs: Controlled Experiments 45
  Stefan Hanenberg

To Merge or Not to Merge: Managing Software Product Families......... 73
  Julia Rubin

DSLs in Robotics: A Case Study in Programming
Self-reconfigurable Robots 98
  Ulrik Pagh Schultz, Mirko Bordignon, Kasper Stoy, Arne Nordmann,
  Nico Hochgeschwender, and Sebastian Wrede

People Analytics in Software Development 124
  Leif Singer, Margaret-Anne Storey, Fernando Figueira Filho,
  Alexey Zagalsky, and Daniel M. German

Structured Program Generation Techniques 154
  Yannis Smaragdakis, Aggelos Biboudis, and George Fourtounis

Refactoring Tools and Their Kin................................. 179
  Friedrich Steimann

Implementing a Linear Algebra Approach to Data Processing............ 215
  Rogério Pontes, Miguel Matos, José Nuno Oliveira,
  and José Orlando Pereira

STRAF: A Scala Framework for Experiments in Trace-Based
JIT Compilation 223
  Maarten Vandercammen, Quentin Stiévenart, Wolfgang De Meuter,
  and Coen De Roover

Author Index 235

Probabilistic Program Analysis

Matthew B. Dwyer[1]([✉]), Antonio Filieri[2], Jaco Geldenhuys[4], Mitchell Gerrard[1],
Corina S. Păsăreanu[3], and Willem Visser[4]

[1] University of Nebraska – Lincoln, Lincoln, USA
dwyer@cse.unl.edu
[2] Imperial College London, London, UK
[3] Carnegie Mellon Silicon Valley and NASA Ames Research Center,
Santa Clara, USA
[4] University of Stellenbosch, Stellenbosch, South Africa

Abstract. This paper provides a survey of recent work on adapting
techniques for program analysis to compute probabilistic characterizations of program behavior. We survey how the frameworks of data flow
analysis and symbolic execution have incorporated information about
input probability distributions to quantify the likelihood of properties of
program states. We identify themes that relate and distinguish a variety
of techniques that have been developed over the past 15 years in this
area. In doing so, we point out opportunities for future research that
builds on the strengths of different techniques.

Keywords: Data flow analysis · Symbolic execution · Abstract interpretation · Model checking · Probabilistic program · Markov decision
processes

1 Introduction

Static program analyses calculate properties of the possible executions of a program without ever running the program, and have been an active topic of study
for over five decades. Initially developed to allow compilers to generate more
efficient output programs, by the mid-1970s [29] researchers understood that
program analyses could be applied to fault detection and verification of the
absence of specific classes of faults.

The power of these analysis techniques, and what distinguishes them from
simply running a program and observing its behavior, is their ability to reason
about program behavior without knowing all of the details of program execution (e.g., the specific input values provided to the program). This tolerance of
uncertainty allows analyses to provide useful information when users don't know
exactly how a program will be used.

Static analyses model uncertainty through the use of various forms of abstraction and symbolic representation. For example, symbolic expressions are used to
encode logical constraints in symbolic execution [46], to define abstract domains

J. Cunha et al. (Eds.): GTTSE 2015, LNCS 10223, pp. 1–25, 2017.
DOI: 10.1007/978-3-319-60074-1_1

in data flow analysis [18,45], and to capture sets of data values that constitute reachable states via predicate abstraction [36]. Nondeterministic choice is another widely used approach, for instance, in modeling branch decisions in data flow analysis. While undeniably effective, these approaches sacrifice potentially important distinctions in program behavior.

Consider a program that accepts an integer input representing a person's income. A static analysis might reason about the program by allowing any integer value, or, perhaps, by applying some simple assumption, i.e., that income must be non-negative. Domain experts have studied income distributions and find that incomes vary according to a generalized beta distribution [57,82]. With such a distribution the program can now be viewed as a *probabilistic program* and, beginning with Kozen's seminal work in the early 1980s, the semantics of such programs has long been studied [44,47,48,62].

For non-probabilistic programs, it was just over six years from Floyd's foundational work on program semantics [28] to Kildall's widely-applicable static analysis framework [45]. Sophisticated extensions of Kildall's work are prevalent today, e.g., [51,52], and form the basis for modern software development environments. For probabilistic programs, however, the development of static analysis frameworks has taken decades and they have not yet reached the level of applicability of their non-probabilistic counterparts.

What would such analyses have to offer? Researchers have explored the use of probabilistic analysis results to assess the security of software components [56] and to measure side-channel leakage [3,65], to assess program reliability [26], to measure program similarity [31], to characterize fault propagation [63], and to characterize the coverage achieved by an analysis technique [21]. We believe that there are many more applications for cost-effective and widely-applicable static analysis frameworks for probabilistic programs.

In recent years, the term "probabilistic program" has been generalized beyond Kozen's definition in which programs draw inputs from probability distributions. This more general setting permits the conditioning of program behavior by allowing certain program runs to be rejected. These programs can be viewed as expressing computations over probability distributions rather than inputs drawn from a distribution. While recent work has just begun to explore the foundations of analysis for this more general setting [15,35], in this paper we consider Kozen's original definition and analysis frameworks targetting such programs.

More specifically, we survey work on adapting data flow analysis and symbolic execution to use information about input distributions. We begin with background that provides basic definitions related to static analysis and probabilistic models. Section 2.2 exposes some of the key intuitions and concepts that crosscut the work in this area. The following two Sects. 3.1 and 3.2, survey work on probabilistic data flow analysis and probabilistic symbolic execution. While we focus on analysis of imperative programs, we note that principles exposed in our survey apply to analysis frameworks for functional programs as well. Section 3.3 discusses approaches that have been developed to reason about the probability of program-related events, e.g., executing a path, taking a branch, or reaching a state. We conclude with a set of open questions and research challenges that we believe are worth pursuing.

2 Overview

2.1 Scope and Background

This paper focuses on programs that draw input variables from given probability distributions, or, equivalently, that make calls on functions returning values drawn from given distributions. The left side of Fig. 1 shows a method, m, that we will use to illustrate concepts in this paper. It takes an integer variable, x, as input, then based on the results of drawing values from a Bernoulli distribution, it either performs its computation (which is unspecified and denoted with...) or triggers an assertion. For the example, we might be interested in reasoning about the lack of assertion violations.

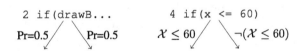

```
1   m(int x) {
2     if(drawBernoulli(0.5) == 1) {
3       if(drawBernoulli(0.5) == 1) {
4       if(x <= 60)
5         ...
6       else
7         assert false
8       } else {
9       if(x <= 30)
10        ...
11      else
12        assert false
13      }
14    } else {
15      if(x <= 55)
16        ...
17      else
18        assert false
19    }
20  }
```

Fig. 1. Example: source code (left) and control flow graph (right)

2 if(drawB...   4 if(x <= 60)

Pr=0.5 / \ Pr=0.5 $x \le 60$ / \ $\neg(x \le 60)$

Fig. 2. Probabilistic choice (left) and symbolic choice (right)

Programs and Program Analyses. There are many different ways to represent the execution behavior of a program to facilitate analysis. Immediately to the right of the code in Fig. 1, we show the control flow graph (CFG), which explicitly represents control successor relationships between statements. A CFG models choice among successors as nondeterministic choice – depicted by the lack of labels on the edges.

We will also consider models that include probabilistic choice, e.g., defining the probability that a branch is taken. The left side of Fig. 2 shows edge probabilities that reflect the outcome of the Bernoulli draw on line 2. Thus the probability of taking the *then* branch is 0.5; the probability of taking the *else* branch is also 0.5. In addition, we will consider models where the choice of successor is defined by the semantics of the branch condition. The right side of Fig. 2 shows a logical condition that reflects the fact that the value of parameter x must be less than or equal to 60 for control to traverse the true branch at line 4.

A key concept in the program analysis frameworks we survey is *symbolic abstraction*. A symbolic abstraction is a representation of a set of states. Abstractions can be encoded in a variety of forms, e.g., logical formulae [79], binary decision diagrams [10], or custom representations [2]. For example, the set of negative integer values can be defined by a predicate $lt0 \equiv \lambda x.x < 0$ which returns true for all values in the set. Logical combinations of such predicates can be used to define an abstract domain, $\mathcal{A}$, whose elements describe sets of possible states of the program.

While abstractions encode sets of states, *abstract transformers* compute the effect of a program statement on a set of states. For example, the fact that the sum of any pair of negative values is negative is encoded as $lt0 +^\# lt0 = lt0$, where $\#$ denotes an abstract transformer for $+$ that operates on symbolic encodings of sets.

Analyses that seek to prove the satisfaction of properties generally define abstractions that *overapproximate* the set of program states, whereas those that seek to falsify properties generally define abstractions that *underapproximate* the set of program states.

Data Flow Analysis. Data flow analysis [45] provides a framework for computing properties shared by sets of program traces reaching a program state. It is common for such analyses to group together the states that share a common control location; the computed properties attempt to characterize the invariants over those states.

Data flow analyses are solved using a fixpoint computation which allows properties of all program paths to be safely approximated. Model checking [16] is a popular verification technique which also relies on an underlying fixpoint computation. Moreover, data flow analyses operate on symbolic abstractions of program states that can be defined by abstract interpretation [18]. In fact, it is now well-understood that data flow analysis can be viewed as model checking of abstract interpretations [75].

An abstract interpretation is a non-standard interpretation of program executions over an abstract domain. The semantics of program statements are lifted to operate on a set of states, encoded as an element of the abstract domain, rather than on a single concrete state. Generating the set of traces for non-trivial programs is impractical; instead, abstract states can be combined, via a meet operation, wherever traces merge in the control flow, and loops are processed repeatedly to compute the maximum fix point (MFP).

Data flow analysis tools and toolkits exist for popular languages, e.g., [27, 52, 84], and have been used primarily for program optimization and verifying program conformance with assertional specifications.

Symbolic Execution. Like data flow analysis, symbolic execution [17, 46] performs a non-standard interpretation of program executions using a symbolic abstraction of program states. Symbolic execution records symbolic expressions encoding the values of program memory for each program location. A *path condition* accumulates symbolic expressions that encode branch constraints taken along an execution.

Sequences of program statements are interpreted by applying the operation at each program location to update the values of program variables with expressions defined over symbolic variables. An operation that reads from an input generates a fresh symbolic variable which represents the set of possible input values. When a branching statement is encountered, the symbolic expression, c, encoding the branch condition is computed and a check is performed to determine whether the current trace—encoded by the path condition—can be extended with c or c's negation. This is done by formulating the constraints as a satisfiability query; if the formula encoding branch constraints is satisfiable, then there must exist an input that will follow the trace. The trace is extended following the feasible branch outcomes, usually in a depth-first manner.

In the example of Fig. 1, on the leftmost path through the control flow graph, when symbolic execution reaches the final branch it records the condition $\mathcal{X} \leq 60$, where $\mathcal{X}$ models the unknown value of input x. This condition describes the set of input values that trigger execution of this path—as long as both Bernoulli trials yield a value of 1.

In practice symbolic execution computes an underapproximation of program behavior. Programs with looping behavior that is determined by input values may result in an infinite symbolic execution. For this reason, symbolic execution is typically run with a (user-specified) bound on the search depth, thus some paths may be unexplored. Moreover, there may be path constraints for which efficient satisfiable checking is not possible. Variants of symbolic execution [34,76,78], called concolic execution, address this problem by replacing problematic constraints with equality constraints between variables and values collected while executing the program along the trace.

Symbolic execution tools and toolkits exist for many popular languages [11,34,41,66] and have been used primarily for test generation and fault detection.

Probabilities and Probabilistic Models. There is an enormous literature on probabilistic reasoning and statistics that can be brought to bear in program analysis. In this paper, we consider two types of discrete time probabilistic models: Markov chains and Markov decision processes [69].

Both models rely on the concept of a probability distribution. A *probability distribution* is a function that provides the probability of occurrence of different possible outcomes in an experiment. The sum of the probabilities for all outcomes is 1.

A Markov chain is a labeled transition system that, given some state, defines the probability of moving to another state, according to a probability distribution. The probability of executing a sequence of states is then the product of the transition probabilities between the states. The model fragment in the upper right corner of Fig. 1 depicts a Markov chain fragment. It defines, for the set of states that are at the first line in the program, a 0.5 probability of transitioning to the state representing the beginning of the then block, and similarly for the beginning of the else block. The distribution indicates a 0 probability of moving to any other state.

For this small example, if we were to assume a probability distribution on the input x, then it would be possible to compute the probability of taking every edge in the CFG. This would be a Markov chain model of m and it would replace all nondeterministic choices in the CFG with probabilistic choices.

There are many situations where the removal of nondeterministic choices is impractical or undesirable. For example, if the input distribution of x is unknown, then retaining nondeterministic choices for the conditionals which test that value would yield a faithful program model. In addition, it may be desirable, for efficiency of analysis, to abstract program behavior, and that abstraction may make it impossible to accurately compute the probability of a transition.

Including nondeterminism in a probabilistic state transition model yields a Markov decision process (MDP). An MDP adds an additional structure, A, that defines a set of (internal) actions which are used to model the selection among a set of possible next-state probability distributions. When traversing a path in an MDP, in each state, a choice from A must be made in order to determine how to transition, probabilistically, to a next state. That sequence of choices is termed a *policy* for the MDP. Given a policy, an MDP reduces to a Markov chain.

2.2   Extending Program Analyses with Probabilities

The literature on incorporating probabilistic techniques into program analysis is large and growing, technically deep, and quite varied. In this paper, our intention is to expose key similarities and differences between families of approaches and, in so doing, provide the reader with intuitions that are often missing in the detailed presentation of techniques.

Where Do the Probabilities Come From? There are two perspectives adopted in the literature. Programs are *implicitly* probabilistic because the distributions from which input values are drawn are not specified in the program, but are characteristics of the execution environment. Alternately, programs are *explicitly* probabilistic in that the statements within the program define the input probability distributions.

It is possible to transform explicit probabilistic constructs by introducing auxiliary input variables and then specifying their distributions. For the example, this would result in the addition of two integer input variables

```
m(int x, int b1, int b2) {...
```

where the two instances of `drawBernoulli(0.5)` expressions would be replaced by `b1` and `b2`, respectively. The input distribution for each auxiliary input would then be specified as a set of pairs, $\{\ldots,(-1,0),(0,0.5),(1,0.5),(1,0),\ldots\}$ where the first component defines a value and the second defines its probability.

Section 3.1 discusses approaches where probabilities governing specific branch outcomes, as opposed to input values, are built into the program model from knowledge the developer has at hand, while Sects. 3.2 and 3.3 describe techniques for computing such probabilities from information about the program semantics and input distribution.

What Does the Analysis Compute? There are again two perspectives adopted in the literature. One can view a probabilistic program as a transformer on probability distributions; the analysis computes the probability distribution over the concrete domain which holds at a program state. Alternatively, one can view a probabilistic program as a program whose inputs happen to vary in some principled way; the analysis computes program properties—properties of sets of concrete domain elements—along with a characterization of how these properties vary with varying input. Within these approaches, there are different types of approximations computed for probabilities. It is common to compute upper bounds on probabilities for program properties, but lower bounds can be computed as well. In addition, it is possible to estimate the probability within some margin of error—an approach that several techniques explore—and it is even possible to compute the probability *exactly*, if certain restrictions hold on the program and its distributions.

Conceptually, there are two pieces of information that are necessary to reason probabilistically about a set of values: a quantity that approximates the probability of each value in the set and the number of values in the set. Early probabilistic static analysis techniques did not explicitly capture this latter quantity, but more recent work discussed in Sect. 3.2, using the techniques of Sect. 3.3, does capture this quantity, as do other recent approaches [56].

Mixing Abstraction with Probabilities. Any analysis that hopes to scale will have to approximate behavior. As explained earlier, in static analyses it is common to model such overapproximation using nondeterministic choice. Across all of the analysis techniques we survey, MDPs have been used when there is a need to mix probabilistic and nondeterministic choice. An important consequence of using MDPs is that it is no longer possible to compute a single probabilistic characterization of a property. Instead, analyses can compute, across the set of all possible sequences of nondeterministic choice outcomes, the minimal and maximal probabilities for a property to hold.

3   Probabilistic Approaches to Program Analysis

This section introduces probabilistic variants of data flow analysis and symbolic execution. Several of these variants either exploit, or could be adapted to exploit, recent advances in methods for quantifying or estimating constraint solution spaces which we discuss at the end of this section.

3.1   Probabilistic Data Flow Analysis

The key challenge in probabilistic data flow analysis is determining how probabilities are incorporated into the control and data abstractions upon which it is based.

Control Flow Probabilities. Early work in extending data flow analysis techniques with probabilities did not consider the influence of control and data flow on probabilities. Instead, user-defined probabilities were attached to nodes in the program's control flow graph. This allowed the analysis to estimate the probability of an expression evaluating to some value or type at runtime, which was used to enable program optimization.

This approach begins with a control flow graph where each edge is mapped to the probability that it is taken during execution. The left side of Fig. 3 shows the probabilistic CFG for the example of Fig. 1, given that input x is uniformly distributed in the range $[1, 100]$. This program is simple enough that the branch probabilities can be easily computed—because the probabilities for each branch along a path are independent.

The sum of all probabilities leaving any control flow node must be 1 (except for the exit node). The probability of executing a path is the product of edge probabilities along the path. Thus, the probability of reaching a program state is the sum of the probabilities of traces that reach that state.

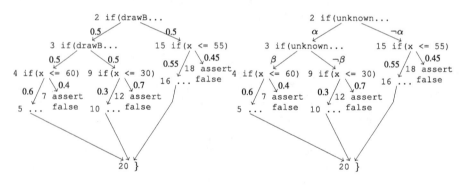

Fig. 3. Probabilistic CFG (left) and MDP (right)

To compute the probability of a data flow fact holding at a program point, Ramalingam uses a slightly modified version of Kildall's dataflow analysis framework [70]. Instead of the usual semilattice with an idempotent meet operation, a non-idempotent addition operator is used. The usual properties of the meet operation can be relaxed, because instead of computing an invariant dataflow fact, we only want the summation of probabilities of all traces reaching a certain point. The expected frequencies may now be computed as the least fixpoint using the traditional iterative data flow algorithm; the quantity becomes a *sum-over-all-paths* instead of a *meet-over-all-paths*.

Ramalingam's sum-over-all-paths approach is reminiscent of the approach taken in probabilistic model checking of Markov chains. In the latter approach, a system of equations is formulated whose solution yields the probability of some property holding—so-called *quantitative* properties in PRISM [49]. Ramalingam's analysis effectively solves an equivalent system of equations.

These techniques rely on being able to annotate branch decisions in the program with probabilities. When the input distributions governing branches is unknown or when the branches along a path are dependent the techniques described above cannot be applied. The discussions below on non-determinism and in Sects. 3.2 and 3.3 describe ways to address this problem.

Abstract Data Probabilities. Researchers have incorporated probabilistic information directly into the semantics of a program and then abstracted over those semantics [19,59,77] to construct probabilistic data flow analyses. This is typically done using a variation on Kozen's probabilistic semantics [47] alongside abstract interpretation and data flow techniques. Embedding probabilities into the semantics allows both control flow and data values to influence the property probabilities computed during the analysis.

Abstracting Probability Distributions. The pioneering work in this area, by Monniaux [59,60], developed the key insights that other work has built on. The goal is to exploit the rich body of work on developing abstract domains and associated transformers, and to extend this work so as to record bounds on probability measures for the concrete values described by domain elements.

Monniaux's work takes the view that probabilistic programs effectively transform an input distribution into an output distribution. More generally, probabilistic programs compute a distribution that characterizes each state in the program. He develops a probabilistic abstract domain, $\mathcal{A}_p$, as a collection of pairs, $\mathcal{A} \times [0,1]$. The intuition is that a classic abstract domain is paired with a *bounding probability weight* that is used to compute an upper bound on the values mapped by that domain. Consider a probabilistic abstract state, $pa \in \mathcal{A} \times [0,1]$, an upper approximation of the probability of a value v in that state is given by $Pr(v) \leq \sum_{(a,w) \in pa \wedge c \in \gamma(a)} w$, where γ is maps a symbolic abstraction to the set of values it describes.

In Monniaux's work, multiple abstract domain elements can map onto a given concrete value; each of these abstract domain elements' weights must be totalled to bound the probability of the given concrete value. As an example, let $\mathcal{A}$ be the interval abstraction applied to a single integer value and let $pa = \{([1,5], 0.1), ([3,7], 0.1), \ldots\}$. For a value of 2, only the first pair would apply, since $2 \notin [3,7]$, contributing 0.1 to the bound on $Pr(2)$. For a value of 3, both pairs would apply and contribute their sum of 0.2 to the bound on $Pr(3)$.

To clarify, these weight components are *not* bounds on the probability of the abstract domain as a whole, but rather are bounds on the probability of each concrete element represented by the abstract domain. This simplifies the formulation of the probabilistic abstract transformers, e.g., the extension of $+^{\#}$ to account for $\mathcal{A}_p$, but it means that additional work is required to compute the probability of a property holding. In essence, this requires estimating the size of the concretization of the abstract domain element and then multiplying by the computed bound for each concrete value.

It is important to note that an upper or lower bound on a probability distribution is not itself a distribution, since the sum across the domain may be greater than 1. This poses challenges for modular probabilistic data flow analyses.

We will see that the techniques from Sect. 3.3 can be applied to the problem of counting the concretization of an abstract domain element that is encoded as a logical formula. This may offer a potential connection between data flow analyses formulated over distributions and those formulated over abstract states—which we discuss below.

The design of probabilistic abstract transformers can be subtle. For statements that generate variables drawn from a probability distribution, an upper approximation of the distribution for regions of the abstract domain is required. For sequential statements, weight components are propagated and abstract domain elements are updated by the underlying transformer.

For conditionals, the transformer can be understood as filtering the abstract domain between those execution environments which satisfy the conditional and those which falsify the conditional. The probabilistic abstract transformer need only apply that filter to the first component of the tuple (the elements of the underlying abstract domain), leaving the weight unchanged. For instance, consider the abstract domain of an interval of integers defined by the tuple, $([-5, 5], 0.1)$. If this domain holds before a conditional $\text{if}(x < 0)\{...\}$, then applying the filter on the true branch results in $([-5, -1], 0.1)$ and applying the filter on the false branch results in $([0, 5], 0.1)$. The space is reduced; the weights remain the same.

Finally, reaching fixpoints for rich probabilistic abstract domains appears to require widening [22, 59] to be cost-effective. These can be challenging to define and, generally, lead to a loss in precision.

Probability for Abstract States. Computing bounds on the probability of a state property has been well-studied. Di Pierro et al. [20] develop analyses to estimate the probability of an abstract state, rather than bound it or its probability distribution. They formulate their analysis using an abstract domain over vector spaces, instead of lattices, and use the Moore-Penrose pseudo-inverse instead of the usual fixpoint calculation.

Abstract states encode variable domains as matrices, e.g., a 100 by 100 matrix would be needed to encode the input x for the example in Fig. 1. While very efficient matrix algorithms can be employed, the space consumed by this representation can be significant when scaling to real programs. Transfer functions operate on these matrices to filter values and update probabilities along branches and, as in Ramalingam's work, weighted sums are used to accumulate probabilities at control flow merge points. Di Pierro et al.'s early work was limited to very small programs, but more recent work suggests approaches for abstracting the matrices to significantly reduce time and space complexity.

Handling Nondeterminism. When abstraction of program choice is required or when there is no basis for defining an input distribution, it is natural to use nondeterminism to account for the uncertainty in program behavior.

In Monniaux's semantics [61] choices that can be tied to a known distribution are cleanly separated from those that cannot. A nondeterministic choice allows for independent outcomes, and this is modeled by lifting the singleton outcomes of deterministic semantics to powersets of outcomes. In the probabilistic setting, the elements of this powerset are tuples of the abstract domain and the associated weight, defined above. So for any nondeterminstic choice, the resulting computation is safely modeled by one of these tuples. The challenge in the analysis is to select from among those tuples to compute a useful probability estimate.

More recent work on abstraction in probabilistic data flow analysis, as well as in model checking, takes a different approach. In the MDP on the right side of Fig. 3 α and β are used to denote the outcomes of nondeterministic choices—modeling for instance unknown branch conditions—and their values comprise the MDP policy. There are three policies for this example: (α, β), $(\alpha, \neg\beta)$, and $(\neg\alpha)$. For a given program state, we can formulate an alternating game that seeks to determine values for α and β which maximize (or minimize) the probability of reaching that state. Probabilistic model checkers such as PRISM and PASS use this approach to formulate MDP-based analyses.

The reachability of line 5 in the MDP is only possible under the policy (α, β). Thus, that policy maximizes the probability of reaching that state at 0.6—the product of the probabilities along the path. Any other policy will minimize the probability of reaching line 5 at 0. Bounding the probability of violating an assertion in a call to m requires considering all three policies. The maximal probability is 0.7 under policy $(\alpha, \neg\beta)$, whereas the minimal probability is 0.4 under policy (α, β).

Abstract interpretation can be applied to the data states in such approaches [22,50,86] to improve efficiency. These abstractions are, however, independent of the probabilistic choices implicit in the semantics, and must be specified by the developer in some way—as in the case of Ramalingam's work.

Theoretical advances in the analysis of stochastic processes [68] and coalgebraic semantics [38,64] may provide new pathways towards the definition of more advanced analysis methods that combine nondeterministic and probabilistic choice.

3.2 Probabilistic Symbolic Execution

Probabilistic symbolic execution extends traditional symbolic execution with the ability of computing probabilities of reaching certain target states in a program. The computation is based on *quantifying* the solution spaces of the path conditions computed by symbolic execution.

We illustrate probabilistic symbolic execution using the example in Fig. 4, where we introduce variables b_0 and b_1 to model the two drawBernoulli distributions from Fig. 1; the domains of those variables consist of 10 values and the

```
// b0, b1 in 0..9
m(int x, int b0, int b1) {
  if(b0<5) {
    if(b1<5) {
      if(x <= 60)
        ...A
      else
        assert false
    } else {
      if(x <= 30)
        ...B
      else
        assert false
    }
  } else {
    if(x <= 55)
      ...C
    else
      assert false
  }
}
```

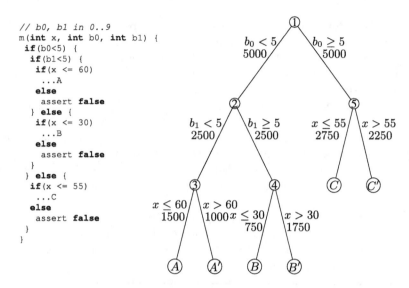

Fig. 4. Illustration of probabilistic symbolic execution

tests check for half of the domain, corresponding to the 0.5 parameter in the Bernoulli distribution. Note that this program now has 3 inputs and an input domain size of $10 \times 10 \times 100 = 10000$. The domain of variables, which is finite and discrete, is denoted by D. Figure 4 illustrates the six symbolic paths generated by a symbolic execution of the example program. The path condition describing each path is the conjunction of the constraints along the path; for example the leftmost path will have $b_0 < 5 \land b_1 < 5 \land x \leq 60$ as its path condition.

Algorithm 1. $pse(l, m, pc)$

---

repeat
  $p \leftarrow symsample(l_0, m_0, true)$
  $processPath(p)$
until $stoppingSearch(p)$

Algorithm 2. $symsample(l, m, pc)$

---

if $stoppingPath(pc)$ **then**
  return pc
end if
while $\neg branch(l)$ **do**
  $m \leftarrow op(l)(m)$
  $l \leftarrow succ(l)$
end while
$c \leftarrow cond(l)(m)$
if $selectBranch(c, pc)$ **then**
  return $symsample(succ_t(l), m, pc \land c)$
else
  return $symsample(succ_f(l), m, pc \land \neg c)$
end if

Algorithm *pse* (Algorithm 1) illustrates probabilistic symbolic execution; it is a modification of traditional symbolic execution to process symbolic paths one at a time using procedure *symsample*. The selection of each path can be done systematically (e.g. using depth-first search as in traditional symbolic execution) or statistically, guided by branch probabilities as in [24]. Our description accommodates many of the advances in the recent literature [24,26]. The processing of each path involves the calculation of probabilities as described in the next section.

At a high level, procedure *symsample* is called from the initial state of the program; it returns a single path which is then processed. After each path, procedure *stoppingSearch* is called to check if the analysis is complete or some other termination criterion is met, and the analysis can stop. Within procedure *symsample* we first check if the search for a path needs to be stopped; otherwise, we symbolically execute the program up to the next branching point and decide which of the next branching statements must be taken.

Procedure stoppingPath uses a stopping criterion (limit on search depth) to avoid exploration of infinite or very long paths, that are due to loops conditioned on input variables. Since some paths might now be truncated before reaching a target property, we introduce three types of paths, (1) *success* paths, which reach and satisfy the target property, (2) *failure* paths, which reach and falsify the property, and (3) *grey* paths, which are truncated before reaching the property. These paths form three disjoint sets; we calculate the cumulative probability of success $Pr(success)$ (i.e., the *reliability* of the code), failure $Pr(failure)$ and grey paths $Pr(grey)$. Grey paths can be handled optimistically (grouped with the success paths), pessimistically (grouped with the failure paths) or kept separate and be used as a measure for how confident we are in our estimates (for example, if the grey paths probability is very low, we are more confident).

Procedure selectBranch selects which branch to execute next; this can be done either systematically or probabilistically, according to the probability of satisfying the corresponding branch conditions. This is computed based on the number of solutions for each path condition as follows. At each branching point, we count the number of solutions for the path condition at that branching point ($\sharp(pc)$) and the number of solutions for the path condition for both branches ($\sharp(pc \wedge c)$ and $\sharp(pc \wedge \neg c)$). Assuming a uniform distribution of the inputs, the probability for the true branch is then simply $Pr(succ_t(l)) = \sharp(pc \wedge c)/\sharp(pc)$; similarly for the false branch, $Pr(succ_f(l)) = \sharp(pc \wedge \neg c)/\sharp(pc)$. Techniques for counting the number of solutions are discussed in Sect. 3.3.

In the example of Fig. 4, when we sample probabilistically at node 3, we have that the path condition at the node is $pc = b_0 < 5 \wedge b_1 < 5$ and $\sharp(pc) = 2500$. The true branch ($b_0 < 5 \wedge b_1 < 5 \wedge x \leq 60$ with a count of 1500) will thus be taken with probability $1500/2500 = 0.6$ and the false branch will be taken with probability 0.4.

Procedure processPath calculates the probability for the path being processed and checks whether the path falls into the success, failure or grey set. Note that many of these calculations have already been performed during the selectBranch, and caching can be used to eliminate redundant work.

Again in the example of Fig. 4, the paths ending at the labels A', B' and C' indicate assertion failures, and thus the probability of failure will be $1500/10000 + 1750/10000 + 2250/10000 = 0.55$. Since there are no loops in the example, the rest of the paths indicate success, which will have probability 0.45.

Furthermore, the procedure can handle sampling without replacement—to guarantee an exhaustive analysis even when certain behaviors have very small probability. In [24] we describe how we leverage the counts we store for each path condition to ensure no path is sampled twice. Whenever a path has been explored completely, we subtract the final path condition count from all the counts along the current path back up to the root. Note that these counts are being used by *selectBranch* to calculate the conditional probabilities at a branch, and thus they change with each sample. If a count becomes zero, the corresponding branch will no longer be selected. The more paths of the program are analyzed, the more counts propagate up the tree until the root node's count becomes zero, at which point all paths have been explored.

Procedure stoppingSearch uses either a measure of confidence based on the percentage of the input domain that has been explored, or it uses a statistical measure of confidence. Enough confidence exists about the portion of the input domain that has been analyzed when $1 - Pr(success) + Pr(failure) < \epsilon$. If we treat grey paths separately, this means $Pr(grey) < \epsilon$. The parameter ϵ is provided by the user, and is typically very small. Note that although we show, for simplicity, that procedure *stoppingSearch* takes the path as input, in practice it just reuses the results computed by procedure *processPath*.

Handling Nondeterminism. Handling nondeterminism within the systems being analyzed has been studied in previous work [26] in the context of scheduling choices in concurrent programs. The approach was to determine the schedule giving the highest (or lowest) reliability. More recently, an approach based on value iteration learning was presented [54] to handle the problem in a more general fashion.

3.3   Computing Program Probabilities

Computing probabilities for probabilistic symbolic execution and other program analyses reduces to computing the probability of satisfying a boolean constraint over the program variables. This operation is performed within the *selectBranch* function. Given the path condition PC reaching a branching point and the condition c of the conditional statement, the goal is to compute the probability of satisfying $PC \wedge c$ and, consequently, $PC \wedge \neg c$. Depending on the theory the constraints are expressed in, different techniques can be used to quantify the solution space of the constraints and, in turn, their probability of being satisfied. In this section introduce the basics of some of these techniques.

Assume the program under analysis has input variables $V = \{v_1, v_2, \ldots, v_n\}$, where v_i has domain d_i and comes with a probability distribution $\mathcal{P}_i : d_i \rightarrow [0, 1]$. The input domain D is the Cartesian product of the domains d_i, while the input distribution $\mathcal{P}$ is the joint distribution over all the input variables $\prod_i \mathcal{P}_i(\bar{v}_i)$. For a constraint $\phi : V \rightarrow \{true, false\}$, the goal is to compute the probability $Pr(\phi)$ of satisfying ϕ given the input domains and probability distributions.

Exact and Numeric Computation

Finite domains. If the input domain is finite, the computation of $Pr(\phi)$ reduces to a counting problem as already mentioned (assume for now all inputs are uniformly distributed, i.e. they are equally likely):

$$Pr(\phi) = \frac{\sharp(\phi \wedge D)}{\sharp(D)} \tag{1}$$

Here $\sharp(\cdot)$ counts the number of inputs satisfying the argument constraint; D has been overloaded to represent the finite domain as a constraint; $\sharp(D)$ is a short form for the size of the domain[1]. For example, considering a single integer input variable x taking values between 1 and 10 uniformly, $\sharp(D) = 10$ and $\sharp(x \leq 5 \wedge D) = 5$, leading to a 0.5 probability of satisfying the constraint.

The computation of $\sharp(\cdot)$ can be performed efficiently for linear integer arithmetic (LIA) constraints. A LIA constraint defines a multi-dimensional lattice bounded by a convex polytope [5]. To count the number of points composing this structure, an efficient solution has been proposed by Barvinok [4]. This algorithm uses generating functions suitable for solving the counting problem in polynomial time, with respect to the number of variables and the number of constraints. Notably, besides the number of bits required to represent the numerical values, the complexity of this algorithm does not depend on the actual size of the variable domains. This makes the computation feasible for very large input domains, allowing its application to probabilistic program analysis [23,26,31]. Several implementations of this algorithm are available, the most popular being LattE [83] and Barvinok [85].

Other finite domains, such as bounded data structures [23] and regular languages [1,55], are active topics of study in applied model counting. The problem of counting the number of distinct truth assignments for a propositional formula is called #SAT, or propositional model counting. There are a number of tools that can efficiently solve many cases of #SAT, including sharpSAT [81] and Cachet [74].

---

[1] More precisely, Eq. (1) represents the probability of satisfying the constraint ϕ conditioned on the fact that the input is within the prescribed domain D.

Handling input distributions. For finite domains, assume, without loss of generality, the input distribution to be specified on a finite partition $D^1, D^2, \ldots, D^n$ of the input domain D (i.e., $\cup_i D^i \equiv D$ and $D^i \cap D^j \neq \emptyset \implies i = j$) via the probability function $Pr(D^i)$. Assume elements within the same set D^i to have the same probability. The case of uniform distribution described so far corresponds to the partition with cardinality 1, i.e., the whole domain.

Since the elements of the partition are disjoint by construction, we can exploit the law of total probability to extend Eq. (1) to include the information about the input distribution:

$$Pr(\phi) = \sum_i \frac{\sharp(\phi \wedge D^i)}{\sharp(D^i)} \cdot Pr(D^i) \tag{2}$$

Here D^i has again been overloaded to represent the constraint of an element belonging to D^i.

Formalizing the input distribution on a finite partition of the input domain is general enough to capture every valid distribution on the inputs, including possible correlations or functional dependencies among the input variables. However, the finer the specification of the input distribution, the more complex the computation of Eq. (2).

Floating-point numbers. Floating-point numbers are often abstracted as real numbers for analysis purposes. Computing the probability of satisfying a constraint over reals requires refining Eq. 1 to cope with the density of the domain. In particular, the counting function $\sharp(\phi)$ is replaced by the integration of an indicator function on ϕ, i.e., a function returning 1 for all the inputs satisfying ϕ [9]. This integration can be performed exactly only when symbolic integration is possible, but in general only numerical integration is possible. A number of commercial and open-source tools can be used for this purpose. However, numerical computations are accurate only up to a certain bound, and they do not scale to large cardinalities. In the latter case, sampling-based methods are preferable.

Sampling-Based Methods. Exact methods can suffer from two main limitations: (1) generality with respect to input domains and constraint classes and (2) scalability, either due to the intrinsic complexity of the algorithm used or to the discretization of the input distributions. Sampling-based methods may be used to address these limitations.

In this section we will present sampling-based methods for quantifying the probability of satisfying arbitrarily complex floating-point constraints. We will briefly discuss how to generalize to other domains at the end of the section.

Sampling-based methods estimate the probability of satisfying a given constraint using a Monte Carlo approach [72]. For simplicity, we will focus on the simplest, though general, method suitable for our purpose: hit-or-miss Monte Carlo.

Hit-or-miss Monte Carlo. We assume first a uniform input distribution over bounded, real domains (we relax this assumption later). Consider the constraint $x \leq -y \wedge y \leq x$, where both $x, y \in [-1, 1] \cap \mathbb{R}$. In probabilistic terms, this can be seen as a Bernoulli experiment, i.e., an experiment having only two mutually exclusive outcomes, *true* or *false*, where the probability of the *true* outcome is the parameter p of a Bernoulli distribution [67] (the probability of the *false* outcome is in turn $1-p$). Our goal is to estimate the parameter p, from n random samples over the input domain.

Figure 5 plots the solution space for the example constraint (x and y on the x- and y-axis, respectively); the value p we aim to estimate is the ratio between the shadowed area, enclosing all the points satisfying the constraint, and the input domain (i.e., the outer box).

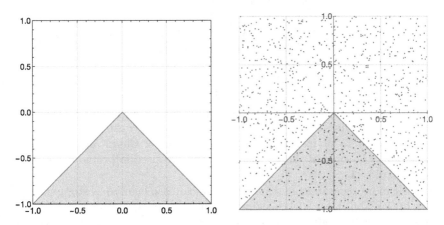

Fig. 5. Sampling-based solution space quantification for $x \leq -y \wedge y \leq x$, $x, y \in [-1, 1]$.

The hit-or-miss Monte Carlo method consists in taking n independent random samples uniformly within the domain; if a sample s_i satisfies the constraint, we assign $s_i = 1$, otherwise, $s_i = 0$. This process is called a Binomial experiment with n samples. The maximum likelihood estimate for p is then $\hat{p}$ [67]:

$$\hat{p} = \frac{\sum_{i=1}^{n} s_i}{n} \qquad\qquad \sigma(\hat{p}) = \sqrt{\frac{\hat{p} \cdot (1 - \hat{p})}{n}} \qquad\qquad (3)$$

The right part of Eq. (3) shows the standard deviation σ of $\hat{p}$ [67]. The standard deviation is an index of the convergence of the estimate. Notably, it decreases with the square root of the number of samples; when the number of samples grows to infinity, the standard deviation goes to 0, making the estimation converge to the actual value of p.

Despite the convergence of $\hat{p}$ to p can be proved only in the limit, given the value of $\hat{p}$, its standard deviation σ, and a desired confidence level $0 < \alpha < 1$, it is possible to define a confidence interval for the unknown value p. In particular:

$$Pr\left(\hat{p} - z_{\frac{\alpha}{2}} \cdot \sqrt{\frac{\hat{p} \cdot (1 - \hat{p})}{n}} \leq p \leq \hat{p} + z_{\frac{\alpha}{2}} \cdot \sqrt{\frac{\hat{p} \cdot (1 - \hat{p})}{n}}\right) = 1 - \frac{\alpha}{2} \qquad (4)$$

where $z_{\frac{\alpha}{2}}$ is the $1 - \frac{\alpha}{2}$ quantile of the standard Gaussian distribution [67].

Equation (4) is constructed using the central limit theorem, under the assumption that a large number of samples n have been collected (as a rule of thumb, hundreds of samples or more are almost surely a good fit for this assumption). The width of the interval, which is an index of the accuracy of the estimate, can be arbitrarily reduced by increasing the number of samples n; thus, Eq. (4) can be used as stopping criteria for the estimation process.

In our example, in a run with $n = 10000$ samples, we obtained $\hat{p} = 0.2512$ with standard deviation $\sigma(\hat{p}) = 0.00433703$; thus, with 99% confidence, we can conclude $p \in [0.248126, 0.254274]$. From Fig. 5, it is easy to see that $p = 0.25$, which falls within the computed interval.

Note that hit-or-miss methods may require a large number of samples to converge to a high accuracy (small interval). This is even worse when the actual value of p is close to its extremes (0 or 1). Improvements on the convergence rates can be achieved using more complex sampling procedures such as quasi-Monte Carlo sampling [72], or importance sampling, Markov Chain Monte Carlo, or slice sampling [7]; some of these methods have been used in probabilistic model checking [42,43,53].

Further more accurate confidence intervals can also be used as stopping criteria [67]; in probabilistic model checking, the most commonly used is the Chernoff-Hoeffding's bound [39,40,53]. Bayesian estimators can also be used, allowing for the inclusion of prior knowledge on the expected result (when available) [32,71]; the use of Bayesian methods led to faster convergence rate in many probabilistic verification problems [87]. Finally, a hybrid approach, that exploits interval constraint propagation and compositional solving has been proposed for probabilistic program analysis in [8,9].

Distribution-aware sampling. The hit-or-miss Monte Carlo method we described offers a straightforward way to handle input distributions: the samples for the Binomial experiment can be simply drawn from the known distribution. Efficient sampling algorithms exist for the most common continuous and discrete distributions, with off-the-shelf implementations for several programming languages (e.g., [80] for Java). A comprehensive survey of random number generation is beyond the scope of this paper (see e.g. [33]). We describe here one of the simplest and most general techniques for this task: *inverse CDF sampling.*

Assume our goal is to take a sample from a distribution D, e.g., a Gaussian distribution describing the inputs received by a temperature sensor. This distribution has a cumulative distribution function $CDF_D(x)$ representing the probability of observing a value less than or equal than x [67]. The value of the CDF is bounded between 0 and 1, for $x \to -\infty$ and $x \to \infty$, respectively. Furthermore, assuming every possible outcome has a strictly positive probability, as it is the case for most distributions used in practice, the CDF is strictly monotonic and invertible; let us denote its inverse $CDF_D^{-1}(\cdot)$.

Inverse CDF sampling reduces sampling from D to sampling from a Uniform distribution via the following three steps:

1. generate a random sample u from the Uniform distribution on $[0, 1]$
2. find the value x such that $CDF_D(x) = u$, i.e., $CDF_D^{-1}(u)$
3. return x as the sample from D

For example, to generate a sample from a Gaussian distribution $\mathcal{N}(10, 3)$, we first generate a sample u from the uniform distribution in $[0, 1]$, let's say 0.83; then, we compute $CDF_{\mathcal{N}(10,3)}^{-1}(0.83) = 12.8625$, which is our sample input.

The computation of the CDF and its inverse is efficient for most univariate distributions used in practice, and implementations are available for all common programming languages. Multivariate distributions are usually more challenging, with only a few cases allowing direct solutions. Nonetheless, more complex computation methods exist (e.g., Gibbs sampling [73]), covering most of the practically useful distributions. Multivariate distributions are indeed useful to capture statistical dependence among input variables, whether this is know in the application domain or inferred from the data. Finally, the discretization method described in Sect. 3.3 remains a viable general, approximate solution; however, distribution-aware sampling scales significantly better, especially when high accuracy is required [8].

Beyond numerical domains. Sampling-based methods are theoretically applicable for any input domain, provided a procedure for generating unbiased samples (according to the input distribution) is available. Solutions have been proposed for model counting of SAT problems (e.g., in [6,13,58], also with distribution-aware approaches [12]) and SMT problems (e.g., in [14]), while stochastic grammars can be used to generate random strings according to specified distributions [30].

4   Conclusions and Future Directions

In this paper we have provided a survey on work to adapt two powerful program analysis frameworks, data flow analysis and symbolic execution, to incorporate probabilistic reasoning. This work has already motivated exciting advances in model counting and solution space quantification as discussed in Sect. 3.3.

As in other areas of program analysis, a mutually-reinforcing cycle of developments in algorithms, tools, and applications is poised to spur further advances. We believe that efforts to focus probabilistic program analyses techniques on applications will reveal new opportunities for adapting algorithms to be more efficient and effective. This will, in turn, inspire researchers to identify additional applications of these techniques. Towards this end we describe several areas where application of probabilistic program analyses has potential and identify opportunities for cross-fertilization among probabilistic analysis techniques.

1. Program understanding has been touched on in [23,31] where errors are found by observing unexpected probabilities for certain behaviors. This provides a means of quantifying the notion of "bugs as deviant behavior" that underlies much work on fault detection. While numeric characterizations of distributions may be difficult for developers to interpret, visualizations of those distributions might allow them to spot unexpected patterns to focus their attention on.
2. Probabilistic symbolic execution is particularly well-suited for quantifying the difference between two versions of a program [25]. This makes it an ideal approach to rank how close a program is to a given oracle program, which has applications in mutation analysis, program repair, approximate computing or even in marking student assignments. Note that this provides a route to a semantic ranking of programs as opposed to more syntactic rankings, e.g., by measuring the shared syntactic structure.
3. It would be interesting to explore the extent to which the computation of branch probabilities—which annotate models in tools like PRISM [50] and PASS [37]—could be achieved, in part, by using path condition calculation and solution space quantification techniques drawn from probabilistic symbolic execution.
4. Hybrid approaches that mix probabilistic symbolic execution and data flow seem promising. The unanalyzed portion of a program's symbolic execution tree defines a "residual" program. If that program can be extracted, via techniques like slicing, then it could be encoded for analysis with data flow techniques. The results of the precise-but-slow, and faster-but-less-precise, analysis, could then be combined.
5. Probabilistic symbolic execution could be extended to support the more general notion of probabilistic program treated by Gordon et al. [35]. The semantics of `observe(e)` statements condition input on a boolean expression e by aborting the path if the expression is false and renormalizing the output distribution. Most existing symbolic execution frameworks already support `assume` and `assert` statements to check and enforce predicates at program points. Extending this to support `observe` requires that the probability estimates of aborted paths be accumulated to permit renormalization at the end of the symbolic execution. We note that relative to existing probabilistic symbolic execution approaches this adds negligible overhead.
6. Probabilistic program analysis has many promising applications in the security domain; for example it can be used in quantitative information flow analysis [3], where the goal is to detect vulnerabilities and compute the leakage (in number of bits of the secret) using information theory metrics. A program can be viewed as a probabilistic function that maps a high security input to an *observable* output. An adversary tries to guess the secret by observing the output. The leakage of a (deterministic) program can be expressed as classical Shannon entropy: $Leakage(P) = -\sum_{i=1,n} p(o_i) \log_2 p(o_i)$, where $p(o_i)$ denotes the probability of observing o_i and can be computed with the techniques discussed in this article.

References

1. Aydin, A., Bang, L., Bultan, T.: Automata-based model counting for string constraints. In: Proceedings of the 27th International Conference on Computer Aided Verification, CAV 2015, Part I, San Francisco, CA, USA, 18–24 July 2015, pp. 255–272 (2015)
2. Bagnara, R., Hill, P.M., Zaffanella, E.: The parma polyhedra library: toward a complete set of numerical abstractions for the analysis and verification of hardware and software systems. Sci. Comput. Program. **72**(1), 3–21 (2008)
3. Bang, L., Aydin, A., Phan, Q., Pasareanu, C.S., Bultan, T.: String analysis for side channels with segmented oracles. In: Proceedings of the 24th ACM SIGSOFT International Symposium on Foundations of Software Engineering, FSE 2016, Seattle, WA, USA, 13–18 November 2016, pp. 193–204 (2016)
4. Barvinok, A.I.: A polynomial time algorithm for counting integral points in polyhedra when the dimension is fixed. Math. Oper. Res. **19**(4), 769–779 (1994)
5. de Berg, M.: Computational Geometry: Algorithms and Applications. Springer, Heidelberg (2008)
6. Biere, A., van Maaren, H.: Handbook of Satisfiability. Frontiers in Artificial Intelligence and Applications. IOS Press, Amsterdam (2009)
7. Bishop, C.: Pattern Recognition and Machine Learning. Information Science and Statistics. Springer, New York (2006)
8. Borges, M., Filieri, A., d'Amorim, M., Păsăreanu, C.S.: Iterative distribution-aware sampling for probabilistic symbolic execution. In: Proceedings of the 10th Joint Meeting of the European Software Engineering Conference and the ACM SIGSOFT Symposium on the Foundations of Software Engineering, ESEC/FSE 2015. ACM (2015)
9. Borges, M., Filieri, A., d'Amorim, M., Păsăreanu, C.S., Visser, W.: Compositional solution space quantification for probabilistic software analysis. In: Proceedings of the 35th ACM SIGPLAN Conference on Programming Language Design and Implementation, pp. 123–132. ACM (2014)
10. Bryant, R.E.: Symbolic boolean manipulation with ordered binary-decision diagrams. ACM Comput. Surv. (CSUR) **24**(3), 293–318 (1992)
11. Cadar, C., Dunbar, D., Engler, D.R.: Klee: Unassisted and automatic generation of high-coverage tests for complex systems programs. In: OSDI, vol. 8, pp. 209–224 (2008)
12. Chakraborty, S., Fremont, D.J., Meel, K.S., Seshia, S.A., Vardi, M.Y.: Distribution-aware sampling and weighted model counting for SAT. In: Twenty-Eighth AAAI Conference on Artificial Intelligence (2014)
13. Chakraborty, S., Meel, K.S., Vardi, M.Y.: A scalable approximate model counter. In: Schulte, C. (ed.) CP 2013. LNCS, vol. 8124, pp. 200–216. Springer, Heidelberg (2013). doi:10.1007/978-3-642-40627-0_18
14. Chistikov, D., Dimitrova, R., Majumdar, R.: Approximate counting in SMT and value estimation for probabilistic programs. In: Baier, C., Tinelli, C. (eds.) TACAS 2015. LNCS, vol. 9035, pp. 320–334. Springer, Heidelberg (2015). doi:10.1007/978-3-662-46681-0_26
15. Claret, G., Rajamani, S.K., Nori, A.V., Gordon, A.D., Borgström, J.: Bayesian inference using data flow analysis. In: Proceedings of the 2013 9th Joint Meeting on Foundations of Software Engineering, pp. 92–102. ACM (2013)
16. Clarke, E.M., Grumberg, O., Peled, D.: Model Checking. MIT Press, Cambridge (1999)

17. Clarke, L., et al.: A system to generate test data and symbolically execute programs. IEEE Trans. Software Eng. **3**, 215–222 (1976)
18. Cousot, P., Cousot, R.: Abstract interpretation: a unified lattice model for static analysis of programs by construction or approximation of fixpoints. In: Proceedings of the 4th ACM SIGACT-SIGPLAN Symposium on Principles of Programming Languages, pp. 238–252. ACM (1977)
19. Cousot, P., Monerau, M.: Probabilistic abstract interpretation. In: Seidl, H. (ed.) ESOP 2012. LNCS, vol. 7211, pp. 169–193. Springer, Heidelberg (2012). doi:10. 1007/978-3-642-28869-2_9
20. Di Pierro, A., Wiklicky, H.: Probabilistic data flow analysis: a linear equational approach. arXiv preprint arXiv:1307.4474 (2013)
21. Dwyer, M.B.: Unifying testing and analysis through behavioral coverage. In: 2011 26th IEEE/ACM International Conference on Automated Software Engineering (ASE), p. 2. IEEE (2011)
22. Esparza, J., Gaiser, A.: Probabilistic abstractions with arbitrary domains. In: Yahav, E. (ed.) SAS 2011. LNCS, vol. 6887, pp. 334–350. Springer, Heidelberg (2011). doi:10.1007/978-3-642-23702-7_25
23. Filieri, A., Frias, M., Păsăreanu, C., Visser, W.: Model counting for complex data structures. In: Proceedings of the 2015 International SPIN Symposium on Model Checking of Software. ACM (2015)
24. Filieri, A., Păsăreanu, C.S., Visser, W., Geldenhuys, J.: Statistical symbolic execution with informed sampling. In: Proceedings of the 22nd ACM SIGSOFT International Symposium on Foundations of Software Engineering, pp. 437–448. ACM (2014)
25. Filieri, A., Păsăreanu, C.S., Yang, G.: Quantification of software changes through probabilistic symbolic execution. In: Proceedings of the 30th IEEE/ACM International Conference on Automated Software Engineering (ASE) - Short Paper, November 2015
26. Filieri, A., Păsăreanu, C.S., Visser, W.: Reliability analysis in symbolic pathfinder. In: Proceedings of the 2013 International Conference on Software Engineering, pp. 622–631. IEEE Press (2013)
27. Fink, S., Dolby, J.: WALA-The TJ watson libraries for analysis (2012)
28. Floyd, R.W.: Assigning meanings to programs. In: Mathematical Aspects of Computer Science, pp. 19–32 (1967)
29. Fosdick, L.D., Osterweil, L.J.: Data flow analysis in software reliability. ACM Comput. Surv. (CSUR) **8**(3), 305–330 (1976)
30. Fu, K., Huang, T.: Stochastic grammars and languages. Int. J. Comput. Inform. Sci. **1**(2), 135–170 (1972)
31. Geldenhuys, J., Dwyer, M.B., Visser, W.: Probabilistic symbolic execution. In: Proceedings of the 2012 International Symposium on Software Testing and Analysis, pp. 166–176. ACM (2012)
32. Gelman, A., Carlin, J., Stern, H., Dunson, D., Vehtari, A., Rubin, D.: Bayesian Data Analysis, 3rd edn. Chapman & Hall/CRC Texts in Statistical Science, Taylor & Francis (2013)
33. Gentle, J.: Random Number Generation and Monte Carlo Methods. Statistics and Computing. Springer, New York (2013)
34. Godefroid, P., Klarlund, N., Sen, K.: DART: directed automated random testing. In: ACM Sigplan Notices, vol. 40, pp. 213–223. ACM (2005)
35. Gordon, A.D., Henzinger, T.A., Nori, A.V., Rajamani, S.K.: Probabilistic programming. In: Proceedings of the on Future of Software Engineering, pp. 167–181. ACM (2014)

36. Graf, S., Saidi, H.: Construction of abstract state graphs with PVS. In: Grumberg, O. (ed.) CAV 1997. LNCS, vol. 1254, pp. 72–83. Springer, Heidelberg (1997). doi:10. 1007/3-540-63166-6_10
37. Hahn, E.M., Hermanns, H., Wachter, B., Zhang, L.: PASS: abstraction refinement for infinite probabilistic models. In: Esparza, J., Majumdar, R. (eds.) TACAS 2010. LNCS, vol. 6015, pp. 353–357. Springer, Heidelberg (2010). doi:10.1007/ 978-3-642-12002-2_30
38. Hasuo, I., Jacobs, B., Sokolova, A.: Generic trace theory. Electron. Notes Theor. Comput. Sci. **164**(1), 47–65 (2006)
39. Hérault, T., Lassaigne, R., Magniette, F., Peyronnet, S.: Approximate probabilistic model checking. In: Steffen, B., Levi, G. (eds.) VMCAI 2004. LNCS, vol. 2937, pp. 73–84. Springer, Heidelberg (2004). doi:10.1007/978-3-540-24622-0_8
40. Hoeffding, W.: Probability inequalities for sums of bounded random variables. J. Am. Stat. Assoc. **58**(301), 13–30 (1963)
41. Jamrozik, K., Fraser, G., Tillman, N., Halleux, J.: Generating test suites with augmented dynamic symbolic execution. In: Veanes, M., Viganò, L. (eds.) TAP 2013. LNCS, vol. 7942, pp. 152–167. Springer, Heidelberg (2013). doi:10.1007/ 978-3-642-38916-0_9
42. Jegourel, C., Legay, A., Sedwards, S.: Cross-entropy optimisation of importance sampling parameters for statistical model checking. In: Madhusudan, P., Seshia, S.A. (eds.) CAV 2012. LNCS, vol. 7358, pp. 327–342. Springer, Heidelberg (2012). doi:10.1007/978-3-642-31424-7_26
43. Jegourel, C., Legay, A., Sedwards, S.: Importance splitting for statistical model checking rare properties. In: Sharygina, N., Veith, H. (eds.) CAV 2013. LNCS, vol. 8044, pp. 576–591. Springer, Heidelberg (2013). doi:10.1007/978-3-642-39799-8_38
44. Jones, C.: Probabilistic non-determinism (1990)
45. Kildall, G.A.: A unified approach to global program optimization. In: Proceedings of the 1st Annual ACM SIGACT-SIGPLAN Symposium on Principles of Programming Languages, pp. 194–206. ACM (1973)
46. King, J.C.: Symbolic execution and program testing. Commun. ACM **19**(7), 385–394 (1976)
47. Kozen, D.: Semantics of probabilistic programs. J. Comput. Syst. Sci. **22**(3), 328–350 (1981)
48. Kozen, D.: A probabilistic PDL. In: Proceedings of the Fifteenth Annual ACM Symposium on Theory of Computing, pp. 291–297. ACM (1983)
49. Kwiatkowska, M., Norman, G., Parker, D.: Advances and challenges of probabilistic model checking. In: 2010 Proceedings of the 48th Annual Allerton Conference on Communication, Control, and Computing (Allerton) (2010)
50. Kwiatkowska, M., Norman, G., Parker, D.: PRISM 4.0: verification of probabilistic real-time systems. In: Gopalakrishnan, G., Qadeer, S. (eds.) CAV 2011. LNCS, vol. 6806, pp. 585–591. Springer, Heidelberg (2011). doi:10.1007/978-3-642-22110-1_47
51. Lam, P., Bodden, E., Lhoták, O., Hendren, L.: The Soot framework for Java program analysis: a retrospective. In: Cetus Users and Compiler Infrastructure Workshop, Galveston Island, TX, October 2011
52. Lattner, C., Adve, V.: LLVM: a compilation framework for lifelong program analysis & transformation. In: Proceedings of the International Symposium on Code Generation and Optimization: Feedback-Directed and Runtime Optimization (2004)

53. Legay, A., Delahaye, B., Bensalem, S.: Statistical model checking: an overview. In: Barringer, H., Falcone, Y., Finkbeiner, B., Havelund, K., Lee, I., Pace, G., Roşu, G., Sokolsky, O., Tillmann, N. (eds.) RV 2010. LNCS, vol. 6418, pp. 122–135. Springer, Heidelberg (2010). doi:10.1007/978-3-642-16612-9_11
54. Luckow, K., Păsăreanu, C.S., Dwyer, M.B., Filieri, A., Visser, W.: Exact and approximate probabilistic symbolic execution for nondeterministic programs. In: Proceedings of the 29th ACM/IEEE International Conference on Automated Software Engineering, pp. 575–586. ACM (2014)
55. Luu, L., Shinde, S., Saxena, P., Demsky, B.: A model counter for constraints over unbounded strings. In: Proceedings of the 35th ACM SIGPLAN Conference on Programming Language Design and Implementation, pp. 565–576. ACM (2014)
56. Mardziel, P., Magill, S., Hicks, M., Srivatsa, M.: Dynamic enforcement of knowledge-based security policies using probabilistic abstract interpretation. J. Comput. Secur. 21(4), 463–532 (2013)
57. McDonald, J.B.: Some generalized functions for the size distribution of income. Econometrica J. Econometric Soc. 52, 647–663 (1984)
58. Meel, K.S.: Sampling techniques for boolean satisfiability. CoRR abs/1404.6682 (2014). http://arxiv.org/abs/1404.6682
59. Monniaux, D.: Abstract interpretation of probabilistic semantics. In: Palsberg, J. (ed.) SAS 2000. LNCS, vol. 1824, pp. 322–339. Springer, Heidelberg (2000). doi:10.1007/978-3-540-45099-3_17
60. Monniaux, D.: Backwards Abstract Interpretation of Probabilistic Programs. In: Sands, D. (ed.) ESOP 2001. LNCS, vol. 2028, pp. 367–382. Springer, Heidelberg (2001). doi:10.1007/3-540-45309-1_24
61. Monniaux, D.: Abstract interpretation of programs as markov decision processes. Sci. Comput. Program. 58(1), 179–205 (2005)
62. Morgan, C., McIver, A., Seidel, K.: Probabilistic predicate transformers. ACM Trans. Program. Lang. Syst. (TOPLAS) 18(3), 325–353 (1996)
63. Murta, D., Oliveira, J.N.: A study of risk-aware program transformation. Sci. Comput. Program. 110(C), 51–77 (2015)
64. Oliveira, J.N., Miraldo, V.C.: "Keep definition, change category" — a practical approach to state-based system calculi. J. Logical Algebraic Methods Program. 85(4), 449–474 (2016)
65. Pasareanu, C.S., Phan, Q., Malacaria, P.: Multi-run side-channel analysis using symbolic execution and Max-SMT. In: IEEE 29th Computer Security Foundations Symposium, CSF 2016, Lisbon, Portugal, 27 June–1 July 2016, pp. 387–400 (2016)
66. Păsăreanu, C.S., Rungta, N.: Symbolic pathfinder: symbolic execution of Java bytecode. In: Proceedings of the IEEE/ACM International Conference on Automated Software Engineering, pp. 179–180. ACM (2010)
67. Pestman, W.R.: Mathematical Statistics: An Introduction, vol. 1. Walter de Gruyter, Berlin (1998)
68. Puggelli, A., Li, W., Sangiovanni-Vincentelli, A.L., Seshia, S.A.: Polynomial-time verification of PCTL properties of MDPs with convex uncertainties. In: Sharygina, N., Veith, H. (eds.) CAV 2013. LNCS, vol. 8044, pp. 527–542. Springer, Heidelberg (2013). doi:10.1007/978-3-642-39799-8_35
69. Puterman, M.L.: Markov Decision Processes: Discrete Stochastic Dynamic Programming. Wiley, New York (1994)
70. Ramalingam, G.: Data flow frequency analysis. In: ACM SIGPLAN Notices, vol. 31, pp. 267–277. ACM (1996)
71. Robert, C.: The Bayesian Choice: From Decision-Theoretic Foundations to Computational Implementation. Springer Texts in Statistics. Springer, New York (2007)

72. Robert, C., Casella, G.: Monte Carlo Statistical Methods. Springer, New York (2013)
73. Robert, C.P., Casella, G.: Monte Carlo Statistical Methods. Springer, New York (2005)
74. Sang, T., Beame, P., Kautz, H.: Heuristics for fast exact model counting. In: Bacchus, F., Walsh, T. (eds.) SAT 2005. LNCS, vol. 3569, pp. 226–240. Springer, Heidelberg (2005). doi:10.1007/11499107_17
75. Schmidt, D.A.: Data flow analysis is model checking of abstract interpretations. In: Proceedings of the 25th ACM SIGPLAN-SIGACT Symposium on Principles of Programming Languages, pp. 38–48. ACM (1998)
76. Sen, K., Marinov, D., Agha, G.: CUTE: A concolic unit testing engine for C (2005)
77. Smith, M.J.: Probabilistic abstract interpretation of imperative programs using truncated normal distributions. Electron. Notes Theor. Comput. Sci. **220**(3), 43–59 (2008)
78. Song, D., et al.: BitBlaze: a new approach to computer security via binary analysis. In: Sekar, R., Pujari, A.K. (eds.) ICISS 2008. LNCS, vol. 5352, pp. 1–25. Springer, Heidelberg (2008). doi:10.1007/978-3-540-89862-7_1
79. Thakur, A., Elder, M., Reps, T.: Bilateral algorithms for symbolic abstraction. In: Miné, A., Schmidt, D. (eds.) SAS 2012. LNCS, vol. 7460, pp. 111–128. Springer, Heidelberg (2012). doi:10.1007/978-3-642-33125-1_10
80. The Apache Software Foundation: Commons math. http://commons.apache.org/proper/commons-math/. Accessed 16 Dec 2014
81. Thurley, M.: sharpSAT – counting models with advanced component caching and implicit BCP. In: Biere, A., Gomes, C.P. (eds.) SAT 2006. LNCS, vol. 4121, pp. 424–429. Springer, Heidelberg (2006). doi:10.1007/11814948_38
82. Thurow, L.C.: Analyzing the American income distribution. Am. Econ. Rev. **60**, 261–269 (1970)
83. UC Davis, Mathematics: LattE. http://www.math.ucdavis.edu/latte
84. Vallée-Rai, R., Co, P., Gagnon, E., Hendren, L., Lam, P., Sundaresan, V.: Soot-a Java bytecode optimization framework. In: Proceedings of the 1999 Conference of the Centre for Advanced Studies on Collaborative Research, p. 13. IBM Press (1999)
85. Verdoolaege, S.: Software package barvinok (2004). http://freshmeat.net/projects/barvinok
86. Wachter, B., Zhang, L.: Best probabilistic transformers. In: Barthe, G., Hermenegildo, M. (eds.) VMCAI 2010. LNCS, vol. 5944, pp. 362–379. Springer, Heidelberg (2010). doi:10.1007/978-3-642-11319-2_26
87. Zuliani, P., Platzer, A., Clarke, E.M.: Bayesian statistical model checking with application to simulink/stateflow verification. In: Proceedings of the 13th ACM International Conference on Hybrid Systems: Computation and Control, pp. 243–252. ACM (2010)

How Ontologies Can Help in Software Engineering

Cesar Gonzalez-Perez[✉]

Incipit CSIC, Avda. de Vigo, s/n, 15705 Santiago de Compostela, Spain
cesar.gonzalez-perez@incipit.csic.es

Abstract. Ontologies are often understood as having a historical background quite different to that of software engineering, which has caused a number of issues when trying to use them in this context. However, recent works have characterized ontologies as being closely related to models and metamodels, thus allowing for an inclusive treatment and use. In this work I describe how ontologies are understood today within software engineering, how they relate to models and metamodels, and how they are useful to software and systems engineering over different lifecycle phases, in different domains, and in relation to standards such as those from ISO/IEC JTC1 SC7.

Keywords: Ontologies · Models · Conceptual modelling · Domain-specific modelling · Metamodelling · Modelling languages · Standards

1 Context and Motivation

In philosophy, *ontology* is the science of being [82]. That is, ontology is the branch of philosophy concerned with the study of what is and how it is, regardless of what we may know about it. As a countable noun, *an ontology* is a theory of the world in terms of what exists and how, again regardless of what our knowledge about it may be. In turn, the study of knowledge (including belief, truth and justification) is part of *epistemology*, a different branch of philosophy [83 "Epistemology"].

Outside philosophy and in the computing realm, the word "ontology" is often used with a different but related meaning; in 1993, Gruber [28], a researcher in artificial intelligence and knowledge engineering, famously defined an ontology as "a formal specification of a conceptualization". There are two especially relevant differences between this definition and the philosophical view described above:

- In computing, ontologies are formal, i.e., they are expressed in a formal or at least semi-formal language, through which relevant concepts and their properties and relationships are captured. In philosophy, however, ontologies are often presented in natural language; see e.g. [10].
- In computing, an ontology captures a conceptualization, that is, some knowledge as held by one or more people. This brings computing ontologies closer to epistemology (the science of knowledge) than philosophical ontology (the science of knowledge-independent being), as noted by [31].

© Springer International Publishing AG 2017
J. Cunha et al. (Eds.): GTTSE 2015, LNCS 10223, pp. 26–44, 2017.
DOI: 10.1007/978-3-319-60074-1_2

Despite these differences, we can still claim that computing ontologies are theories of (a part of) the world, because they describe what a portion of reality looks like (although many anti-realists would disagree). In this regard, and according to Gregor [27], they are analytical (i.e., type 1) theories, since they describe the target domain without attempting to explain causal phenomena or predict future observations.

Two additional points must be made in relation to Gruber's definition and its context. First of all, the definition provided by Gruber, and especially the way in which it has been applied since, correspond mostly to what today we call *domain ontologies*, i.e., ontologies that describe a particular subject or field of work such as genomics [2], lexical structures [66] or cultural heritage [52]. In addition to domain ontologies, however, the literature has also studied *upper ontologies*, which, rather than describing a specific area of reality, aim to establish what reality is like in general, making statements that should be valid for any domain or application. For example, a domain ontology about lexical structures may contain concepts such as "Determiner" or "Adjective", which are only relevant within that domain; similarly, a domain ontology for genomics may contain concepts such as "Gene" or "Transposon". An upper ontology, however, may contain concepts that describe the very fabric of reality, such as "Type", "Property" or "Role"; see, e.g., BORO [76], DOLCE [62] or UFO [34]. The relationship between domain ontologies and upper ontologies is that of *conformance*, i.e., a domain ontology conforms to a particular upper ontology, very much as a model conforms to a metamodel. This fact and its consequences are explored in Sect. 2.

Secondly, Gruber, as well as other authors who adopted and further developed the application of ontologies in computing [29, 32, 38], were part of the artificial intelligence (AI) community, which since the 1970s had been pressed to find a good manner to describe states of affairs in the world on which machines were able to apply automatic reasoning. Agent technologies, which became a fashionable research theme in the late 1990s and early 2000s, also pushed in this direction [12], and ontologies (as in computing rather than philosophy) were developed as a solution to this problem. At the same time, the software engineering community was developing solutions to cope with the increasing complexity of the systems that were being developed, and introducing a wide range of modelling languages and approaches over the 1980s and 1990s [14, 26, 61, 79]. As a result, the same problem (namely, representing the world in a suitable fashion) was being addressed by two communities at the same time and with not much exchange of information [46], and focusing on very different aspects of the problem. As pointed out by [31], "AI researchers seem to have been much more interested in the nature of reasoning rather than in the nature of the real world". The solutions thus obtained by the two communities (ontologies and modelling approaches) share some commonalities, but also differ in significant ways, which are explored in Sect. 2. In particular, in software engineering we use models for two major purposes: to describe domains and to specify systems [21]. A model used to describe a domain looks much like a domain ontology, and the relationship between models and ontologies is also explored in Sect. 2.

Finally, it is worth mentioning that ontologies have become quite typical in the semantic web [7] field, particularly through World Wide Web Consortium (W3C) specifications such as the Web Ontology Language (OWL) [86] and the Simple Knowledge Organization System (SKOS) [85]. SKOS and most especially OWL use a very computation-oriented notion of what ontologies are and focus on web-based solutions, which introduces significant "implementation noise" that makes these approaches barely usable outside their niche. This is also discussed in Sect. 2.

Over the following sections, I will focus on how ontologies can be useful in software engineering; for this reason, the discussion will be centred on software engineering and, in general, I will use software engineering terms and concepts. Terminology and concepts that are specific of the ontologies field are explicitly flagged.

In particular, the following sections describe three major aspects on how ontologies can be useful in software engineering. First, ontologies help obtain a better philosophical grounding of the software engineering discipline and practice, solving some issues that often pass unnoticed. Second, ontological thinking allows us to carry out better domain modelling by contributing aspects often neglected by traditional modelling technologies. Third, ontologies constitute an excellent basis for the standardisation of the software engineering field, especially within the work carried out by organizations such as ISO.

2   Ontologies and Models

Ontologies are intuitively close to models in software engineering, as described above. However, before I discuss ontologies and their relationship to models, some concepts must be fixed. This section provides some base concepts and terms, and then discusses the differences and commonalities between ontologies and models.

2.1   Base Concepts in Models, Metamodels and Modelling Languages

A **model** is "an abstraction that represents some view on reality, necessarily omitting details, and for a specific purpose" [39], or "an abstraction of a (real or language-based) subject allowing predictions or inferences to be made" [59, 60], or "a statement about a given subject under study (SUS), expressed in a given language" [23], or even "a description of (part of) a system written in a well-defined language" [18]. In any case, a model always involves the following [43]:

- Something that is represented, i.e., the modelled subject. (Mapping)
- An abstraction process, which eliminates irrelevant details of the former to keep only what is relevant to a particular purpose. (Simplification)
- An ability to reason on the model and then apply the conclusions of the reasoning to the modelled subject, i.e., a proxy function. (Application)

As seen above, representation plays a central role in models. A model can represent the subject through mappings of three different kinds [21]:

- **Isotypical**, by which an element in the model maps straightforwardly to an entity in the modelled subject. For example, an architectural plan of a house usually represents the real house isotypically, since it maps to that house and only that house. Also, an object in an object-oriented model or running process usually represents the real entity it refers to isotypically.

- **Prototypical**, by which an element in the model maps to a set of entities in the modelled subject given by example; in other words, the element in the model exemplifies the kind of subject entities that are being represented. For example, a model car placed next to a cardboard model house to illustrate where cars are expected to park represents cars prototypically, since the model car does not map to any particular real car, but just to an example car.
- **Metatypical**, by which an element in the model maps to a set of entities in the modelled subject given declaratively; in other words, the element in the model is a description of the properties that subject entities must comply with in order to be represented. For example, the technical specifications of the windows to install in the house from our previous example constitute a metatypical representation, since they do not depict a specific window or exemplify a set of allowed windows, but declare what properties any window must possess in order to be acceptable. A class in an object-oriented model or computer program also represents the real entities it refers to metatypically.

Models that work in an isotypical manner have been called in the literature token models, and those who represent metatypically have been called type models [60]. This distinction is old, having been introduced by philosopher Charles Sanders Peirce in the late 19th century, and plays an important role in contemporary ontological thinking [83 "Types and Tokens"]. However, and since different elements in one model can work in different manners (isotopically, prototypically or metatypically), I prefer the more precise granularity of the latter rather than the simplistic classification into token and type models.

A **metamodel**, in turn, is a particular kind of model, as indicated by the qualifier "meta-"; a metamodel is a "model of models" [68] or "a model of a set of models" [18]. Either case, it is clear that a metamodel is a model for which the modelled subjects are also models. The relationship between a metamodel and the models that it represents is one of conformance [39], i.e., a model *conforms to* a metamodel.

Also, and very importantly, since metamodels are a specific type of models, everything that we state about models also applies to metamodels, including their ability to represent their subjects (i.e., other models) isotypically, prototypically or metatypically.

Defining what a **modelling language** is proves harder. For some authors, a modelling language is "a set of models" [18], i.e., a language is the set of all possible models that may be possibly expressed in that language. According to this view, a specification (or model) of that language constitutes a metamodel, since we said that a metamodel is a model of a set of models. This is analogous to saying that English is the set of all possible sentences that may be possibly uttered in this language, and that a specification (or model) of English constitutes its grammar (cf. metamodel).

Other authors, however, place no emphasis in this difference between metamodels and languages, and define a modelling language as "an organised collection of model unit kinds that focus on a particular modelling perspective" [23, 56 clause 7.1.18], where model unit kinds are the primitives that this language uses to express models, e.g., "Class" or "Association" in UML [69].

2.2 Base Concepts in Ontologies

As stated earlier, an **ontology** is "a formal specification of a conceptualization" [28, 29], or "a formal, explicit specification of a shared conceptualization" [15]. Also, "an ontology defines a set of representational primitives with which to model a domain of knowledge or discourse. The representational primitives are typically classes (or sets), attributes (or properties), and relationships (or relations among class members)" [30]. However, it is often emphasised in the literature that ontologies do not need to be composed of type-level elements only, and they may also contain instance-level elements such as objects, often called "individuals" in ontology parlance [15, 86], as well as axioms [15, 86] that further constrain the semantics of the involved types and instances.

Furthermore, ontologies are usually described as containing knowledge rather than data [28], that is, they work at the *knowledge level*, a concept introduced by [67] in the 1980s. Knowledge and data, together with the intermediate level of information and the top level of wisdom, compose the Ackoff "pyramid" [1] of increasing abstraction. Thus, by representing the world in terms of knowledge rather than data, ontologies are supposed to be more abstract than, say, database schemata, and provide better support for semantics, especially in the context of the semantic web [7]. According to [39], ontologies were introduced and popularised within the software engineering community from the early 2000s and onwards, as shown by the increasing literature on the subject, the availability of specific tools (such as Protégé protege.stanford.edu or Swoogles-woogle.umbc.edu) and ontology repositories, and the number of projects devoted to ontologies. Still, some authors have pointed out that the promise of semantic knowledge, especially on the web, is still unrealised [84].

Another essential aspects of ontologies in computing, hinted at above, is that they must be formal and, more precisely, understandable by a computer or "codified in a machine interpretable language" [15]. In fact, automatic (i.e., algorithmic) reasoning is often presented as a key motivation to develop ontologies [31, 86]. To this purpose, ontology languages such as CycL [33] or OWL [86] have been developed that focus on rigorous implementation of formal logic. The amount of detail required to create an ontology, as well as the associated "implementation noise", are usually quite large; this is a contradiction with the principle of minimal encoding bias [29], which states that a good ontology should be expressed at the knowledge level and be as free from encoding details as possible. In addition, this means that creating an ontology by hand (on paper or on a whiteboard, for example) and dynamically exploring alternatives is extremely difficult, and specialised tools are obligatory.

Finally, a clear distinction must be made between upper, or foundational, ontologies and domain ontologies, as introduced in previous sections. An **upper ontology** is an "axiomatic account of high-level domain-independent categories about the real world" [80], or one that "defines a range of top-level domain-independent ontological categories, which form a general foundation for more elaborated domain-specific ontologies" [36]; this means upper ontologies should be valid across domains and contain very abstract concepts only. In turn, a **domain ontology** is a "specific theory about a material domain (e.g., law, medicine, archaeology, molecular biology, etc.)" or "a shared conceptual specification of the domain" [34]. Developing a domain ontology requires a deep understanding of the particular domain of application; however, developing an upper ontology requires a deep understanding of reality and the commitment to specific meta-ontological choices as exemplified by [75], such as the nature of categorisation or the structure of time.

This has several consequences. Firstly, it seems that upper ontologies closely match the field of study of philosophical ontology, whereas domain ontologies are closer to epistemology, since they describe a domain in terms of human-mediated knowledge [31]. Secondly, upper ontologies establish a structure to which domain ontologies can conform, by serving as a starting point to build new (domain) ontologies, asa reference for the comparison of different (domain) ontologies, and as a common framework for (domain) ontology harmonisation and integration [62].

2.3 Differences Between Ontologies and Models

As discussed above, ontologies and models seem to be trying to address the same problems (representing the world in an abstract manner) but do it from very different perspectives. These differences often result in different artefacts, different uses and different possibilities:

- Ontologies are intended for computer processing, whereas models are aimed at human understanding (but see below).
- Ontologies are highly formal and require a logical basis, whereas models can be semi-formal and admit some degree of informality.
- Ontologies are harder to develop, whereas some models can be created quite easily.
- Ontologies aim to represent the world objectively, as it is, whereas models are inherently subjective.
- Ontologies often combine type (i.e., metatypical) and token (i.e., isotypical) representations together, whereas models tend to emphasise the difference.

First of all, the overall motivation for ontologies has been automated, algorithmic reasoning [31, 86] carried out by machines. This has meant that an ontology is usually a computer-oriented artefact, not always easily readable by humans. Contrarily, modelling in software engineering has been motivated since the 1980s by the need to tackle complexity and understand better the world around us as well as obtain better specifications for the systems that engineers will build [44]. This means that models are usually human-oriented artefacts that machines cannot process directly. However, the model-based software engineering (MBSE) approach [9, 81], popularized in the last 15 years, has changed this significantly. These days, models are often constructed as machine-readable artefacts that can be processed by a computer to generate other models or even code through MDA/MDE approaches [68] or languages such as Executable UML [64]. Still, much modelling is still not machine-based and oriented towards humans. From the ontologies side, work in ontology visualization [58] is being carried out to make ontologies more easily understandable to humans. In summary, ontologies and models have very different historical aims, which are now converging.

Since ontologies are traditionally geared towards computers, they are often based on some form of formal logic, and an ontology, as an artefact, is a highly formal one. This is particularly noticeable when looking at ontology languages; for example, CycL [33] is based on first-order logic and has some support for modal operators and higher-order quantification (such as "all" and "exists"); similarly, OWL [86] is a "computational logic-based language" that supports full algorithmic decidability in its OWL-DL (description logic) variant. Contrarily, many modelling languages rarely aim to attain full formality, with the exception of those particular to the formal methods subfield or oriented towards MBSE. Modelling languages, in general and as usually employed in software engineering, are based on meta-specifications such as MOF [70] that make extensive use of natural language and thus leave room for informality. Again, this is changing now, and implementations based on languages such as UML are being successfully used for machine processing.

As a further consequence, ontologies are usually harder to develop than models. An example of this is the fact that ontologies usually require great care when identifying and naming classes; in OWL, for instance, a class is identified by an international resource identifier (IRI), which must be correctly generated and namespaced. In UML [69], however, a class is identified by a simple name in natural language. For reasons like this, it is very easy to informally sketch an exploratory model on a piece of paper or a whiteboard, but it is very hard to do this foran ontology. However, the ontology, once created, will have a degree of formality and a potentiality for automatic processing that the model may lack.

As an additional major difference, ontologies aim to represent the world objectively, as it is, without introducing much subjective bias, whereas models may embrace subjectivity. This is particularly so in the case of upper ontologies, although domain ontologies, given their focus on shared conceptualizations [15], also have this property. According to [31], ontologies constrain the meanings they aim to provide (through axioms, for example), whereas conceptual models offer a fully subjective and pre-interpreted view of the represented subject. In the case of upper ontologies, this is even more so, as illustrated in [80] when describing foundational (i.e., upper) ontologies as being related to "reusable information", "semantic interoperability" and "axiomatic accounts of high-level domain-independent categories". In modelling, to the contrary, a very specific purpose is always taken as a starting point, and it is assumed that this purpose strongly shapes the resultant model; as pointed out by [4], "software engineers have taken a very pragmatic approach to data representation, encoding only the information needed to solve the problem in hand". Also, the statistician George Box is usually credited as the author of the famous aphorism "All models are wrong; some models are useful"; this is often interpreted to mean that models, given the fact that they represent through abstraction, are necessarily discarding details, and are therefore "wrong" or biased in some way as dictated by the guiding purpose [43].

Lastly, ontologies often emphasise that a good account of reality is given by combining classes and instances in the same representation, and usually there is no particular emphasis in differentiating layers or levels. The modelling community, however, has developed strong ideas about the separation of type (i.e., metatypical) and token (i.e., isotypical) representations, such as OMG's strict metamodelling paradigm [3] and, although classes and objects can be mixed together in the same models in, for example, UML, this is very rarely done.

Additional differences between ontologies and models are reported and discussed in [4].

2.4 Commonalities of Ontologies and Models

Despite the differences described in the previous section, numerous works have tried to find commonalities between ontologies and models. This is not surprising, since, as pointed out above, models and ontologies are trying to solve much the same problems, and some common grounds are to be expected. In addition, cross-pollination between disciplines is often seen as a motivation.

In [4], the authors characterize models and ontologies over several key aspects, and observe that "all ontologies are models, but not all models are ontologies", since any information representation that fulfils the necessary conditions to be an ontology also fulfils those to be a model. This means that ontologies are a specific kind of models and that, therefore, everything we say about models should also apply to ontologies. Also, the authors convincingly criticise many of the claims that are usually employed to highlight the differences between models and ontologies. For example, they show that support for reasoning is not a definitional property of ontologies, that there is no requirement for open or closed world assumptions for either models or ontologies, and that it is perfectly possible to create information representations that are not shared (and therefore are not ontologies) using ontology languages. All these facts mean that ontologies and models are extremely similar, much more than often depicted. However, and although the authors state that these strong similarities make many ontology-driven efforts and technologies redundant, this is hard to sustain, since a subtype usually adds details to the super type it derives from, and hence ontologies are likely to possess specific properties (such as those described in Sect. 2.3) that are not present in models. Still, most of the observations in [4] are valid and constitute a strong change of direction to the usual discourse and its emphasis on difference.

A few years later, [39] tackled similar concerns from a different angle. Here, the author relates models to domain ontologies, and metamodels to upper (foundational) ontologies. In both cases, the author points out that other works also coincide in equating or relating domain ontologies and models, such as [19, 47], and upper ontologies with metamodels [34, 35].

It thus seems that ontologies and models, despite being often presented as different technologies, are not that different after all. This is compatible with our experience when, in 2006, we "extracted" a domain ontology for software development methodologies [22] from an existing model of the same domain [56] with little effort. Apparently, the same representation could be easily cast as either a software engineering model or a domain ontology; this made us realise that ontological thinking may be applicable to software engineering as a fruitful contribution.

3   Using Ontologies

Previous sections have described ontologies, models, and the relationships between them, focussing on differences and similarities. At the end of the last section, I concluded that ontologies and models are not too different, and that, for this reason, bringing over ontological thinking into software engineering should be feasible. In this section, I explore three major areas where ontologies have proven useful to software engineering over the last few years: philosophical grounding, domain modelling and standardisation.

3.1   For Philosophical Grounding

It is interesting to observe how software engineering has focussed so much in representing reality, but invested so little in understanding the implications of these representations [46, 77]. Often, we make representational choices without being too conscious of the consequences, and some choices are never made because we cannot even think of them. Philosophy, however, has been dealing with the issue of representing reality for some time, and can help. Thus, the philosophical grounding of modelling has become the theme of some recent works in software engineering, in which ontologies (especially upper) play an important role.

My colleagues and I have devoted some time to searching for answers to questions such as "What are conceptual models made of?", "What do classes in class models actually represent?" or "What is the relationship between conceptual models, mental models and physical reality?" [46, 77]. Take, for example, the second question. Assuming that classes in class models represent categories of things, often called "universals" in philosophy, do they stand for universals-as-they-are or rather universals-as-we-know-them? In other words, do classes directly represent things in the world (ontological, direct representation) or do they represent mental concepts, which in turn represent things in the world (epistemic, mediated representation)? If the latter, and assuming that mental concepts may be different from an individual to the next, how are we sure that a class in a model stands for the "right" concept? How do we eliminate subjectivity and ambiguity so that a shared understanding is achieved?

This line of reasoning has also been used to analyse specific aspects of modelling, such as whole/part relationships in object-oriented models [41, 73, 74] or the UML itself [72]. In [41], the authors characterize whole/part relationships by ontological analysis and describe a number of primary (necessary, Boolean) and secondary (classificatory, not necessarily Boolean) characteristics of these relationships. In [73, 74], the authors continue to differentiate resultant and emergent properties by using Bunge's ontology [10, 11]; a resultant property is a property of an aggregate that is a direct result of properties of its parts (the whole equals the sum of its parts), whereas an emergent property of an aggregate is one that is not provided by any properties of its parts, but rather emerges from their interaction (the whole is greater than the sum of its parts). For example, a car engine is an aggregate of individual mechanical parts: the engine has a resultant "Weight" property, directly obtained from its members' properties, as well as an emergent "Peak Power" property, which materialises from the interactions of its members rather than being contributed directly by the members' properties. The authors in [73, 74] conclude that an aggregate (the "whole" in a whole/part relationship) must possess at least a resultant and an emergent property; otherwise, it would not be a true aggregate.

A similar ontological analysis based on the Bunge-Wand-Weber approach [78] has been carried out by [72] on the UML itself, resulting in a comprehensive set of recommendations to enhance UML. Some of the improvement areas include:

- Distinguishing between physically impossible and humanly disallowed events.
- Achieving better separation between the description of the domain and the specification of the system.
- Introducing additional modelling primitives to avoid overloading, i.e., the fact that some existing modelling constructs are used for several different purposes.

Precisely, ontological analysis has been especially useful to explicitly clarify and solve some obscure areas of modelling. For example, it has been long known that the "is-a" construct in modelling was being used with little rigour to represent very different semantics; in fact, [32] discusses the problem of "ISA overloading" back in 1998, and proposes an initial framework to avoid it. We have observed that the problem is compounded by the fact that the copula *to be* in English, very much like in most other Indo-European languages, is extremely overloaded with meaning. We have identified at least five senses in which the verb *to be* is regularly used in the modelling literature:

- **Existence**, by which something is said to exist, e.g., "There is a person".
- **Identity**, by which two entities are said to be the same, e.g.,"Isabel is my wife".
- **Predication**, by which a property is associated to an entity, e.g., "Isabel is tall".
- **Classification**, by which an entity is assigned to a type or class, e.g., "Isabel is a person".
- **Generalisation**, by which a type or class is said to be subsumed by a more abstract one, e.g., "A person is a living being".

In modern-day object oriented languages, existence of an entity is conveyed by the existence of the corresponding object; identity is not conveyed but delegated to the real-world entity; predication is easily conveyed through attribute values; classification is conveyed through the object's "instance-of" relationship towards its class; and generalisation is conveyed through generalisation/specialisation relationships between classes. Thus, I do not see any problem with "is-a" overloading today as long as a well-defined language is used that supports object identification, attribute values, instantiation relationships and generalisation/specialisation relationships as separate modelling primitives.

Ontological reasoning is sometimes confronted with linguistic or epistemic thinking, especially when discussing alternative ways of representing. In [5], for example, "logical" and "physical" representations are described: when we say that a particular book object in a library management system *is a book*, we are using a logical representation; when we say that this object *is an object*, we are using a physical representation. As discussed by [23], physical models represent ontologically, using concepts from what we have called upper or foundational ontologies, such as "Object". Contrarily, logical models represent epistemically, using concepts from what we have called domain ontologies, such as "Book". Although some authors insist that physical and logical modelling (sometimes confusingly named linguistic and ontological modelling, respectively, such as in [6]) are orthogonal manners of representing the same reality, it is easily seen that they are not, and in fact logical models conform to physical models, very much like domain ontologies conform to upper ontologies, and therefore a linear (rather than orthogonal) chain of models arises as proposed by [23].

An additional area where ontological thinking has been used in software engineering is that of language development. ConML is a conceptual modelling language designed for users with no previous exposure to information technologies and especially oriented towards domains in the humanities and social sciences [20, 48]. Although ConML superficially resembles UML, it contains some aspects that are worth mentioning. One of them is that of symmetric unary associations. Most associations are binary (i.e., they link two types together) or even higher-arity, but some are unary, which link a type back to itself. Of these, some entail an asymmetric relation between the instances they connect, whereas others establish a symmetric relation. UML and other conventional languages provide no support to model this latter kind of associations, despite being extremely common in real life: for example, a place and its neighbouring places, a person and his/her spouse, an author and his/her co-authors, a mathematical function and its inverse, an archaeological-site and all those others that are visible from it. Since these associations involve a single role (for both "ends") attached to a single class, and UML requires that every association end attached to a type has a different qualified name, these associations cannot be expressed in UML. The solution adopted by ConML is straightforward, namely allowing for associations with a single "end" [48 clause 5.6.9], and its novelty does not reside so much in the adopted solution as in the detection of the need and the insight to differentiate between symmetric and asymmetric unary associations.

Also in relation to ConML, ontological thinking allowed us to improve the usual treatment of null semantics that is found in most languages. Usually, "null" means no data, but no distinction is made between ontological and epistemic reasons for this absence. For example, if the "Name" column in a "Persons" table contains "null" for a particular row, does this mean that this person lacks a name (ontological absence) or rather that we do not know it (epistemic absence)? This is easy to determine for some properties, which by nature cannot be ontologically absent (e.g., "Age" in the above mentioned table), but impossible for others. For this reason, ConML uses *null* to indicate ontological absence of information (i.e., "this data does not exist") and *unknown* to indicate epistemic absence of information (i.e., "this data exists but we do not know about it") [44 Problem 5, 48 clause 5.6.8]. This allows for more precise semantics and a better representation of the domain.

3.2   As Domain Models

Regarding the second area of ontology use in software engineering, it is worth noting that a number of domain-specific models have been published as the result of consensus building in particular areas of discourse. Some examples include the Semantics of Business Vocabulary and Business Rules (SBVR) [71], which focuses on "documenting the semantics of business vocabularies and business rules for the exchange of business vocabularies and business rules among organizations and between software tools"; or the International Council of Museums (ICOM) International Committee for Documentation (CIDOC) Conceptual Reference Model (CIDOC CRM) [13, 52], which "provides definitions and a formal structure for describing the implicit and explicit concepts and relationships used in cultural heritage documentation"; or the Cultural Heritage Abstract Reference Model (CHARM) [25, 51]. Models like these are highly specialised in a technical area, have been created after more or less elaborate processes of consensus building among experts in the field, are published to a wide audience for shared reference, and often are provided in a machine-readable format that may allow automated processing by computer. Therefore, and according to our discussion in previous sections, they qualify as domain ontologies. Whether actual ontological thinking has been used to construct these models is sometimes difficult to say, either because this fact is not captured in the published documentation or because of the blur between ontologies and conceptual modelling that we have previously described. Some of these models, however, explicitly mention the fact that they are conceived as ontologies; for example, ISO 21127:2014 [52], the standard version of CIDOC CRM, states in the Introduction that "ISO 21127 is an ontology for cultural heritage information".

The field of software engineering itself has also been described through a domain ontology, at least partially, by e.g. [22], which is strongly based on the ISO/IEC 24744 [56] standard "Software Engineering – Metamodel for Development Methodologies".

Having a published, shared ontology of a domain can be enormously useful in software engineering, especially in situations where a software system is to be built in a specific domain. First of all, the domain ontology provides a readily available and common vocabulary and conceptualization for the communication during requirements elicitation and analysis. Despite no empirical studies have been carried out about this as far as I know, our experience is that software developers learn about a domain much faster and make fewer mistakes when supported by a domain ontology rather than mere input and discussion with domain experts.

Secondly, the domain ontology can be used as a starting point on which to develop the system's domain model, along the lines proposed by domain-driven design (DDD) [17]. Usually, systems cover only a specific area of a domain, and often in a manner that is highly particular to the customer of future users; this means that, whatever ontology is taken as a base, it will likely have to be "pruned" and refined. The degree to which domain ontologies support extension and tailoring is highly variable, this being a factor with a large impact on the applicability of a domain ontology to the practice of software engineering (see below). Some kinds of systems go one step beyond and, instead of being based on a particular ontology, assume that there will be an ontology serving as conceptual basis for the processes that take place inside, but that this ontology is not fixed. These systems model the concept of ontology as part of the system's conceptual model; it is the case, for example, of agent-based systems developed by using the FAME Agent-Oriented Modelling Language (FAML) [8]. In FAML, "Ontology" is a language primitive which, together with others such as "Agent" or "Role", allows the system developer to organize a community of agents that exchange information in terms of an ontology, but leave the specific contents of the ontology open to be dynamically evolvable at run time. In other words, under FAML, ontologies are not constructed in design-time and then used in run-time; rather, they are constructed, used and even dynamically re-constructed at run-time.

Thirdly, the domain ontology can be used as a reference model for the interchange of information between systems. Even if the system is not built according to the ontology, it may be designed so that it can import and/or export data that conforms to it, thus enhancing its interoperability. Some domain ontologies, in fact, are heavily oriented towards this, such as CIDOC CRM, which is described in [13] as intended to "provide the 'semantic glue' needed to mediate between different sources of cultural heritage information".

Some remarks are worth about the extension and tailoring of domain ontologies. Although the knowledge captured by a domain ontology is supposed to be shared, it sometimes happens that certain users of the ontology wish to alter specific aspects to suit their particular views on reality, accommodate technical constrains, or simply add detail to an abstract conceptualization. As we mentioned above, the degree to which different ontologies cater for extension and tailoring varies greatly. Some, such as CHARM [50], are explicitly conceived as abstract reference models, and *must* be extended before they are used through a series of well documented extension guidelines [49]. The fact that these ontologies are expressed in an explicit and documented language contributes to the ease of extension, since formal support makes it easier to establish the extension rules and validate whether an ontology is a true extension of the base one or simply a different ontology. As a counterexample, CIDOC CRM [52] is expressed in a language that is not named, described or documented, which makes extension difficult and, what is worse, makes it impossible to verify whether a CIDOC CRM-looking ontology is a true extension of the standard or not.

3.3   For Standardisation of Software Engineering

The third and last area of use of ontologies in software engineering is concerned with the field of software engineering itself. Practice in this field is varied and colourful, including approaches that range from the very rigorous of formal methods and high-ceremony methodologies to the hacker ethics of some agile approaches and "extreme" styles. At different points along this spectrum, different standardisation organizations have been working to produce guidelines and recommendations that may help the community to improve the ways in which we develop software systems. A good example is the SWEBOK ontology [65], based on the Software Engineering Body of Knowledge (SWEBOK), initially developed by the IEEE Computer Society and then made into an international standard as ISO/IEC TR 19759:2005 [57]. Another interesting case is that of the International Organization for Standardization (ISO), Joint Technical Committee 1, Sub-Committee 7 (JTC1/SC7), named "Software and systems engineering". This subcommittee has been working since 1987 in the "standardization of processes, supporting tools and supporting technologies for the engineering of software products and systems". ISO JTC1/SC7 has produced a number of standards in the areas of process lifecycles, process assessment, system architecture, open distributed processing, methodologies, testing or user documentation. Unfortunately, different standards, especially when coming from different working groups, tend to use a different conceptualization of the software engineering field, very often overlapping but incompatible [40]. For example, ISO/IEC 12207 "Software life cycle processes" [54] and ISO/IEC 15504

"Process assessment" [53] use substantially different conceptualizations of what a software process is; this is remarkable, given the fact that 15504 is supposed to establish a manner in which processes such as those defined by 12207 are to be assessed. In some cases, even standards coming out of the same working group present noticeable differences in their conceptualization; it is the case, for example, of ISO/IEC 15288 "System life cycle processes" [55] and the previously mentioned ISO/IEC 12207, which present very different views on how processes are organized and composed of smaller units. These discrepancies between standards make interoperation and communication very difficult.

To mitigate this, and after the problem had been identified and described by several key actors [40, 63], ISO JTC1/SC7 initiated a study group in 2012 with the aim to "evaluate the feasibility of preparing an ontology (a conceptual model) of the domains of interest of SC7 and its standards". After some exploratory work, this group proposed that the major challenged to be tackled was to provide a solution to the ongoing tension between standardisation and customisation. In other words:

- standards already exist and are being actively applied by industry, so they should not be changed arbitrarily;
- at the same time, reconciling differences necessarily means that somehow standards must change.

The proposed solution was based on the idea of the gradual refinement of models, already employed for CHARM [24]. According to this idea, a definitional elements ontology (DEO) would be created to work as a very abstract representation of all the SC7 concerns and concepts. The DEO would be so abstract that it could not be applied straight away; it would need to be refined into a configured definitional ontology (CDO) whenever is needed through a set of well-defined mechanisms, such as removal of unwanted areas or extension with new concepts [42]. CDOs can be also "chained" an arbitrary number of levels by further refining a CDO into a more concrete CDO, in order to add detail in a piecemeal fashion, often to match the organizational and operational needs of the community [45]. For example, a CDO could be created from SC7's DEO for each of the major scope areas in which SC7 works; from these first-level CDOs, each working group could derive its own particular CDO, and even a more specific CDO could be constructed for each family of standards when needed. Finally, a standard domain ontology (SDO) is an instance of a CDO that suits the needs of a particular standard, providing its conceptual foundation.

The study group proposed a proof-of-concept DEO to SC7 in late 2014, consisting of 26 classes plus associations, which are strongly based on ISO/IEC 24744 [56] and related work.

4   Outlook

In the previous sections I have described ontologies and ontological thinking from the perspective of software engineering, and in particular in relation to modelling and meta-modelling. Although ontologies have been introduced in the software engineering field for some time now, and are being effectively used for some purposes, there are still a number of areas where much work is to be done. The hybridisation of the two fields (ontologies and software engineering, see Sect. 1) also poses new challenges. This is particularly so in the area of philosophical grounding (Sect. 3.1), where specific aspects of upper ontologies are being re-examined and questioned in recent works, such as those about physical vs. logical modelling [16], alternative modelling primitives [37], or the notion of identity [42]. This is a complex and difficult area of research where very few studies exist with a strong empirical or logical backing, and for this reason more advances are to be expected in the near future.

In the domain modelling and standardisation areas (Sects. 3.2 and 3.3), in turn, the major challenge resides in finding a suitable manner to alleviate the tension between the need for standardisation and that for customisation. The proposal from the ISO JTC1/SC7 study group, described in Sect. 3.3, is being tested in the field and will hopefully produce results in the next few years. Other approaches may also be proposed. Also in this area and connected to the previous, a significant challenge is that of consensus building. Since an ontology working as shared domain model, especially if it is to be a standard, is supposed to be accepted by a large community, agreement must be reached on what this model contains and how it represents reality. Although this is primarily a social rather than technical issue, ontology and modelling technologies must be developed so that they can accommodate the incremental construction of models and exploratory developments as required by this situation.

In conclusion, ontologies have contributed very valuable insights to the theory and practice of software engineering, especially in the subfield of conceptual modelling. But they have also created a new area of inquiry, bringing up new questions and old problems that will take long to settle.

Acknowledgements. Thank you to Brian Henderson-Sellers for the revision of a draft of this work and for his contributions to the ideas presented here.

References

1. Ackoff, R.L.: From data to wisdom. J. Appl. Syst. Anal. **16**, 3–9 (1989)
2. Ashburner, M., Ball, C.A., Blake, J.A., Botstein, D., Butler, H., Cherry, J.M., Davis, A.P., Dolinski, K., Dwight, S.S., Eppig, J.T., Harris, M.A., Hill, D.P., Issel-Tarver, L., Kasarskis, A., Lewis, S., Matese, J.C., Richardson, J.E., Ringwald, M., Rubin, G.M., Sherlock, G.: Gene ontology: tool for the unification of biology. Nat. Genet. **25**, 25–29 (2000)
3. Atkinson, C.: Supporting and applying the UML conceptual framework. In: Bézivin, J., Muller, P.-A. (eds.) UML 1998. LNCS, vol. 1618, pp. 21–36. Springer, Heidelberg (1999). doi:10.1007/978-3-540-48480-6_3
4. Atkinson, C., Gutheil, M., Kiko, K.: On the relationship of ontologies and models. In: Proceedings of the 2nd International Workshop on Meta-Modelling (WoMM). LNI 96, Karlsruhe, Germany, pp. 47–60 (2006)
5. Atkinson, C., Kühne, T.: Rearchitecting the UML infrastructure. ACM Trans. Model. Comput. Simul. **12**(4), 290–321 (2002)
6. Atkinson, C., Kühne, T.: Model-driven development: a metamodeling foundation. IEEE Softw. **20**(5), 36–41 (2003)

7. Berners-Lee, T., Hendler, J., Lassila, O.: The semantic web. Sci. Am. **284**, 29–37 (2001)
8. Beydoun, G., Low, G., Henderson-Sellers, B., Mouratidis, H., Gomez-Sanz, J.J., Pavon, J., Gonzalez-Perez, C.: FAML: a generic metamodel for MAS development. IEEE Trans. Softw. Eng. **35**(6), 841–863 (2009)
9. Bézivin, J.: On the unification power of models. Softw. Syst. Model. **4**(2), 171–188 (2005)
10. Bunge, M.: Treatise on Basic Philosophy - Ontology I: The Furniture of the World, vol. 3. Reidel, Boston (1977)
11. Bunge, M.: Treatise on Basic Philosophy - Ontology II: A World of Systems, vol. 4. Reidel, Boston (1979)
12. Castel, F.: Ontological computing. Commun. ACM **45**(2), 29–30 (2002)
13. CIDOC. The CIDOC Conceptual Reference Model (web site) (2011). http://www.cidoc-crm.org/. Accessed 26 Nov 2012
14. Coleman, D., Arnold, P., Bodoff, S., Dollin, C., Gilchrist, H., Hayes, F., Jeremaes, P.: Object-Oriented Development: The Fusion Method. Prentice-Hall, Englewood Cliffs (1994)
15. Corcho, O., Fernández-López, M., Gómez-Pérez, A.: Ontological engineering: principles, methods, tools and languages. In: Ruiz González, F., Calero, C., Piattini, M. (eds.) Ontologies for Software Engineering and Software Technology, pp. 1–48. Springer, Heidelberg (2006)
16. Eriksson, O., Henderson-Sellers, B., Ågerfalk, P.J.: Ontological and linguistic metamodelling revisited: a language use approach. Inf. Softw. Technol. **55**(12), 2099–2124 (2013)
17. Evans, E.: Domain-Driven Design: Tackling Complexity in the Heart of Software. Addison-Wesley Professional, Boston (2003)
18. Favre, J.-M.: Foundations of meta-pyramids: languages vs. metamodels - Episode II: story of thotus the baboon. In: Bézivin, J., Heckel, R. (eds.) Language Engineering for Model-Driven Software Development, Dagstuhl Seminar Proceedings, 04101. IBFI, Dagstuhl (2005)
19. Gašević, D., Kaviani, N., Hatala, M.: On metamodeling in megamodels. In: Engels, G., Opdyke, B., Schmidt, Douglas C., Weil, F. (eds.) MODELS 2007. LNCS, vol. 4735, pp. 91–105. Springer, Heidelberg (2007). doi:10.1007/978-3-540-75209-7_7
20. Gonzalez-Perez, C.: A conceptual modelling language for the humanities and social sciences. In: Rolland, C., Castro, J., Pastor, O. (eds.) Sixth International Conference on Research Challenges in Information Science (RCIS), pp. 396–401. IEEE Computer Society (2012)
21. Gonzalez-Perez, C., Henderson-Sellers, B.: A representation-theoretical analysis of the OMG modelling suite. In: The 4th International Conference on Software Methodologies, Tools and Techniques, 28–30 September 2005. Frontiers in Artificial Intelligence and Applications 129. IOS Press, Amsterdam, pp. 252–262 (2005)
22. Gonzalez-Perez, C., Henderson-Sellers, B.: An ontology for software development methodologies and endeavours. In: Ruiz González, F., Calero, C., Piattini, M. (eds.) Ontologies for Software Engineering and Software Technology, pp. 123–151. Springer, Heidelberg (2006)
23. Gonzalez-Perez, C., Henderson-Sellers, B.: Modelling software development methodologies: a conceptual foundation. J. Syst. Softw. **80**(11), 1778–1796 (2007)
24. Gonzalez-Perez, C., Martín-Rodilla, P.: Integration of archaeological datasets through the gradual refinement of models. In: Giligny, F., et al. (eds.) 21st Century Archaeology: Concepts, Methods and Tools - Proceedings of the 42nd Annual Conference on Computer Applications and Quantitative Methods in Archaeology, pp. 193–204. Archaeopress (2015)
25. Gonzalez-Perez, C., Parcero Oubiña, C.: A conceptual model for cultural heritage definition and motivation. In: Zhou, M., et al. (eds.) Revive the Past: Proceeding of the 39th Conference on Computer Applications and Quantitative Methods in Archaeology, pp. 234–244. Amsterdam University Press (2011)

26. Graham, I., Henderson-Sellers, B., Younessi, H.: The OPEN Process Specification. The OPEN Series. Harlow. Addison-Wesley Longman, Essex (UK) (1997)
27. Gregor, S.: The Nature Of Theory In Information Systems. MIS Q. **30**(3), 611–642 (2006)
28. Gruber, T.: A translation approach to portable ontology specifications. Knowl. Acquisition **5**(2), 199–220 (1993)
29. Gruber, T.: Toward principles for the design of ontologies used for knowledge sharing? Int. J. Hum Comput Stud. **43**(5–6), 907–928 (1995)
30. Gruber, T.: Ontology. In: Liu, L., Özsu, M.T. (eds.) Encyclopedia of Database Systems. Springer, New York (2009)
31. Guarino, N.: Formal ontology, conceptual analysis and knowledge representation. Int. J. Hum Comput Stud. **43**(5–6), 625–640 (1995)
32. Guarino, N.: Some ontological principles for designing upper level lexical resources. In: Rubio, A., et al. (eds.) Proceedings of First International Conference on Language Resources and Evaluation, Granada (1998)
33. Guha, R.V., Lenat, D.B.: Cyc: a midterm report. In: Buchanan, B.G., Wilkins, D.C. (eds.) Readings in Knowledge Acquisition and Learning, pp. 839–866. Morgan Kaufmann, New York (1993)
34. Guizzardi, G.: Ontological Foundations for Structural Conceptual Models. University of Twente, The Netherlands (2005)
35. Guizzardi, G., Wagner, G.: On the ontological foundations of agent concepts. In: Grundspenkis, J., Kirikova, M. (eds.) CAiSE 2004 Workshops in Connection with The 16th Conference on Advanced Information Systems Engineering, pp. 265–279. Riga Technical University (2004)
36. Guizzardi, G., Wagner, G.: A unified foundational ontology and some applications of it in business modeling. In: Missikoff, M. (ed.) Enterprise Modelling and Ontologies for Interoperability, CEUR Workshop Proceedings, vol. 125. CEUR-WS.org (2004)
37. Guizzardi, G., Zamborlini, V.: Using a trope-based foundational ontology for bridging different areas of concern in ontology-driven conceptual modeling. Sci. Comput. Program. **86**, 417–443 (2014)
38. Heller, B., Herre, H.: Ontological categories in GOL. Axiomathes **14**(1), 57–76 (2004)
39. Henderson-Sellers, B.: Bridging metamodels and ontologies in software engineering. J. Syst. Softw. **84**(2), 301–313 (2011)
40. Henderson-Sellers, B.: Standards harmonization: theory and practice. Softw. Syst. Model. **11**(2), 153–161 (2012)
41. Henderson-Sellers, B., Barbier, F.: What is this thing called aggregation? In: TOOLS 29, May 1999. IEEE Computer Society (1999)
42. Henderson-Sellers, B., Eriksson, O., Ågerfalk, P.J.: On the need for identity in ontology-based conceptual modelling. In: Saeki, M., Kohler, H. (eds.) Proceedings of 11th Asia-Pacific Conference on Conceptual Modelling (APCCM 2015), CRPIT, Sydney, Australia, pp. 9–20 (2015)
43. Henderson-Sellers, B., Gonzalez-Perez, C.: Multi-level meta-modelling to underpin the abstract and concrete syntax for domain specific modelling languages. In: Reinhartz-Berger, I., et al. (eds.) Domain Engineering: Product Lines, Conceptual Models, and Languages, pp. 291–316. Springer, Heidelberg (2013)
44. Henderson-Sellers, B., Gonzalez-Perez, C., Eriksson, O., Ågerfalk, P.J., Walkerden, G.: Software modelling languages: a wish list. In: Gray, J., et al. (eds.) IEEE/ACM 7th International Workshop on Modeling in Software Engineering (MiSE). IEEE Computer Society (2015)

45. Henderson-Sellers, B., Gonzalez-Perez, C., McBride, T., Low, G.: An ontology for ISO software engineering standards: 1) Creating the infrastructure. Comput. Stand. Interfaces **36**(3), 563–576 (2014)

46. Henderson-Sellers, B., Gonzalez-Perez, C., Walkerden, G.: An application of philosophy in software modelling and future information systems development. In: Franch, X., Soffer, P. (eds.) CAiSE 2013. LNBIP, vol. 148, pp. 329–340. Springer, Heidelberg (2013). doi: 10.1007/978-3-642-38490-5_31

47. Hesse, W.: From conceptual models to ontologies. In: Delcambre, L., Kaschek, R.H., Mayr, H.C. (eds.) Dagstuhl Seminar on The Evolution of Conceptual Modeling. Schloss Dagstuhl, Dagstuhl (2008)

48. Incipit. ConML Technical Specification. Incipit, CSIC (2016). http://www.conml.org/Resources_TechSpec.aspx

49. Incipit. CHARM Extension Guidelines. Incipit, CSIC (2016). http://www.charminfo.org/Resources/Technical.aspx

50. Incipit. CHARM Web Site (web site) (2016). http://www.charminfo.org. Accesed 30 May 2016

51. Incipit. CHARM White Paper. Incipit, CSIC (2016). http://www.charminfo.org/Resources/Technical.aspx

52. ISO. Information and documentation – a reference ontology for the interchange of cultural heritage information. ISO 21127:2014 (2014)

53. ISO/IEC. Software Process Assessment - Part 1: Concepts and Vocabulary. ISO/IEC 15504-1:2004 (2004)

54. ISO/IEC. Systems and software engineering – software life cycle processes. ISO/IEC 12207:2008 (2008)

55. ISO/IEC. Systems and software engineering – system life cycle processes. ISO/IEC 15288:2008 (2008)

56. ISO/IEC. Software Engineering - Metamodel for Development Methodologies. ISO/IEC 24744:2004 (2014). http://www.iso.org/iso/home/store/catalogue_tc/catalogue_detail.htm?csnumber=62644

57. ISO/IEC. Software Engineering - Guide to the software engineering body of knowledge (SWEBOK). ISO/IEC TR 19759 (2015). http://www.iso.org/iso/home/store/catalogue_tc/catalogue_detail.htm?csnumber=67604

58. Katifori, A., Halatsis, C., Lepouras, G., Vassilakis, C., Giannopoulou, E.: Ontology visualization methods — a survey. ACM Comput. Surv. **39**(4), 10 (2007)

59. Kühne, T.: Clarifying matters of (meta-) modeling: an author's reply. Softw. Syst. Model. **5**(4), 395–401 (2006)

60. Kühne, T.: Matters of (meta-) modeling. Softw. Syst. Model. **5**(4), 369–385 (2006)

61. Martin, J., Odell, J.: Object-Oriented Analysis and Design. Prentice-Hall, Englewood Cliffs (1992)

62. Masolo, C., Borgo, S., Gangemi, A., Guarino, N., Oltramari, A.: Ontology Library. Laboratory For Applied Ontology - ISTC-CNR (2003). http://www.loa.istc.cnr.it/old/Papers/D18.pdf

63. McBride, T., Henderson-Sellers, B.: The Growing Need for Alignment, N5507. ISO/IEC JTC1 SC7 (2012)

64. Mellor, S.J., Balcer, M.: Executable UML: A Foundation for Model-Driven Architectures. Addison-Wesley, Boston (2002)

65. Mendes, O., Abran, A.: Software engineering ontology: a development methodology. Metrics News. **9**, 68–76 (2004)

66. Miller, G.A., Beckwith, R., Fellbaum, C., Gross, D., Miller, K.: WordNet: an on-line lexical database. Int. J. Lexicogr. **3**, 235–244 (1990)

67. Newell, A.: The knowledge level. Artif. Intell. **18**(1), 87–127 (1982)
68. OMG. MDA Guide, omg/2003-06-01. Object Management Group (2003)
69. OMG. Unified Modelling Language Specification: Infrastructure. formal/05-07-05 (2006)
70. OMG. OMG Meta Object Facility (MOF) Core Specification. formal/2013-06-01 (2013). http://www.omg.org
71. OMG. Semantics of Business Vocabulary and Business Rules (SBVR). formal/2015-05-07 (2015). http://www.omg.org/spec/SBVR/
72. Opdahl, A.L., Henderson-Sellers, B.: Ontological evaluation of the UML using the Bunge-Wand-Weber model. Softw. Syst. Model. **1**(1), 43–67 (2002)
73. Opdahl, A.L., Henderson-Sellers, B., Barbier, F.: Erratum to "ontological analysis of whole-part relationships in OO models". Inf. Softw. Technol. **43**(9), 577 (2001)
74. Opdahl, A.L., Henderson-Sellers, B., Barbier, F.: Ontological analysis of whole-part relationships in OO models. Inf. Softw. Technol. **43**(6), 387–399 (2001)
75. Partridge, C.: A Couple of Meta-ontological Choices for Ontological Architectures. LADSEB-CNR, Padova (2002)
76. Partridge, C.: Business Objects: Re-Engineering for Re-Use. 2nd edn. The BORO Centre, 412 p. (2005)
77. Partridge, C., Gonzalez-Perez, C., Henderson-Sellers, B.: Are conceptual models concept models? In: Ng, W., Storey, Veda C., Trujillo, Juan C. (eds.) ER 2013. LNCS, vol. 8217, pp. 96–105. Springer, Heidelberg (2013). doi:10.1007/978-3-642-41924-9_9
78. Rosemann, M., Green, P.: Developing a meta model for the Bunge-Wand-Weber ontological constructs. Inf. Syst. **27**(2), 75–91 (2002)
79. Rumbaugh, J., Blaha, M., Premerlani, W., Eddy, F., Lorensen, W.: Object-Oriented Modeling and Design. Prentice-Hall, Englewood Cliffs (1991)
80. Schneider, L.: How to build a foundational ontology. In: Günter, A., Kruse, R., Neumann, B. (eds.) KI 2003. LNCS, vol. 2821, pp. 120–134. Springer, Heidelberg (2003). doi: 10.1007/978-3-540-39451-8_10
81. Selic, B.: The pragmatics of model-driven development. IEEE Softw. **20**(5), 19–25 (2003)
82. Simons, P., Cameron, R.: A short glossary of metaphysics. In: Le Poidevin, R., et al. (eds.) Routledge Companion to Metaphysics, pp. 578–599. Routledge, London (2009)
83. Stanford University. Stanford Encyclopedia of Philosophy (2015). http://plato.stanford.edu/. Accessed 23 July 2015
84. Uschold, M.: Where are the semantics in the semantic web? AI Mag. **24**(3), 25–36 (2003)
85. World Wide Web Consortium. SKOS Simple Knowledge Organization System Primer (2009). http://www.w3.org/TR/2009/NOTE-skos-primer-20090818/
86. World Wide Web Consortium. OWL 2 Web Ontology Language (2012). http://www.w3.org/TR/2012/REC-owl2-overview-20121211/

Empirical, Human-Centered Evaluation of Programming and Programming Language Constructs: Controlled Experiments

Stefan Hanenberg[(⊠)]

Paluno – The Ruhr Instistute for Software Technology,
University of Duisburg-Essen, Essen, Germany
stefan.hanenberg@uni-due.de

Abstract. While the application of empirical methods has a long tradition in domains such as performance evaluation, the application of empirical methods with human subjects in order to evaluate the usability of programming techniques, programming language constructs or whole programming languages is relatively new (or, at least, running such studies is becoming more common). Despite the urgent need for such usability studies, few researchers are well-versed in such techniques, certainly when compared to the large number of researchers inventing new programming techniques or formal approaches. The main goal of this text is to introduce empirical methods for evaluating programming language constructs, with a strong focus on quantitative methods. The paper concludes with by explaining how and why a series of controlled experiments were gradually designed to study the usability of type systems.

1 Introduction

Over the decades, a number of researchers and authors have argued about the need for empirical studies in software science[1] in general and quantitative, human-centered studies in particular (see [14,37,38,44,46]). While the common statement of these authors is, that there is a lack of empirical knowledge in general, the domain of programming and programming language construction is no exception (see for example [15,41])[2]: While new programming language constructs appeared over the last decades, it is unclear (or at least not explicitly documented) which of those constructs are actually usable by programmers and

---

[1] According to Hanenberg [14] the phrase *software science* is being used in order to describe the research related to software artifacts in general. While the term *software engineering* is used much more often, especially the programming language community or people doing performance measurements feel that this term does not adequately describe their domains. We think that the term software science, although originally used by Halstead [12] for something different, is more appropriate to describe the whole domain of software-related research.

[2] Sheil called the study of programming as practiced by computer science even '*an unholy mixture of mathematics, literary criticism, and folklore.*' 1 [37, p. 102].

J. Cunha et al. (Eds.): GTTSE 2015, LNCS 10223, pp. 45–72, 2017.
DOI: 10.1007/978-3-319-60074-1_3

which ones are not. The study by Kaijanaho showed even that between 1973 and 2012 only 22 studies were performed that analyzed the usability of programming language and that meet basic evidence standards (see [22]).

And these days, the number of new language constructs in main stream programming languages seems to increase even more while there is typically no evaluation of such language constructs. For example lambda expressions were just recently added to languages such as Java or C++. However, it is not clear whether such constructs are helpful to developers or whether they do harm on software development. Of course, there are a number of people that argue for or against such constructs. In the case of lambda expressions, people in favor for functional programming language argue that there was always the need for such constructs. Or people in favor for object-oriented languages that provided lambda expressions since decades (such as for example Smalltalk programmers) see in such a trend the confirmation that such language constructs should have been in these main stream languages since years.[3]

However, the general problem of this line of argumentation is that software has been written with previous versions of these main stream languages before. I.e., there is no obvious need for such new language constructs. Of course, it is possible that such new constructs make it easier to write software, i.e. it is possible that the developers' performance is better with such new constructs. However, it is also possible that the developer performance will be reduced:

1. It could be possible that the semantics of the construct is not clear to developers. In such a case, there is a need to think about ways to improve the training for these constructs by giving better documentation, examples, etc.
2. It could be the case that developers use the construct frequently in situations where it was not intended to be used and where the resulting software becomes harder to write. Again in such a situation there is the need to think about different ways to communicate under what circumstances the language construct should be used.
3. It could be possible that the construct's semantics is so complex that developers inherently either misunderstand it or do errors whenever they use it. In such a situation it is at least worth to think about whether the introduction of the language construct into the language was really an improvement of the language.

Of course, it is also possible that the new language construct actually does help developers. But without having evidence that at least under certain circumstances a language construct is able to help developers, there is the risk that new languages or new language constructs finally harm developers and the software they write.

Unfortunately, the question of whether or not a language construct is actually usable by developers requires a different perspective on the research process than

---

[3] It should be noted that just recently a study appeared which was not able to reveal a measurable benefit of lambda expressions in C++. Instead, the study showed at least for non-professional programmers a measurable disadvantage (see [45]).

what's mostly practiced and taught today. While computer scientists are quite well-trained in formal methods as well as in mathematical reasoning on formal methods, the introduction of empirical methods into the field software science is still not main-stream.[4] Additionally, the field of empirical methods is quite large: there is a huge number of different quantitative and qualitative methods. In order to apply these methods, there is a need to get substantial knowledge about them.

This text gives a general introduction into the field of empirical studies in software science and focuses on quantitative methods in general and controlled experiments in particular. The text consists of two parts. The first part gives a general introduction into the idea of human-centered studies and introduces two concrete studies that apply such kind of studies, the second part describes a series of controlled trials on the programming language constructs type system.

For the first part, we introduce the general idea of empirical studies in comparison to alternative approaches (Sect. 2). Then, we introduce the basic concepts of human-centered controlled experiments including experimental designs, etc. in Sect. 3. Afterwards, Sect. 4 illustrates two examples for experiments following the idea of human-centered studies. In the second part (Sect. 5), we give a more detailed description of one experiment series on type systems in order to illustrate the process of knowledge gathering using human-centered controlled experiments. Finally, we summarize and conclude this work in Sect. 6.

2   An Short Introduction into Empirical Studies in Software Science

While the phrases 'empirical studies' or 'empirical approaches' in software science are nowadays quite often used, the meaning of such phrases is not completely precise. Hence, we start with a short description of research methods in software science, followed by a description of different human-centered studies.

2.1   A Classification of Research Methods in Software Science

The scientific approaches in software science can be classified in the following ways (se Fig. 1):

- **Classical approaches:** Classical approaches are based on mathematical and logical reasoning. Examples for such approaches are the formal reasoning on type systems in programming language design (see for example [32]).
- **Stochastic approaches:** Stochastic approaches are similar to the classical approaches, but have an underlying stochastic model upon which mathematical/logical reasoning is performed. Such approaches can be for example often found in the field of dependability of computer systems (see for example [26]).

---

[4] Again, to get an impression of how less it is main-stream: according to Kaijanaho the number of randomized controlled trials on human-factors comparative evaluation of language features up to 2012 was 22 (see [22, p. 143]).

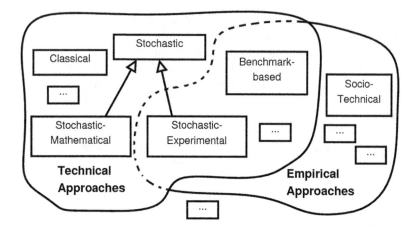

Fig. 1. Categorization of research approaches (taken from [14]

- **Empirical approaches:** In contrast to the mathematical/logical approach, empirical approaches make use of observations. I.e., the insights, which are the result of research, are based on occuring phenomena.
  - **Benchmark-based / Stochastic-experimental approaches:** Stochastic-experimental and benchmark-based approaches are both based on observing technical entities. A benchmark-based approach tests one unit (programming language, virtual machine, etc.) against some pre-defined elements (such as programs). Likewise, a stochastic-experimental approach checks a stochastic statement in an experimental way (see for example [10] for examples of benchmark-based approaches).
  - **Human-centered (socio-technical) approaches:** In contrast to all previously mentioned approaches, human-centered (or socio-technical) approaches try to achieve progress by using humans as part of the research approach. I.e. the human-centered approach either directly observes humans or considers the results of things produced by humans (examples for this approach will be explained in more detail throughout this paper).

2.2 Different Human-Centered Approaches

Although the phrase human-centered approach sounds like a unique approach, it is a term that subsumes a number of different approaches where all have in common that they either directly observe the behavior of humans or they study the result of some human behavior. Both kinds of approaches are based on observations, but different things are observed:

- **Behavioral Studies:** When the behavior of humans is the focus of a research method, the researcher is interested in what people are actually doing. If for example a researcher is interested in the way how people are using a certain technique, they observe humans while they are using the technique. Under what situation the technique is being used plays in such studies rather a minor role.

- **Product Studies:** When the result of humans' behavior is observed, it means that something that is produced by humans is analyzed. This typically means a concrete piece of software that is analyzed, or a concrete programming task performed by developers, or the result of some questionnaire given to developers.

While the previous classification distinguishes between what is being observed and analyzed, it does not say how this observation is being practiced.

In empirical research, it is common practice to distinguish between two different kinds of approaches: the qualitative and the quantitative approaches. Unfortunately, both term are not completely well-defined. The following tries to articulate how both terms are mostly used.

- **Quantitative Approaches:** Quantitative approaches are based on measurements that can be directly gathered from observations and which can be directly expressed in quantities. The analysis of this data is performed using corresponding statistical methods.
- **Qualitative Approaches:** Qualitative approaches are based on data collections that cannot (necessarily) be expressed in terms of quantities.

The most typical example of a quantitative study is a controlled experiment where a set of developers either uses a programming language A or a programming language B in order to solve a certain programming task. In such a scenario, a possible measurement is the development time required to solve the task. Literature such as by Wohlin et al. [46] or the paper by Ko et al. [25] describe how controlled experiments are performed in software science in general.[5]

In general, the idea of controlled experiments are closely related to the philosophical approach of the *critical rationalism* by Karl Popper [33] where a predefined hypothesis is being tested by corresponding trials. The controlled studies on type systems which are described later in this paper are examples of such quantitative studies.

A typical example for a qualitative study is the application of *grounded theory* by Glaser and Strauss [11], an approach that originates from the social sciences. Based on that, a data collection is performed by for example interviewing developers that are applying a certain technique. Then the researcher uses techniques called *open coding* and *memoing* that identify the key elements from the interviews. Afterwards (after some incremental steps) the researcher performs a *theoretical coding* that consists of formulating hypotheses to be integrated into a theory which is finally written up. The study by Hoda et al. [19] is a detailed description of applying grounded theory to software engineering in order to study self-organization in Agile teams.

---

[5] Additionally, the paper collection of Victor Basili by Boehm et al. [1] gives a larger set of examples about performed controlled trials.

In contrast to quantitative approaches, whose methods seem to be quite similar and at least related to controlled experiments, there is a large variety of different qualitative methods where grounded theory is just one among it. The paper by Seaman [35] gives a more detailed description of different data collection techniques using qualitative methods in software engineering.

Although the previous classification seemed to indicate that there is a very strict distinction between qualitative and quantitative approaches, it turns out that in software engineering it is often the case that a quantitative study still contains some qualitative elements: For example, if developers are asked to perform a simple modeling task, it is often the case that someone involved in the experiment checks whether the task has been fulfilled. Most often, even in such cases researchers speak about a quantitative, human-centered study, although at least to a certain extent qualitative elements are part of the study.

3   An Short Introduction into Controlled Experiments (with Human Subjects)

Before speaking about concrete experiment about programming languages, we need to introduce first the whole idea of defining and executing controlled experiments. This section explains the line of reasoning using controlled experiments and the basic terminology in controlled experiments and it sketches how experimenters actually define experiments.

3.1   Introduction into Hypotheses Testing

Controlled experiments can be directly motivated by the philosophy by Karl Popper [33]. According to this, a scientific statement should not only express a scientist's perspective or belief about a certain topic. Instead, the researcher should provide evidence that the statement actually holds, i.e. the statement should be backed up by more than just the researcher's personal conviction: *"Thus I may be utterly convinced of the truth of a statement; certain of the evidence of my perceptions; overwhelmed by the intensity of my experience: every doubt may seem to me absurd. But does this afford the slightest reason for science to accept my statement? Can any statement be justified by the fact that K. R. P. is utterly convinced of its truth? The answer is, 'No'"* [33, p. 24].

In order to provide such evidence, the starting point of controlled experiments is a *hypothesis*, i.e. a statement that can be tested by the researcher running the experiment, respectively researchers that doubt about the correctness of a given hypothesis they have in mind, or which they found in literature: *"The objectivity of scientific statements lies in the fact that they can be intersubjectively tested"* [33, p. 22].

According to Popper, a hypothesis is a testable all-quantified statement. This statement implies (i.e., predicts) a number of phenomena that can be observed.

Controlled experiments are a method to test such hypotheses. In general, the line of argumentation of controlled experiments is, that if a hypothesis predicts a certain phenomenon, but the experiment does not reveal the predicted phenomenon, the hypothesis is wrong.

The following Boolean expression reveals the logic of hypothesis testing:

$$((Hypothesis \rightarrow Observation) \wedge \neg Observation) \rightarrow \neg Hypothesis$$

While this general idea is quite easy and plausible, the application of controlled experiments in software science turns out to be not that trivial. The main reason for it is that developers (respectively the developers' behavior) can typically not be described by a Boolean formula and unfortunately different developers (typically) do not behave in absolutely the same way. And unfortunately, there is a large variation among developers. In the literature, it is often mentioned that developers can vary by the factor of 10, which is known as the 10x-problem [28] (although it should be mentioned that this factor 10 is not really the result of a detailed study so far, but just some kind of metaphor describing that there is a large difference between developer performance). The 10x problem describes in general that two comparable developers can differ in the time they require to solve a given problem by the factor 10: one developer might require 10 min while another one requires 100 min.

3.2 Basics of Experimentation

The following terms need to be known before going into details about concrete experiments (see [21] for a more detailed description):

- **Independent variable:** The independent variable is the thing to be tested. For example, if we want to compare a programming language A and a programming language B, the independent variable is the programming language. Of course, it is possible that there is more than one independent variable. For example, it is possible that an experiment has the independent variable 'programming language' and the independent variable 'IDE'.
- **Treatment:** A treatment is one specific setting of the independent variable. For example, the previously mentioned independent variable programming language has the two treatments programming language A and programming language B.
- **Dependent variable (also called response variable):** A dependent variable is the measurement being performed within the experiment. For example, if we want to compare the number of errors in language A and B, the dependent variable is the number of errors. In order to retrieve the dependent variable, a corresponding **measurement technique** is necessary, i.e. a description of the way of the measurement is performed.
- **Confounding factors:** The confounding factors are those parts of an experiment that (potentially) influence the experiment in an undesired way, i.e. that have an accidental influence on the dependent variable.
- **Null-Hypothesis / Alternative Hypothesis:** The null hypothesis is the hypothesis that is actually tested. The hypothesis (typically) says that under all treatments the dependent variable is the same, i.e. the null-hypothesis is a falsifiable statement about the relation between the dependent and the independent variable. For example, an experiment that tests the influence of

the programming language A and the language B on the number of errors states that the means of the dependent variable under the treatment A is the same as the mean under the treatment B: $\mu_A = \mu_B$. The alternative hypothesis is the negation of the null-hypothesis, i.e. for the given example it is $\mu_A \neq \mu_B$.

- **Threats to validity:** Threats to validity are concerns that potentially influence the experiment as a whole in an undesired way such as in the possible flawed conclusions drawn from the experiment. The threats to validity are documented by the experimenter in order to identify potential weaknesses in the experimental setup.

If a hypothesis is given, it is an experimenter's task to find an appropriate experimental design.

3.3 Experimental Designs

While there is a large variety of different experimental designs (see for example [23] among a large variety of literature from the behavioral sciences), experiments in software science just use a small number of different experimental design (see for example [21, 46]) that will be briefly introduced here. The reason for this small number of used designs is (probably) caused by the 10x-problem, because a large variation between subjects makes it hard to detect differences at all.

All of the mentioned designs are so-called randomized controlled trials, which means that there is a random assignment from subjects to the corresponding groups.

Each of the experimental designs comes with one or more analysis technique based on inference statistics, i.e. each experimental design determines the way how it can be analysed. The analysis techniques are the so-called *significance tests* which are applied to the combination of dependent and independent variable in order to determine whether (or not) the null-hypothesis holds. Each significance tests comes with a number of preconditions that need to be fulfilled.

Instead of giving a detailed description of the tests, we just mentioned the names of the tests to be applied. Details about the tests can be found in corresponding literature on experimental design (see for example [23]) and are implemented in standard statistical software such as SPSS[6] or R[7].

A summary of the experimental designs and the corresponding analysis techniques is given in Table 1.

One-Factor Design with Two Alternatives (AB-Between-Subject). An one-factor design with two alternatives is commonly called an AB-between-subject experiment. It is a randomized trial with one independent variable and two treatments. The subjects are randomly assigned to one of two groups and one treatment is assigned to each group. The design checks the hypothesis explained

---

[6] www.ibm.com/software/analytics/spss/.
[7] https://www.r-project.org/.

above, i.e. it checks whether the mean of the dependent variable under treatment A is the same as the mean under the treatment B. An AB-between-subject design is analyzed using a so-called t-test or a Mann-Whitney-U-test.

One-Factor Design with N Alternatives. A variation of the AB experiment is the one-factor design with N alternatives, i.e. the independent variable has n treatments. The subjects are assigned to one of the n groups. Typically, such a design is analyzed using a analysis of variance (ANOVA). Another alternative is to compare all groups individually with the previously mentioned t-test or U-test and do a correction of the alpha-error (such as the Bonferroni-correction). Another alternative is to run a so-called post-hoc test on an ANOVA that compares each alternative with one another.

Multi-Factor Designs. Multi-factor designs are applied whenever more than one independent variable needs to be tested. The most common case (and the easiest multi-factor design) is the 2×2 factor design. The 2×2 factor design is based on 2 independent variables, each with two treatments. The design requires 4 groups (one group for each combination of treatments of both independent variables). The tested hypothesis of a 2×2 design is, that neither the first factor nor the second factor influences the dependent variable. A 2×2 design is analyzed with a 2×2 ANOVA that additionally determines, whether there is an interaction between both factors, i.e. whether the combination of factors influences the dependent variable in a significant way.

Paired One-Factor Design (AB-Within-Subject Design). A paired one-factor design is given, whenever a single subject is measured on all treatments of an independent variable, i.e. the dependent variable is measured multiple times for a single subject (every time under a different treatment). The simplest design is the AB-within-subject design where one subject is measured for both treatments of the independent variable. An AB-within-subject design is typically counterbalanced, i.e. it consists of two groups. The first group measures a subject under the treatment A and then under the treatment B, the second group measures a subject first under treatment B and then under treatment A. An AB-within-subject design is analysed using a paired t-test or a Wilcoxon-test.

Paired One-Factor Design with N Alternatives. The paired one-factor design with N alternatives means that there are n treatments for the independent variable and the subject is measured under all alternatives. This design is typically analysed using a repeated-measures ANOVA.

AB-BA-Crossover Trial. The AB-BA-crossover trial is a special version of the AB-within-subject design. The grouping of subjects is the same as in a the AB-within-subject design with counterbalancing. However, the AB-BA-crossover trial explicitly takes into account that there are possible so-called carry-over effects when a subject switches from one treatment to the other. Such carry-over effects might be learning effects, etc. (see [36] for a detailed discussion of possible crossover effects and [43] for a more detailed description of such effects in one specific programming experiments). The analysis of an AB-BA crossover-trial is a combination of a non-paired t-tests (in order to check for the possible carry-over effect), and either a paired t-test (in case no carry-over -effects were found) or a non-paired t-test applied only to the first measurements.[8]

Table 1. Standard designs and corresponding analysis techniques

Design	Analysis technique
AB-Between-Subject	T-Test (U-Test)
One-Factor Design With N Alternatives	ANOVA
Multi-Factor-Designs	Multi-Factor ANOVA
Paired One-Factor Design (AB-Within-Subject Design)	Paired T-Test (Wilcoxon-Test)
Paired One-Factor Design with N Alternatives	Repeated-Measures ANOVA
AB-BA-Crossover Trial	T-Test

3.4 Analysis of Experiments, the Problem of Non-Significant Results

It has been previously stated that the significance tests check the hypothesis. However, this must be explained in more detail.

The significance checks the alpha error, i.e. the probability to reject the hypothesis although it is true. This approach is the standard approach in experimentation, although it should be mentioned that there are authors that criticize this focus on the alpha error (see [18]).

The resulting p-value is compared to a previously defined alpha-level, which is commonly accepted .05 in software science.[9] In case the p-value is less than .05, a significant difference has been found. Otherwise, the alpha-error it too high and the common interpretation is, that no significant difference has been found.

However, not finding a (significant) difference does not imply that there is no difference. Experimenters usually state that an experiment that does not reveal significant differences – experimenters call such experiments *null experiments* – has

---

[8] The corresponding non-parametric tests [5] are valid here, too, i.e. it is possible to analyse the crossover trial using a U-test and a Wilcoxon-test.

[9] The rather arbitrary choice of .05 is probably commonly used because it has been originally proposed by Fisher [8] although some other disciplines use a different alpha level.

failed for the following reason. As previously mentioned, experimenters in software science are aware of the 10x-problem, i.e. they typically assume that there is a large deviation among developers. However, a large deviation directly influences the statistical tests: the higher the deviation between two samples (assuming the same difference in means between both samples), the larger is the p-value for the comparison of equality between both samples. I.e. if the deviation is high enough, no difference will be detected. This implies that revealing no difference just means that the experiment was not able to reveal a difference – independent of whether there is or is not such a difference.

Experimenters are aware of this problem and consider this problem in the experimental design. One approach to address this problem is to increase the sample size. The other alternative is to enforce in an experiment a situation where the expected difference in means is higher (or experimenters choose a different experimental design that either reduces the deviation or whose analysis technique has a larger statistical power).

In addition to the p-value, experimenters are interested in the effect size (although it is not that often reported in experimental papers). For example, a typical effect size for the t-test is Cohen's D [4], which divides the difference in means of two samples by its standard deviation.

3.5   Experiment Design from the Experimenter's Perspective

As described in [17], experimenters try to reject a null-hypothesis, i.e. they try to design experiments explicitly in way that permits to reveal a difference between two treatments (under the assumption of an AB-experiment). Whether or not they are finally able to reveal such a difference depends on a number of choices.

- **Hypothesis:** It is quite usual that the experimenter himself needs to define the hypothesis to be tested. Unfortunately, it is quite common that new techniques in software science appear without a precise definition of the phenomena they imply. As a consequence, experimenters typically need to search on their own for situations where there might be differences between techniques to be tested and formulate a corresponding hypothesis.
- **Experimental setup:** Once a hypothesis has been found, experimenters need to define a scenario under which this hypothesis can be tested. This scenario consists of the programming tasks that could be given to subjects, additional documentation given to subjects, etc.
- **Experimental design:** Section 3.3 might have given the impression that the experimental design is directly implied by the hypothesis. However, this is not the case. Typically, experimenters need to ask themselves, whether subjects should be tested under multiple treatments. Additionally, in that phase experimenters ask themselves, whether some variables that potentially have an influence, should be explicitly considered as a separate factor, etc.
- **Measurement:** While the hypothesis already contains some description of measurements (such a hypothesis 'the number of errors increases using programming language A in comparison to B'), the experimenter has to define

how precisely the measurement needs to be done. For example, it might be possible that an error is a run-time error, a compile-time error, an error in the design of the program, a 'conceptual error' (misuse of a construct), etc.
- **Subjects:** Typically, the experimenter decides what subjects should be used. The choice of subjects probably has an influence on the experiment's results (for example, if arbitrary persons are chosen, it seems plausible that the deviation becomes even larger). Additionally, the experimenter decides how many subjects are required at least in the experiment and he needs to define the kind of training given to the subjects.

All of these choices depend on the expected effect size of the factors and the deviation among the subjects in the experiment – which is the reason why the experimenter runs a number of small-scale studies in the experiment design phase, so-called pilot trials.

4 Example Studies: Empirical Evaluations of Programming Languages

This section introduces two different studies that quantitatively evaluate programming languages or programming languages features from different perspectives: a code repository study that actually is based on all previously introduced ideas and a rather classical human-centered controlled trial.

4.1 Repository Study: Usage of the Programming Language Feature 'OptionalTyping' [39]

The study by Souza and Figueiredo is based on code repositories. The focus of the study is on type systems: it addresses the question, how in a programming language that provides optional typing [2], i.e. the ability to let the developer decide whether or not an expression should be statically typed, this features is actually used. The programming language studied by Souza and Figueiredo is Groovy.

The authors define a corpus consisting of about 7000 Groovy projects and define the following research questions:

- Do programmers use types more often in the interface of their modules?
- Do programmers use types less often in test classes and scripts?
- Does the experience of programmers with other languages influence their choice for typing code?[10],[11]

Based on these research questions, the authors define how the data is being collected: For fields, constructor parameters, method parameters, method returns

---

[10] The points are word-by-word citatations from Souza and Figueiredo [39].
[11] Two other questions are formulated, which are skipped were for reasons of simplification.

and local variables it is counted for each project, how often they make use of static types. I.e. the situation is, that five treatments of the independent variable (declaration kind) are defined. The dependent variable is the occurrence of the static types. Hence, a one-way ANOVA is applied that states, that the factor declaration kind is significant ($p < .001$). Next, a post-hoc test is applied that compares all treatment one another. This test reveals significant differences between each treatment with one exception: method parameters and returns are not different (which can be interpreted that if people statically type the parameters in a method definition, they also declare a type for the return). The main outcome of the pairwise comparison is, that local variables are the least often statically typed declarations ($p < .001$). Method parameters turn out to be the declarations that are most often statically typed.

The same analysis is performed on test-classes. There the result is, that again returns are most often statically typed.

Then, the same analysis is performed on script files, with the result that hardly anything is statically typed in script files – which significantly differs from usual classes ($p < .05$) except for local variables ($p > .3$).

Next, the authors check, whether the declared visibility (public, protected, private) has an influence on the declaration with the result, that (again) with the interesting observation that protected fields are most often statically typed, followed by public fields (again, $p < .001$). In addition to the p-values the authors give some descriptive numbers as well which state that about 75% of all protected methods are statically typed.

With respect to the developers' backgrounds, the authors determine from the developers contributing to the repository whether they have a background in a statically typed language, in a dynamically typed language or both. Again, the test reveals significant differences between all groups except the group that uses statically and dynamically typed languages in comparison to the group that uses only dynamically typed languages.

The essential contribution of the study is, that is shows there are a number of influencing factors that determine whether or not static types are used in a language that provides optional typing. First, it depends on the kind of declaration whether or not it will be statically typed, it depends on the kind of code (ordinary code, test classes and scripts) and it depends on the developer's experience whether or not he makes use of static typing.

Hence, this repository mining study essentially uses all parts of controlled experiments (hypotheses, data collection, data analysis using inference statistics) and gives strong evidence for its claims. Instead of building a controlled experiment, i.e. instead of defining a situation where data should be constructed by human subjects, the study uses existing data from code repositories. What's essential in the study is, that – although the underlying research question (how do developers use static typing) seems quite trivial – the resulting study is quite complex, because it turns out that the answer is influenced by multiple, different factors.

What the study cannot answer is, whether the choice for or against static types is actually a good one, i.e. it is unclear whether either people or projects who declared static types would have benefited from not using static types, or whether people or projects who used dynamic types would have benefited from using static types. This should not sound as a criticicm of the study itself. It just says that focus of the study is not on the question what the actual effect of static typing on developer or projects is. The focus is on how developers apply the construct.

4.2   Controlled Trial: Study on Programming Language Syntax [42]

The second study used here as an example is a traditional controlled trial by Stefik and Siebert [42]. The controlled trial focuses on the syntax of programming languages and determines what influence keywords (respectively tokens) have on the understandability of a programming language's syntax. One of the main focus of the authors is on non-programmer or novices, because they belong to the group that is addressed by the programming language Quorum written by the authors.

The study consists of three different substudies, altogether approximately 250 subjects participated in the experiment.

First Study: Survey. In the first study (which is in fact not a controlled trial and does not make use of inference statistics[12]) subjects were asked to rate a number of words that are often used in common programming languages (for, if, static, etc.) or commonly used operators (such as + in Java for concatenating strings). The keywords were grouped in six different categories (such as types, control flow, etc.). The participants were grouped according to their expertise into the groups 'programmers' and 'non-programmers'. Then, for both groups the best and the worst rated words are being described. An interesting observation is, that there seems to be some large disagreement between non-programmers and programmers. For example, words such as 'String' do not seem to be intuitive for non-programmers while they are for programmers (for obvious reasons). Another interesting observation is, that for loops the worst rated words are foreach (for non-programmers as well as for programmers) and while (for non-programmers). It is also interesting that for operators such as 'not equal' both groups preferred tokens such as 'not=' (while != only made sense to programmers).

Again, the results of this survey need to be handled with care. The authors argue (and they are probably right) that they cannot apply significance tests in order to check whether for example the word 'String' is considered much worse by novices than any other word. But this study gives a first idea about the problem of keywords in programming languages – a first idea that is used in the subsequent studies.

---

[12] It is understandable that the authors do not run inference-statistical methods: a huge number of different words is being tested and it sounds plausible, that traditional approaches from inference statistics would not have revealed differences at all – because of the high number of variables.

Study on Language Intuitiveness. In the second study, subjects were mainly asked about structural elements of the language such as loops, if statements, functions, etc. where different syntactical versions of such constructs in nine different languages (C++, Java, Smalltalk, PHP, Perl, Ruby, Go, Python, and Quorum) were shown to the subjects who rated for each construct how intuitive they consider this construct. Due to the rather low number of alternatives (compared to the first study by the same authors) it is possible to make a hypothesis test on the results.

The authors defined three hypotheses to be tested:

1. In aggregate, programming languages are rated as equally intuitive.
2. All programming language constructs are rated as equally intuitive.
3. Programming experience has no effect on subjective ratings of intuitiveness.

The hypothesis is tested using a 2-factor ANOVA: the first factor is the task with seven treatments (loops, if, etc.), the second factor is the language with nine treatments (C++, Java, etc.). The analysis reveals some amazing results. First, languages are significantly different among all tasks ($p < .001$), again, there were significant differences between programmers ($p < 0.001$). A corresponding post-hoc test revealed that the language invented by the authors of the study "was rated as statistically significantly more intuitive than Go ($p < 0.001$), C++ ($p < 0.001$), Perl ($p < 0.001$), Python ($p < 0.001$), Ruby ($p < 0.024$), Smalltalk ($p < 0.001$), PHP ($p < 0.001$), and approached significance with Java ($p = .055$)" [42, p. 19:21]. With respect to all language constructs (i.e. the variable task), each task was significant. The programming experience mattered on the effect of the rating as well ($p < .001$).

Study on Novices Accuracy Rates. In the third study[13], the authors formulate the following hypotheses:

1. Novices will have equal accuracy rates while programming, regardless of the programming language used.
2. All syntactical variations of programming language constructs (e.g., loops, conditionals) have equal accuracy rates among novices.

In order to check this hypotheses, the authors defined a measurement technique based on a given tool that they defined before. In short, this measurement checks the accuracy for each token to be written by a subject when writing a piece of code. As a reference, subjects were given a sample program in the language they were working on.

Altogether, 6 different programming languages were tested that way (Quorum, Perl, Randomo, Java, Ruby, Python), where Randomo is a language whose syntax is arbitrarily chosen from the ASCII-table. Additionally, 6 different tasks

---

[13] The authors distinguish in his paper between a third and a fourth study that we present here as one, because the hypothesis and applied analysis methods were identical.

were defined. I.e. each subject was measured more than once. Hence, the results were analyzed using a repeated-measures ANOVA. Again, language turned out to be a significant factor ($p < .001$). The following post-hoc test reveals that only the programming languages Quorum, Python and Ruby were significantly different from the randomly created language Randomo – for Java ($p = .922$) and Perl ($p = .573$) this statement does not hold. With respect to the second hypothesis, the corresponding post-hoc test reveals again significant results.

Summary of the Study. Despite the fact, that most programming language designers (and probably even programmers) do not have a big focus on the programming language syntax, this study actually measures (based on the rating of people) that syntax does matter. And among the findings it is rather a tragedy that the syntax of main stream languages such as Java are not considered as intuitive. Another interesting observation is that the intuition changes between novices and programmers which is an indicator that an originally rather non-intuitive syntax construct needs to be explicitly learned first, before it can be understood. This implies that at least some of the nowadays main stream languages have at least some tendency to be harder to learn than other languages.

From the perspective of controlled experimentation this set of studies gives a first idea about the variety of different steps that scientists performing controlled experiments typically do. The authors started with the idea that there might be differences in the intuitiveness of programming language syntax. Instead of starting now with a concrete experiment, the authors started with some survey in order to check, whether they get a first indicator for the validity of their suspicion. After the survey revealed some remarkable differences, the authors were able to concentrate in a follow up study on those elements that constitutes the differences. And finally they ran a controlled experiment in order to check whether their suspicion is actually observable.

5   Empirical Studies on the Usability of Type Systems - An Experience Report

Among the large set of available programming language features, probably the most deeply studied ones are type systems[14] where the author of this paper contributed in a number of studies over the last years. These studies (quantitative, controlled experiments on the usability of type systems) do represent a series of studies that reflect type systems from different perspectives.

In the following, we describe the studies that have been performed over the years. The main focus is on the construction of the hypothesis up to the construction of the experiment design. While we mention only the results of the analysis briefly, we discuss in more detail the possible interpretations of the experiments.

---

[14] At least, this statement can be found in the work by Kaijanaho [22].

5.1 Motivation

The overall motivation for controlled studies on static type systems was that there is a community that considers static type systems (see [3,32]) valuable: Static type systems played a major role in the programming language design of main stream programming languages such as Java or C++. However, over the last decades, programming languages such as PHP, Ruby, Python, and especially JavaScript played a larger role, especially in software development for the web. Additionally, taking into account that static type systems are a relatively well-established technique in programming language research and in software industry it seems appropriate to test whether the application of static type systems has a measurable influence on software development.

5.2 Related Controlled Experiments

The start of the experiment series originated from two other studies that had been performed before. One study by Cannon [9] and one by Prechelt and Tichy [34]:

- The experiment by Gannon from the 70s revealed a positive influence of static type system in comparison to an untyped systems in terms of errors and development time [9].
- After two decades, Prechelt and Tichy ran a study that compared static type checking versus no type checking on procedure arguments (see [34]) based on the languages ANSI C and K&R C with the result that the statically typed group was faster in solving programming tasks.

While we considered both experiments convincing, we thought it is still valuable to run an additional study. Additionally, it should be mentioned that in addition to the study by Souza and Figueiredo, mentioned in the previous section, there are additional studies that check the use of a certain language construct using code repositories (see for example [30]).

5.3 The Start of the Experiment Series [13]

The study by Gannon was performed at a time where software development was quite different from nowadays development. Writing and executing programs where not done using IDEs and it can be assumed that things such as testing frameworks did not play a major role. Next, we were thinking that maybe the choice of ANSI C and K&R in the experiment by Prechelt and Tichy – languages the subjects were possibly familiar with – possibly had an influence on the experiment results. And finally, both experiments required only relatively few time from the subjects (approximately 2 h). We were thinking that an experiment where developers were asked to write a piece of software that requires more time would be more convincing.

In order to overcome these points, our first experiment tried to find a larger task. Additionally, we thought that the process of testing a task should be made easier: instead of taking GUI-code into account (as being done in the Prechelt experiment), we were thinking that software should be found that can be more easily tested. As a result, we decided to give developers the programming task to write a parser for a small subject of Java. Before writing the parser, we decided to ask the subjects to write a scanner.

After a (very small) test, we decided to give developers about 27 hours time to write the parser. In order to overcome the language problem, we decided to write our own language just to be used in the experiment. The resulting language (syntactically a mixture of Java and Smalltalk) was written in two variants: a statically typed and a dynamically typed variant. The language was available only within the experimental environment, i.e. subjects were not able to take any material about the language at home. In order to train the subjects, corresponding teaching material was developed and the language was taught to the subjects within one and a half day. Approximately 50 subjects participated in the study divided into two groups (AB-experiment).

The measurements in the experiment were the time until a subset of the scanner was finished and the percentage of test cases that were fulfilled by the final parser.

The result of the experiment was quite frustrating. While we were able to measure a difference in the development time for the scanner (p < .05), we were not able to measure a difference in the number of successful test cases for the parser (p > .4).

However, the problem with the measurement on the scanner was, that we did not explicitly ask the subjects to write a complete scanner before starting with the parser. As a consequence, it was quite unclear how trustworthy the results of this measurement was. With respect to the parser, the problem was that a parser (at least the one produced by the subjects) was hardly possible to test. The underlying idea to use words from the grammar and test whether these words are accepted turned out to be a bad idea: parser implementations that had problems with recursions hardly accepted any word. We concluded from the experiment mainly the following things: first, the experiment definition was not appropriate because of the chosen tasks, and second, the effort for the experiment (50 student subjects, each about 40 h involved, development of a programming language for the experiment) was much too high. However, we also concluded that the possible benefit of static type systems— in case it does exist— cannot be identified that easily by an experiment which motivated us to continue with the work on controlled experiments on type systems.

5.4   Type Casts [43]

Since we were not able to show the benefit of static type systems in the first experiment, we decided to test a hypothesis from the dynamic programming language community stating, that type casts, a language construct that does not appear in dynamic programming languages, causes serious problems for developers.

We tried to reduce the whole effort for the experiment: the goal was to define an experiment where the subjects were required to work at most one day on the programming task. Additionally, the first experiment revealed too few points of measurements that we were able to reason on. Hence, we decided to give our subjects multiple tasks: each task should be relatively small, but still able to reveal possible differences. In order to reduce teaching, we no longer used a new language, but used a language were we expected that the subjects were familiar with: we used Java (as the statically typed language) and Groovy (as the dynamically typed language) where no special language constructs of Groovy were used in the experiment. Instead, it was only used as a dynamically typed Java. Since IDEs for Groovy and Java seemed to have quite different qualities we decided to run the experiments just in a text editor.

We ended up with five very small programming tasks where the expected number of lines of code were between 5 and 25. In these tasks, subjects using Java had to use a very small API that inherently required them to type cast objects. Such casts were not necessary for the developers using Groovy. Figure 2 illustrates a piece of code that was a possible Java solution for the easiest task.

```java
public void doPoachersGoal (Player p, Keeper t) {
    if ((p instanceof Forward) && (p . number == 9 ) {
        ((Forward) p). poachersGoal ++;
        t . goalsAgainst ++;
    } else
        throw new SoccerException ("...");
}}
```

Fig. 2. Example solution code for Experiment 2 (taken from [43])

As measurements, we still used development time – and used test cases that checked for the correctness of the solutions. We assumed that relatively few subjects would participate in the study. As a reaction on that, we decided to use a counterbalanced AB-within subject design. In order to reduce the possible learning effect, we defined two different APIs. When the subjects switched to the other treatment, they used the other API. Since the tasks were different, we compared the tasks individually, i.e. by running five individual paired tests.

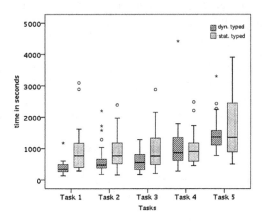

Fig. 3. Results from type cast experiment (taken from [43])

21 subjects (again students) participated in the experiment. Figure 3 illustrates the resulting measurements. For the first three tasks we were able to find significant differences ($p < .01$) while we were not able to find differences for the last tasks ($p > .5$). We concluded from that, that type casts play potentially a role in programming – but only in trivial situations where the LOC of a task is less than 10 lines of code. Hence, from our perspective type casts should not play a major role in the discussion about type systems.

Altogether, we were quite satisfied with the experiment. Although we did not had the feeling that we identified a major issue in type systems, we had the feeling that the experiment design worked quite fine and the reduction of the programming tasks was from our point of view a good decision, despite the fact that the programming tasks now became a major threat to validity (because of their size).

5.5   Types as Documentation in Undocumented APIs ([16, 24, 27])

Based on the two previously executed experiments on type systems, we were more intensively thinking about the question, under what circumstances we would expect to measure differences between static and dynamic types. I.e. we spent a lot of time on defining a possible hypothesis to be tested instead of directly using a given hypothesis. However, a comment from the literature by Pierce, who stated that static types in programming language where the type names appear in the code might help as a documentation [32] gave us some hint in what direction further experiments could go. Hence, our goal was to define programming tasks where we expected that the additional documentation of the static types help developers to understand the code. After some discussions and first measurements in pilot studies, we decided to define programming tasks where developers have to use a completely undocumented API – people with the static type names in the code have an additional source of documentation while developers without these type names have not.

Because of our experiences with the previous study, we (again) defined five programming tasks and again used Java and Groovy as the programming languages. Again, we used an AB-within-subject design. Again, we just used text editors for the experiment.

The experiment was executed on 27 subjects. Figure 4 illustrates the results of the measurements. Altogether, the results were slightly mixed: while we received in three of the five tasks the expected results (the statically typed group performed better), two tasks showed the opposite. Especially the two programming tasks that showed the opposite than what we expected frustrated us: Although we took some additional data into account, it was still unclear to us what made the two tasks special. However, we also had to take into account that there might be some hidden problems in the tasks themselves or the task descriptions.

Because we were not able to explain the phenomena to us, we decided to replicate the experiment: we started from the same starting point (defining an undocumented API, defining corresponding programming tasks on it) and re-ran the experiment [16, 24].

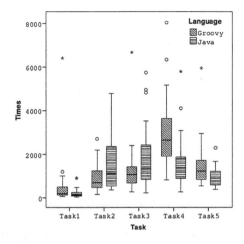

Fig. 4. Results from types as documentation experiment (taken from [27])

33 subjects participated in the replication. And the results were as expected: the statically typed group required less time for using the undocumented API. Additionally, we used the same experiment to double-check a previous (unpublished) experiment where we checked whether debugging type errors requires less time using a static type system, a statement that we were able to confirm [16,24].

5.6 Replication of Previous Findings (Petersen et al. [31])

Although the previous experiment finally revealed the expected results, we (still) had to take into account that the result of the experiment repetition might have been only a matter of luck – taking into account that the first experiment revealed slightly contradictory results. As a consequence, we decided to replicate the experiment once more. But in order to get some (small) new insights, we decided to run now the experiment with some tool support: we used Eclipse for the Java as well as for the Groovy group. Hence, the goal was not only to see whether we are able to replicate the results, the goal was as well to get rid of one threats to validity of previous experiments (the missing IDE). However, we decided to reduce the programming experiment once more: we just used two programming tasks in the experiment. Again, we used an AB-within-subject design.

23 subjects (students) participated in the experiment. Again, we got clear results (see Fig. 5): for both programming tasks subjects using the statically typed programming language required significantly less time to solve the task ($p < .05$).

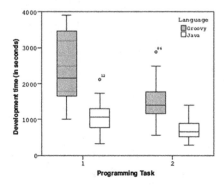

Fig. 5. Results from experiment repetition (taken from [31])

5.7 Types as Pure Syntax Elements (Spiza and Hanenberg 2014 [40])

While we ran in between another experiment that compared generic and raw typed in Java[15], we wanted to put our focus on asking the question about the documentation characteristics of static typed in a slightly different way. In case the static type names help in the code, it is possible that they do help without actually doing any type checking. I.e. it is possible that the type names help (i.e. just the piece of syntax), although the type system itself is not required. However, we rather thought that the type system is necessary as long as the type names in the API are correct. But as soon as the type names are incorrect, we expected that developers might have troubles.

We defined three programming tasks comparable to the ones used in the previous experiments. All type names in the API were correct. We additionally defined one task where one parameter type (in a list of parameter types) was not correct. With respect to the experimental design, we had the tendency that those tasks with correct type names are rather not critical and can be defined in the same way as in previous experiments (AB-within subject). However, we expected the learning effect for the task with the incorrect type to be too high – even if we would have defined a 'similar' programming task. As a consequence, we decided test the task with the incorrect type name between subject.

The programming language used in the experiment was Dart – a language with an optional type system that permitted us to switch off the type checker.

The results of the experiment (20 students participated as subjects) were quite surprising. Again, the static type names helped using the API (for two tasks $p < .05$, non significant results for one task), although the effect was smaller than in previous experiments. However, the task with the wrong type name revealed a significant, negative impact for the group with the (wrong) static type name ($p < .05$).

---

[15] The result of the experient was that the additional type annotations of generic Java helped when using an undocumented API – which (again) confirmed the previous findings– but which also showed a situation where generic types reduced the extensibility of an API (see [20]).

5.8 A First Summary

Although not all experiments revealed clear results (such as the experiment by Mayer et al. [27]), the large majority of experiments revealed that the static type system helps using an undocumented API. Additionally, we got at least one results from a smaller experiment, that a wrong type name could do harm. As a consequence, our interpretation of the experiment series so far is, that the help of the static type system is be caused by the syntactic representation of type names, but the absence of a type check directly negates this effect. Additionally, we know that the type system helps fixing type errors (in comparison to corresponding MessageNotUnderstood errors[16]).

However, even taking into account that there is a significant, positive impact of static type systems, it is not clear how large this effect is in comparison to other effects. Hence, the next steps from here are to define experiments that compare the type system effect with something else.

5.9 Comparing Types and Documentation (Endrikat et al. [6])

A first experiment we performed that tried to compare the effect of type systems with something else was done by Endrikat et al. [6]. Again, the underlying motivation of documentation was still the leading idea for the work. The general question was, how type systems perform when documentation is available. A possible result of this could be that in the presence of documentation the effect of the static type system is directly hidden by the documentation effect. Or the type system effect is still present and can be compared to the documentation effect.

In order to define a controlled trial, we had to decide what kind of documentation should be used in the experiment. We decided to use a kind of documentation that consisted of some free-text explaining certain parts of an API and additional code examples that helped only to a certain extent solving given programming tasks (otherwise, developers with documentation could just copy and paste solutions).

The experiment now speaks about a second factor, the documentation factor with the two treatments 'documentation available' and 'documentation not available'. If we compare it to the factor type system (again with the treatment 'static type system' and 'dynamic type system'), this implies that we have a 2×2 factor design. While almost all previous studies were based on an within-subject measurement, we expected that this is not possible for the here given experiment: we expected (again) that the learning effect using the documentation would be too high. However, we already had enough experience in the previous studies that we felt confident that we are able to design a between-subject experiment that could reveal the effect of the static type system. Consequently, we defined four groups (combinations of the treatments of both factors) and randomly assigned subjects to them. Since we felt that our task definitions are quite stable (from our experience with the previous experiments), we just defined one single programming task. As programming languages, we used the language Dart.

---

[16] Which was the results of the replication study by Kleinschmager et al. [16,24].

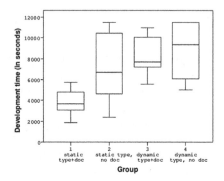

Fig. 6. Results from type vs. documentation experiment (taken from [6])

Altogether, 23 subjects participated in the experiment. Figure 6 illustrates the results of the experiment. The results were quite surprising. First, the factor type system (still) turned out to be a significant factor (p < .05) and second, the factor documentation was just approaching significance (p < .1).

We found the result of this experiment quite fascinating and asked ourselves whether we should search more in this direction (other kinds of documentation, other tasks, etc.) or whether we should go on comparing the results with other factors. We decided to go into the second direction.

5.10 Comparing Types and Code Completion [7]

In the most recent experiment by Fisher and Hanenberg we started comparing the effect of type systems with the effect achieved by code completion techniques. If we want to compare both effect using a 2-factor design, it is necessary to find a code completion technique that is available for a dynamically as well as a statically typed language. We decided to use MS VisualStudio which provides quite good code completion for JavaScript as well as code completion for TypeScript, a statically typed variant of JavaScript. We defined two programming tasks for the computer game PacMan. Again, the code expected to be written was relatively small. In contrast to the previous study, we decided to measure subjects twice: with the static as well as with the dynamic type system. I.e. a subject always worked with or without code completion.

Similar to the previous study, we were again able to see a significant impact of the factor type system (p < .05), but (again) only a close to significant effect of code completion (p < .1).

5.11 Summary and Conclusion of Experiment Series

The goal of the previous experience report was not to discuss too detailed each single experiment. Instead, the goal was to give an idea, how the reasoning process was applied in the presence of actual data. Each step in the experiment series was driven by the results of the previous step. At each step, there were multiple possible following steps where we had to decide, what direction to follow. The experiment series (that was not finished with the mentioned studies but which is still ongoing, see for example [29]) illustrates that human-centered studies do not have the idea in mind that there might be one single study that possibly answers a given research question. Instead, studies should be to a certain extent be replicated, other alternatives should be taken into account and it should be checked, how identified factors can be compared to other factors.

Still, the experiment series gave so far at least one relatively clear result: static type systems do help in comparison to dynamically typed languages. And do far, the experiments gave us the ability (and first evidence for) some working theory that the main part of the static type system that helps is the type names in the code.

6 Summary, Conclusion and Future Work

This paper introduces into the topic of quantitative evaluation of programming languages. It first introduced into the general idea of empirical evaluation and then focused on controlled experiments. In order to see how such studies are actually applied, we introduced first two studies by other authors (one about the use of optional types, the other about the impact of syntax). The first of these studies was actually not a controlled trial but a code repository study. However, the applied techniques were the same: The only difference was that the experimenters did not have influence on the sample itself, i.e., by defining the sample (the used set of projects) corresponding data is already given which is not the case with typical human-centered studies.

Finally, we introduced a series of controlled experiments that we ran. We consider this experiment series quite mature from the perspective that we gain over and over comparable results. The goal for illustrating this experiment series in more detail was to show the reasoning process underlying human-centered controlled experiments. This hopefully gives readers not only the motivation but also first ideas how other programming language constructs could be evaluated. Because one thing seems to be clear: the situation that most programming language constructs are hardly evaluated is a major problem in software science in general that should be solved soon.

References

1. Boehm, B., Rombach, H.D., Zelkowitz, M.V.: Foundations of Empirical Software Engineering: The Legacy of Victor R. Basili. Springer, Heidelberg (2005)
2. Bracha, G.: Pluggable type systems. In: OOPSLA'04 Workshop on Revival of Dynamic Languages (2004)
3. Bruce, K.B.: Foundations of Object-Oriented Languages: Types and Semantics. MIT Press, Cambridge (2002)
4. Cohen, J.: Statistical Power Analysis for the Behavioral Sciences. L. Erlbaum Associates, Hillsdale (1988)

5. Conover, W.J.: Practical Nonparametric Statistics, 3rd edn. Wiley, New York (1998)
6. Endrikat, S., Hanenberg, S., Robbes, R., Stefik, A.: How do API documentation and static typing affect API usability? In: 36th International Conference on Software Engineering, ICSE 2014, Hyderabad, India - 31 May–07 June 2014, pp. 632–642 (2014)
7. Fischer, L., Hanenberg, S.: An empirical investigation of the effects of type systems and code completion on API usability using typescript and javascript in MS visual studio. In: Proceedings of the Dynamic Language Symposium. accepted for publication (2015)
8. Fisher, R.A.: Statistical Methods for Research Workers. Cosmo Study Guides. Cosmo Publications, New Delhi (1925)
9. Gannon, J.D.: An experimental evaluation of data type conventions. Commun. ACM 20(8), 584–595 (1977)
10. Georges, A., Buytaert, D., Eeckhout, L.: Statistically rigorous java performance evaluation. SIGPLAN Not. 42(10), 57–76 (2007)
11. Glaser, B.G., Strauss, A.L.: The Discovery of Grounded Theory: Strategies for Qualitative Research. Aldine Publishing Company, Chicago (1967). Observations
12. Halstead, M.H.: Elements of Software Science (Operating and Programming Systems Series). Elsevier Science Inc., New York (1977)
13. Hanenberg, S.: An experiment about static and dynamic type systems: Doubts about the positive impact of static type systems on development time. In: Proceedings of the ACM International Conference on Object Oriented Programming Systems Languages and Applications, OOPSLA, pp. 22–35. ACM, New York (2010)
14. Hanenberg, S.: Faith, hope, and love: An essay on software science's neglect of human factors. In: Proceedings of the ACM International Conference on Object Oriented Programming Systems Languages And Applications, OOPSLA 2010, pp. 933–946. Reno/Tahoe, Nevada, October 2010
15. Hanenberg, S.: Why do we know so little about programming languages, and what would have happened if we had known more? In: Proceedings of the 10th ACM Symposium on Dynamic Languages, DLS 2014, p. 1. ACM, New York (2014)
16. Hanenberg, S., Kleinschmager, S., Robbes, R., Tanter, É., Stefik, A.: An empirical study on the impact of static typing on software maintainability. Empirical Softw. Eng. 19(5), 1335–1382 (2014)
17. Hanenberg, S., Stefik, A.: On the need to define community agreements for controlled experiments with human subjects - a discussion paper. In: Submitted to PLATEAU 2015 (2015)
18. Harlow, L.L., Mulaik, S.A., Steiger, J.H.: What If There Were No Significance Tests?. Multivariate Applications Book Series. Lawrence Erlbaum Associates Publishers, Hillsdale (1997)
19. Hoda, R., Noble, J., Marshall, S.: Developing a grounded theory to explain the practices of self-organizing agile teams. Empirical Softw. Eng. 17(6), 609–639 (2012)
20. Hoppe, M., Hanenberg, S.: Do developers benefit from generic types? An empirical comparison of generic and raw types in java. In: Proceedings of the 2013 ACM SIGPLAN International Conference on Object Oriented Programming Systems Languages & Applications, OOPSLA 2013, pp. 457–474. ACM, New York (2013)
21. Juristo, N., Moreno, A.M.: Basics of Software Engineering Experimentation. Springer, Heidelberg (2001)
22. Kaijanaho, A.-J.: Evidence-based programming language design: A philosophical and methodological exploration. Number 222 in Jyväskylä Studies in Computing. University of Jyväskylä, Finland (2015)

23. Kirk, R.E.: Experimental Design: Procedures for the Behavioral Sciences Procedures for the Behavioral Sciences. SAGE Publications, Thousand Oaks (2012)
24. Kleinschmager, S., Hanenberg, S., Robbes, R., Tanter, É., Stefik, A.: Do static type systems improve the maintainability of software systems? An empirical study. In: IEEE 20th International Conference on Program Comprehension, ICPC 2012, Passau, Germany, pp. 153–162, 11–13 June 2012
25. Ko, A.J., LaToza, T.D., Burnett, M.M.: A practical guide to controlled experiments of software engineering tools with human participants. Empirical Softw. Eng. **20**(1), 110–141 (2015)
26. Laprie, J.-C.: Dependability of computer systems: concepts, limits, improvements. In: Sixth International Symposium on Software Reliability Engineering, ISSRE 1995, Toulouse, France, 24–27 October 1995, pp. 2–11 (1995)
27. Mayer, C., Hanenberg, S., Robbes, R., Tanter, É., Stefik, A.: An empirical study of the influence of static type systems on the usability of undocumented software. In: Proceedings of the 27th Annual ACM SIGPLAN Conference on Object-Oriented Programming, Systems, Languages, and Applications, OOPSLA 2012, part of SPLASH 2012, Tucson, AZ, USA, 21–25 October 2012, pp. 683–702. ACM (2012)
28. McConnell, S.: What does 10x mean? Measuring variations in programmer productivity. In: Oram, A., Wilson, G. (eds.) Making Software: What Really Works, and Why We Believe It, O'Reilly Series, pp. 567–575. O'Reilly Media (2010)
29. Okon, S., Hanenberg, S.: Can we enforce a benefit for dynamically typed languages in comparison to statically typed ones? A controlled experiment. In: 2016 IEEE 24th International Conference on Program Comprehension (ICPC), pp. 1–10, May 2016
30. Parnin, C., Bird, C., Murphy-Hill, E.R.: Java generics adoption: How new features are introduced, championed, or ignored. In: Proceedings of the 8th International Working Conference on Mining Software Repositories, MSR 2011 (Co-located with ICSE), Waikiki, Honolulu, HI, USA, 21–28 May 2011, pp. 3–12. IEEE (2011)
31. Petersen, P., Hanenberg, S., Robbes, R.: An empirical comparison of static and dynamic type systems on API usage in the presence of an IDE: Java vs. groovy with eclipse. In: 22nd International Conference on Program Comprehension, ICPC 2014, Hyderabad, India, 2–3 June 2014, pp. 212–222 (2014)
32. Pierce, B.C.: Types and Programming Languages. MIT Press, Cambridge (2002)
33. Popper, K.R.: The Logic of Scientific Discovery, Routledge. 1st English Edition: 1959, Original First Edition (German): Logik der Forschung, published 1935 by Julius Springer, Austria, Vienna (2002)
34. Prechelt, L., Tichy, W.F.: A controlled experiment to assess the benefits of procedure argument type checking. IEEE Trans. Softw. Eng. **24**(4), 302–312 (1998)
35. Seaman, C.B.: Qualitative methods in empirical studies of software engineering. IEEE Trans. Software Eng. **25**(4), 557–572 (1999)
36. Senn, S.S.: Cross-over Trials in Clinical Research. Statistics in Practice. Wiley, Chichester (1993)
37. Sheil, B.A.: The psychological study of programming. ACM Comput. Surv. **13**(1), 101–120 (1981)
38. Shneiderman, B., Psychology, S.: Human Factors in Computer and Information Systems. Winthrop Publishers, Cambridge (1980)
39. Souza, C., Figueiredo, E.: How do programmers use optional typing?: An empirical study. In: Proceedings of the 13th International Conference on Modularity, MODULARITY 2014, pp. 109–120. ACM, New York (2014)

40. Spiza, S., Hanenberg, S.: Type names without static type checking already improve the usability of APIS (as long as the type names are correct): An empirical study. In: Proceedings of the 13th International Conference on Modularity, MODULARITY 2014, pp. 99–108. ACM, New York (2014)

41. Stefik, A., Hanenberg, S.: The programming language wars: Questions and responsibilities for the programming language community. In: 2014 Proceedings of the 2014 ACM International Symposium on New Ideas, New Paradigms, and Reflections on Programming & Software, Onward!, pp. 283–299. ACM, New York (2014)

42. Stefik, A., Siebert, S.: An empirical investigation into programming language syntax. Trans. Comput. Educ. **13**(4), 19:1–19:40 (2013)

43. Stuchlik, A., Hanenberg, S.: Static vs. dynamic type systems: An empirical study about the relationship between type casts and development time. In: Proceedings of the 7th Symposium on Dynamic Languages, DLS 2011, Portland, Oregon, pp. 97–106. ACM (2011)

44. Tichy, W.F.: Should computer scientists experiment more? IEEE Comput. **31**, 32–40 (1998)

45. Uesbeck, P.M., Stefik, A., Hanenberg, S., Pedersen, J., Daleiden, P.: An empirical study on the impact of C++ lambdas and programmer experience. In: 38th International Conference on Software Engineering Austin, TX, 14–22 May 2016. to appear (2016)

46. Wohlin, C., Runeson, P., Höst, M., Ohlsson, M.C., Regnell, B., Wesslén, A.: Experimentation in Software Engineering: An Introduction. Kluwer Academic Publishers, Norwell (2000)

To Merge or Not to Merge: Managing Software Product Families

Julia Rubin[(✉)]

The University of British Columbia, Vancouver, Canada
`julia.rubin@ubc.ca`

Abstract. A large number of companies, especially in the automotive, electronics, aerospace and defense domains, develop a portfolio of closely related software products designed to satisfy similar, yet not identical, needs of their customers (a.k.a. a software product line). Even though numerous software product line engineering approaches promise to ease the product line development and maintenance effort, in practice, the adoption of such approaches is still limited. Instead, products are often established ad-hoc, e.g., by copying existing variants and modifying them to fit the requirements of a new customer or market segment.

In this paper, we discuss reasons leading organizations to employ cloning to realize their product lines. We then present two strategies for efficient management of cloned product variants: (1) the unification of the variants into single-copy representations promoted by product line engineering methods and (2) the construction of a management infrastructure on top of existing cloned variants, to mitigate the shortcomings of cloning while leveraging its benefits. We outline existing work that contributes to the implementation of these two strategies and identify opportunities for future research.

1 Introduction

Software surrounds us and drives our lives: most modern systems heavily rely on software. Managing the complexity of these software systems is a challenging task. It is even more challenging for Software Product Lines (SPL) – families of software product variants with similar yet not identical functionality, commonly developed and maintained by companies in the automotive, electronics, aerospace and defense domains.

To deal with the complexity of SPL development, Software Product Line Engineering (SPLE) emerged as a software engineering discipline that promotes predicted and managed software reuse. SPLE relies on capturing *common* and *variable* software artifacts – entities that are part of all products of the product line, and entities that are specific to some, but not all, products, respectively [11,18,27,46,47,65]. Common and variable artifacts are traced to *features*: high-level characteristics of product functionality [5]. The set of all product line features, together with relationships between the features, is specified in a *feature model* [27]. A particular selection of features from a feature model defines a concrete product of an SPL.

© Springer International Publishing AG 2017
J. Cunha et al. (Eds.): GTTSE 2015, LNCS 10223, pp. 73–97, 2017.
DOI: 10.1007/978-3-319-60074-1_4

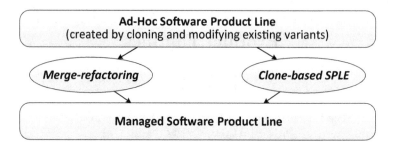

Fig. 1. Approaches for transitioning from ad-hoc to well-managed software product lines.

A set of software artifacts, a feature model, and traceability information between features and their corresponding artifacts constitute an *SPL architecture*. Individual products are specified by a particular feature selection and are *derived* from an SPL architecture.

SPL architectures are largely divided into two categories: *compositional* and *annotative*. *Compositional* SPL architectures group product artifacts into distinct fragments, each corresponding to a particular feature. Derivation of a specific product is then performed by composing a chosen set of fragments. *Annotative* SPL representations rely on one "maximal" product in which annotations indicate the artifacts that realize a particular feature. In such representations, a specific product is derived by removing artifacts corresponding to unselected features [7,30,31]. Intuitively, compositional architectures are similar to the aspect-oriented programming paradigm while annotative architectures are similar to code parameterized with preprocessor directives.

SPLE approaches promise to ease product line development and maintenance; improve time-to-market and quality; reduce portfolio size, engineering costs, and more [11,46]. Yet, *in practice, the adoption of these approaches is still limited and reuse of artifacts between products rather occurs ad-hoc, in an opportunistic manner.* One popular form of ad-hoc reuse is cloning, where an existing product variant is simply copied or placed in a separate branch of a version control system, and later modified to fit the requirements of a new customer or market segment (the "clone-and-own" approach).

In this paper, we outline reasons behind the lack of adoption of advanced SPLE approaches. We then discuss the benefits and shortcomings of cloning and describe two main directions for moving forward (see Fig. 1). The first direction relies on unifying cloned products into single-copy representations proposed by SPLE approaches[1] (we call this a *merge-refactoring* approach). The second direction proposes to build an efficient management infrastructure on top of existing cloned products, mitigating the shortcomings of cloning while leveraging its benefits (we call this a *clone-based SPLE* approach). The management

---

[1] We mostly focus on producing annotative SPL architectures: these architectures appear to be more intuitive to practitioners as they do not require a paradigm shift in the way software is being developed, especially in the embedded domain, where predecessor directives are commonly used [7,49].

infrastructure captures essential product line constructs such as features, dependencies between features, as well as traceability information between the features and their implementation artifacts. As such, it defines a new type of SPL architectures – the one that is built on top of existing clones.

In what follows, we describe these directions in detail, outline existing work in the area, and provide suggestions for future work that leads to more efficient management of cloned product variants. Specifically, the remainder of the paper is structured as follows: Sect. 2 sets the scene by discussing existing SPL cloning practices in industry. Section 3 introduces the annotative SPLE approach. Section 4 focuses on merge-refactorings, while Sect. 5 describes the cloned-based SPLE approach. Section 6 outlines possible future directions. Finally, Sect. 7 summarizes and concludes the paper.

2   Cloned Software Product Lines in Industry

The first step towards improving existing cloning practices is to gain a better understanding of their perceived benefits and shortcomings. We thus start by presenting the results of an empirical study that investigates experiences of developers in six industrial software product lines realized via cloning [15]. We describe the cloning practices using a fictitious, but representative, company GlobalCo that delivers GPS solutions (see Fig. 2).

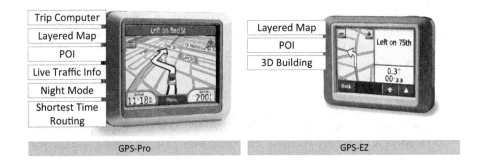

Fig. 2. GlobalCo products.

2.1   Developing SPLs with Clones

GlobalCo develops an advanced product, GPS-Pro, that has the Trip Computer feature for monitoring the vehicle speed and the time to destination, and the Layered Map feature for overlaying graphical objects on the map. As the product has been tested and released to the market, GlobalCo's market analysis reveals the need for a simplified and less expensive product variant, GPS-EZ. Layered Map is determined to be the only essential feature of this product, while Trip Computer should not be included.

The goal of the company now is to release the new product to the market as fast as possible. Efficient management of reuse, although important, is hardly considered a priority. The easiest way for the development team responsible for GPS-EZ to cope with this request is thus to branch the already tested code of GPS-Pro and remove the Trip Computer feature implementation from it.

From this point on, however, the two product variants become independent from each other and their corresponding implementations grow apart. As the number of cloned variants and the differences between their implementations increase, it becomes difficult to keep track of changes made to each of the variants and propagate the changes between them. In our scenario, imagine that the development of GPS-Pro continues, adding the ability to show points of interests (POI) and Live Traffic Info as two additional layers on the map. The team also extends the product with Night Mode and Shortest Time Routing features.

Later, it is decided to borrow the POI feature from GPS-Pro and use it in GPS-EZ as well. The implementation of this feature should then be identified, detached from the rest of the code of GPS-Pro and copied to GPS-EZ. Independently, the development team of GPS-EZ implements the ability to show 3D Buildings as an additional layer on the map. The team also implements an extension to the POI feature copied from GPS-Pro, but cannot immediately propagate the change back to that product because it is currently frozen towards a close release. The two products not only have a different set of features now, but two seemingly identical features have different implementations in the distinct products, challenging the portfolio management task.

Due to a lack of information about the dependencies between features, borrowing the Night Mode and Shortest Time Routing features from GPS-Pro is an additional challenge: the Night Mode feature might not work well with 3D Buildings, because it was not designed to work with that functionality as GPS-Pro does not contain it. Shortest Time Routing depends on the Live Traffic Info feature that is not available in GPS-EZ. Moreover, if GlobalCo now decides to establish a new product variant that has the Layered Map, POI, Night Mode and 3d Buildings features, it is unclear which product should be used as a starting point, and how to remove their unnecessary features while borrowing the required features from other products.

2.2 Main Benefits and Shortcoming of Cloning

Interviews with industrial practitioners participating in the study [15] showed that companies often rely on cloning to realize their SPLs because they do not plan upfront to develop a product family. Instead, as in the GlobalCo example, the companies incrementally grow their product portfolios as they become successful and as new customers require modified variants of already existing products. Companies mostly focus on making sure these individual products are delivered on time and postpone dealing with reuse issues to the future.

In such reality, cloning is perceived to be a simple yet efficient reuse mechanism that saves time and resources: unlike advanced SPLE solutions proposed in the literature, it does not require any upfront investment. Moreover, it allows participants to start the development from an already implemented and veri-fied set of artifacts. At the same time, it provides independence and freedom to change these artifacts as needed.

Yet, adapting cloned artifacts to the new needs might involve a significant effort. The effort in maintaining the artifacts also increases because some tasks need to be performed on each cloned copy. Knowledge about reuse is rarely maintained. Thus, propagating modifications between clones is not a trivial task.

Table 1 summarizes the main benefits and shortcomings of cloning that emerged from the study.

Table 1. Main benefits and shortcomings of cloning [15].

Benefits	Shortcomings
– No upfront investment	Difficult to:
– Rapidly available	– Reconcile changes
– Reuse of verified code	– Share features
– Developer independence	– Establish new variants

2.3 Conclusions

We draw two main conclusions from the study: first, any approach that aspires to be better than cloning has to address the perceived benefits of cloning, such as simplicity, availability, and developer independence. Without such argument, many SPLE approaches fail to convince practitioners that they would yield bet-ter results. Second, even if a company decides to make a transition for cloned to a well-managed SPL approach, such transition is a time- and labor-intensive task by itself; the overhead related to this task should be comparably lower than the overall overhead related to the management of existing clones. Automation plays a crucial role here: providing support for automating the transition will streamline SPLE adoption in practice.

In what follows, we discuss automated approaches for unifying cloned variants into a single-copy SPLE representation (Sect. 4). We also present an alternative approach for building a management infrastructure on top of existing clones, to reduce the overhead of cloning while maintaining its advantages (Sect. 5). Before that, we give a more rigid definition of an annotative SPLE architecture.

3   Software Product Line Engineering

The Software Product Line Engineering paradigm separates two processes: *domain* and *application engineering* (see Fig. 3 taken from [47]). The first process, domain engineering, is responsible for establishing an *SPL architecture* and defining the commonalities and variabilities of a software product line. The second process, application engineering, is responsible for *deriving* individual *products* (a.k.a. *variants* or *applications*) from the SPL architecture established during domain engineering. It exploits the variability of the product line and ensures the correct binding of the variability according to the applications' specific needs. In this paper, we focus on an automated *feature-driven annotative SPL approach* [7,13,30,31] which we describe below.

3.1 Domain Engineering

The SPL architecture created during the domain engineering phase represents all possible products of a product line (a.k.a. a 150% view). As schematically shown in Fig. 4, *artifacts* of the architecture, i.e., requirements, tests, design and implementation elements, are *annotated* by *features*.

The exact type and granularity of artifacts depend on the development process that a specific organization employs. We thus loosely define artifacts as follows:

Definition 3.1. *(Artifact[2]) An* artifact *is a tangible by-product produced during the development of software. Some artifacts, such as class diagrams, requirements, and design documents help describe the architecture and design of software. Other artifacts, such as code elements, executable models and tests are concerned with the implementation and validation of software.*

A feature typically consists of a label and a short description that identifies its functionality [9]. For conciseness, either label or feature description can be dropped when clear from the context. While there is no universal agreement on what a feature is (and what it is not), we adopt the definition by Kang et al. [29]:

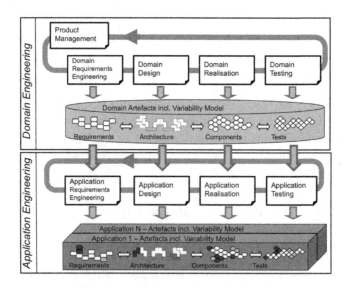

Fig. 3. SPLE: domain and application engineering [47].

---

[2] Adapted from http://en.wikipedia.org/wiki/Artifact_(software_development).

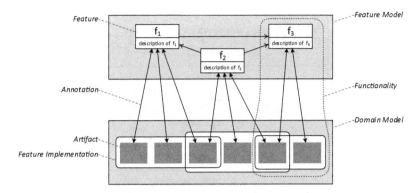

Fig. 4. Feature-driven annotative SPL representations.

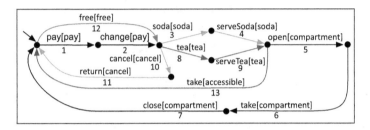

Fig. 5. Vending machine SPL architecture.

Definition 3.2. *(Feature [9,29]) A feature is a distinctively identifiable functional abstraction that must be implemented, tested, delivered, and maintained. A feature consists of a label and a short description that identifies its behavior.*

Annotative product line approaches assume that a feature *annotates* all artifacts that contribute to its implementation. A feature can annotate one or more artifacts; an artifact can be annotated by one or more features. We also say that artifacts are *traced* to the feature they implement. A feature and its implementation constitute a *functionality* of an individual product or an entire product line.

Definition 3.3. *A functionality of a product or a product line is a feature and its corresponding feature implementation – a set of artifacts annotated by that feature.*

It is up to a particular SPL architecture to decide on the granularity of annotations, e.g., whether features annotate complete functions of source code or individual statements. Likewise, in models, features can annotate coarse- or fine-grained artifacts, e.g., complete statecharts or individual states and transitions.

Figure 5 shows an example of a "toy" vending machine SPL architecture taken from [10]. Artifacts of this architecture are states and transitions in a transition system. These artifacts are annotated by seven vending machine features: cancel, soda, tea, pay, free, compartment and accessible. In this example, annotations

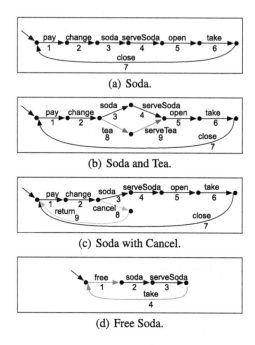

(a) Soda.

(b) Soda and Tea.

(c) Soda with Cancel.

(d) Free Soda.

Fig. 6. Vending machine variants derived from the SPL architecture in Fig. 5.

are represented by appending the feature label in square brackets to the elements annotated by that feature. For instance, transitions #1 and #2 in Fig. 5 are annotated by the feature pay.

The vending machine SPL architecture "encodes" numerous variants. The functionality of each variant is defined by the subset of features that comprise it. Given a feature subset, the corresponding variant is *derived* from the SPL architecture during the application engineering phase, as explained later in this chapter. For example, a vending machine variant in Fig. 6(a) implements functionality defined by the pay, soda, and compartment features. It accepts payment, returns change, allows to select soda, and serves it. It then opens a compartment allowing the user to take the drink, and, when taken, closes the compartment. Another variant of the vending machine that implements functionality defined by the pay, soda, tea, and compartment features is shown in Fig. 6(b). It allows the user to choose either soda or tea and then serves the chosen drink. Yet another variant, in Fig. 6(c), implements functionality defined by the pay, cancel, soda, and compartment features. It allows the user to cancel the purchase before selecting the drink and returns the paid amount. The one in Fig. 6(d) offers free drinks and is fully accessible, i.e., does not open or close the beverage compartment. It implements functionality defined by features free, soda, and accessible.

Obviously, not all functionality combinations are reasonable or desirable. For example, having both pay and free options together, as well as having both compartment and accessible options, do not make sense. Likewise, having a vending

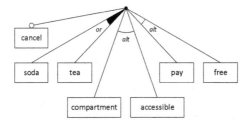

Fig. 7. Vending machine feature model.

machine variant which serves no drinks – neither soda nor tea – is unreasonable. Constraints on valid functionality combinations are expressed in a *feature model* [27]. A feature model is a rooted tree whose nodes are feature labels. Relationships between parent and child features in the tree commonly include:

- *mandatory*: a child feature must be selected when its parent is selected;
- *optional*: a child feature might be selected when its parent is selected;
- *or-group*: at least one of the sub-features must be selected when the parent is selected;
- *xor-group* (a.k.a. *alternatives*): exactly one of the sub-features must be selected when the parent is selected.

In addition to the main hierarchy, cross-tree constraints can be used to describe dependencies between arbitrary features. Commonly used cross-tree constraints are:

- *requires*: if one feature is selected the other needs to be selected as well;
- *excludes*: two features mutually exclude each other.

An example of a feature model for the vending machine product line is given in Fig. 7. It has one optional feature: cancel; an or-group with features soda and tea; and two groups of alternative features: the first includes pay and free while the second – compartment and accessible.

Following [60], a feature model can be represented as a set of features and a Boolean formula that encodes the relationships between these features. For the example in Fig. 7, the formula that represents the relationships between the features is (soda∨tea)∧(pay⊕free)∧(compartment⊕accessible).

A *feature model configuration* is then a subset of features that "respect" the formula, i.e., for which the formula evaluates to *true*. Valid configurations include soda, pay, and compartment (which corresponds to the product in Fig. 6(a)), soda, pay, cancel, and compartment (which corresponds to the product in Fig. 6(c)) and more.

Definitions 3.4 and 3.5 below formally describe the notion of a feature model, feature model configuration and an SPL architecture.

Definition 3.4. *(Feature Model and Configuration – simplified version of [60])*
Given a universe of elements $\mathbb{F}$ *that represent features, a* feature model $\mathcal{FM} =$

$\langle \mathcal{F}, \varphi \rangle$ *is a set of features* $\mathcal{F} \in 2^{\mathbb{F}}$ *and a propositional formula* φ *defined over the features from* $\mathcal{F}$. *A* feature configuration $\widehat{\mathcal{FM}}$ *of* $\mathcal{FM}$ *is a set of selected features from* $\mathcal{F}$ *that respect* φ *(i.e.,* φ *evaluates to* true *when each variable* f *of* φ *is substituted by* true *if* $f \in \widehat{\mathcal{FM}}$ *and by* false *otherwise.)*

Definition 3.5. *(SPL Architecture – simplified version of* [6]*) Given a universe of elements* $\mathbb{A}$ *that represent artifacts at a certain granularity level, an* SPL architecture $\mathcal{PL} = \langle \mathcal{FM}, \mathcal{M}, \mathcal{R} \rangle$ *is a triple, where* $\mathcal{FM}$ *is a feature model,* $\mathcal{M} \in 2^{\mathbb{A}}$ *is a domain model, and* $\mathcal{R} \subseteq \mathcal{F} \times \mathcal{M}$ *is a set of relationships that annotate elements of* $\mathcal{M}$ *by features of* $\mathcal{F}$.

3.2   Application Engineering

As mentioned earlier, individual products are defined by a subset of features that correspond to the desired product functionality – a feature model configuration. Given a feature model configuration, a product is derived from the SPL architecture by removing domain model artifacts annotated by features that are *excluded* from the configuration.

Below, we formally describe the product derivation process. We denote by Δ the mapping between an artifact of the domain model and the corresponding artifact of the derived product. For example, let a refer to transition #12 in Figs. 5 and $\hat{a}$ refer to transition #1 in Fig. 6(d). Then, under the configuration that includes features soda, free, and accessible, $\Delta(a) = \hat{a}$.

Definition 3.6. *(Product Derivation – adapted from* [6]*) Let* $\mathcal{PL} = \langle \mathcal{FM},$ $\mathcal{M}, \mathcal{R} \rangle$ *be an SPL architecture and let* $\widehat{\mathcal{FM}}$ *be one of its feature model configurations. A set of elements* $\hat{M}$ *is* derived *from the architecture* $\mathcal{PL}$ *under the configuration* $\widehat{\mathcal{FM}}$, *denoted by* $\hat{M} = \Delta(\mathcal{PL}, \widehat{\mathcal{FM}})$, *if and only if the following properties hold:*

(a) *An element belongs to the derived product if and only if this element is annotated by a feature of the feature configuration* $\widehat{\mathcal{FM}}$ *(under which the derivation was performed):* $\forall m \in \mathcal{M}, \Delta(m) \in \hat{M} \Leftrightarrow \exists f \in \widehat{\mathcal{FM}} \cdot (f, m) \in \mathcal{R}$.
(b) *Only one element can be derived from a given domain model element:* $\forall m \in \mathcal{M}, \exists! \hat{m} \in \hat{M} \cdot \hat{m} = \Delta(m)$.
(c) *Only derived elements are present in the derived model:* $\forall \hat{m} \in \hat{M}, \exists! m \in \mathcal{M} \cdot \hat{m} = \Delta(m)$.

We rely on concepts established in this section in the remainder of the paper.

4   Merge-Refactoring Approaches

In this section, we focus on merge-refactoring approaches that transform a set of cloned product variants into an annotative SPL representation. For the GlobalCo example presented in Sect. 2, this translates to merging the branches of GPS-Pro and GPS-EZ while unifying commonalities at the code level (i.e., building a domain model – see Sect. 4.1), tracing variabilities to their corresponding features (i.e., building annotations – see Sect. 4.2), and identifying relationships between these features (i.e., building a feature model – see Sect. 4.2).

4.1   Building a Domain Model

Most existing merge-refactoring approaches largely focus on building the domain model (a.k.a. the 150% product line representation). The main goal of this process is to establish correspondences between similar elements in distinct product variants, and then unify these elements so they appear in the domain model only once. Building such representation for the entire product line eliminates duplications and explicates differences between existing variants.

More formally, the domain model construction process identifies *tuples* of elements: sets of elements from distinct variants that are considered similar to each other[3]. Elements of each tuple are then unified. The process relies on a combination of the following three functions [49,53,62]:

- *Compare* is a heuristic function that establishes the similarity degree, a number between 0 and 1, for a tuple of elements[4]. *Compare* is a domain-specific function, i.e., the exact way of calculating the similarity degree between elements is determined by the original domain of these elements. For example, a similarity degree between classes is often calculated as a weighted sum of the similarity degrees of their sub-elements: names, attributes, operations, etc. [67].
  Numerous specific implementations calculate the similarity degree between pairs of input elements by comparing their corresponding sub-elements [32,45, 67]. Some approaches [45] also utilize behavioral properties of the compared elements, e.g., dynamic behaviors of states in the compared state machines, similar to checking bisimilarity. There are also approaches that extend beyond a pairwise comparison of input elements, i.e., establish similarity degrees for tuples longer than two [53,62].
- *Match* is a heuristic function that selects, from the set of all possible tuples, those tuples whose elements are to be unified. It relies on *compare* to judge the "quality" of each considered tuple.
  There are several ways to implement *match*. Some approaches use empirically established *similarity thresholds* to pick "strong" tuples that are good candidates for containing similar elements [45,49,54]. Other approaches strive to produce an "optimal merge"– a disjoint set of tuples with maximal total weight (defined as the sum of weights of all tuples in the set). As this problem is known to be NP-hard, these approaches rely on heuristic algorithms to compute matching solutions [53]. Another set of solutions apply clustering techniques to produce matches by grouping similar elements together, e.g., agglomerative clustering applied by Strueber et al. [62]; clustering algorithms, in turn, rely on results of *compare* to decide on the similarly between elements in a group.
- *Compose* is a function that takes as input a set of tuples produced by *match* (i.e., groups of elements that are considered similar to each other) and unifies

---

[3] We do not allow combining elements from the same variant. Hence, a tuple cannot contain elements from the same variant.

[4] The similarity degree for a tuple is also referred to as the *tuple weight*.

elements in each tuple, ensuring that matched elements appear in the resulting model only once. To produce a target product line representation, identical parts of the matched elements are put together while non-identical parts are annotated with features. Similar to *compare*, *compose* is also a domain-specific function: the granularity of unification, as well as the way in which annotations are represented, is defined by the elements' domain.

4.2   Building a Feature Model and Annotations

Automatically identifying product line features and relationships between these features is a challenging task. The simplest approach adopted by several merge-refactoring techniques [49,54,62] is to define one feature per each input product variant. Domain model elements are then annotated by these features according to the product(s) that contributed them. That is, a feature f_{P_i} annotates all non-common domain model artifacts that originated from the product P_i. All features representing original products are then defined as alternatives to each other. In that way, only the original products can be derived from the constructed product line representation; mixing features from different product is disallowed because that can result in unexpected feature interactions not considered so far.

Automating the identification of "semantic" features bearing a meaning for a human, as well as identifying possible synergies and potential interactions between features that did not appear together in any of the existing products, is still an open research direction. Moreover, multiple possible valid annotative SPL representations are possible, which are varied by the way features are selected and elements are combined [54]. Without further information, it is unclear which of these representations captures the user's intention the best. For that reason, even though there is a number of approaches that attempt to automate the complete merge-refactorings process in the context of industrial product lines [36,49,58,62,69], most existing work provides semi-automated or even manual solutions [3,16,22,25,26,28,34,35].

In reality, "simple" product lines that are easy to re-engineer manually often can also be efficiently managed as clones. Cloning stops scaling when the number of products grows and when these products further grow apart. In such cases, manual merge-refactoring is a time-consuming process that takes several years [22,25,26]. Meanwhile, companies still need to maintain product variants as distinct clones. Hence, focusing on merge-refactorings only is insufficient for addressing the needs of industrial practitioners. Next, we describe the clone-based SPLE approach that aims at improving the management of clones. Such an approach has potential to ease future merge refactorings or even eliminate the need to perform them altogether.

5   A Clone-Based SPLE Approach

In this section, we describe an approach for building a management infrastructure on top of existing cloned product variants, mitigating the shortcomings of cloning while leveraging its benefits. The management infrastructure helps the developers to capture essential product line constructs such as features, dependencies between features, as well as traceability information between the features and their implementation artifacts. For the GlobalCo case, it provides a global view on the set of specific changes performed by each team, making it apparent that the POI feature works differently in GPS-Pro and GPS-EZ, and that the Shortest Time Routing feature requires the Live Traffic Info in order to operate.

The main difference between the clone-based SPLE and the merge-refactoring approaches is that in the former, the information about features, their dependencies, and their relations to product artifacts do not need to be computed "all at once". Instead, this information is collected incrementally, only when needed. Each investment in extending the clone management infrastructure with additional information has "revenue" for the developers, in terms of easing the management of clones. Interestingly, the knowledge collected by the clone management infrastructure can also facilitate future merge-refactoring, if an organization eventually decides to take that direction.

The clone-based SPLE management infrastructure specifies a set of six conceptual operators, which we present next. We also show how the operators can be combined to realize product line development tasks. We discuss possible implementations of the operators and identify the remaining gaps.

5.1   Clone-Based SPLE Management Operators

Formal definitions of the clone-based SPLE management operators [51,55,56] are summarized in Table 2. We discuss and exemplify the operators using the vending machine example in Fig. 6. In what follows, we use the term *feature-oriented system* (a.k.a. *system*) to refer to a feature model and a set of artifacts annotated by features of that model. A feature-oriented system can represent both an SPL architecture and an individual product variant. In the latter case, the feature model only includes those features that were selected when deriving the variant from an SPL architecture.

Table 2. Operators for managing cloned variants.

	Operator	Input	Output
1	findFeatures	*variant*	*set of features*
2.	findFeatureImplementation	$f \times variant \times property$	*feature impl.*
3	dependsOn?	$<f_1, variant> \times <f_2, variant> \times property$	*set of witnesses*
4	same?	$<f_1, variant_1> \times <f_2, variant_2> \times property$	*set of witnesses*
5	interact?	*set of* $< f_i, variant_i > \times property$	*set of witnesses*
6	merge	$system_1 \times \ldots \times system_n \times matches \times resolution$	*system*

1. findFeatures returns a set of features, i.e., <feature label, description> pairs, realized by the given product variant. For the vending machine in Fig. 6(b), the features include <soda, sells soda>, <tea, sells tea> and <pay, allows to pay for the drink being purchased>.

2. `findFeatureImplementation`, commonly known as *feature location*, returns a feature implementation of the given feature f – the set of artifacts that realize the input feature. We say that these artifacts are *traced* to the feature. The exact form of the detected feature implementation depends on the *goal* of feature location: e.g., "detect the artifacts that contribute only to the feature of interest" or "detect all artifacts required for the feature to be executable (including the main method of a program)". We declaratively represent this goal using the input *property* that specifies inclusion and exclusion conditions for the feature location process. For example, transitions 1 and 2 of the vending machine in Fig. 6(b) realize the pay feature w.r.t. the property which disregards transitions contributing to other features, such as soda and tea.

3. `dependsOn?` determines whether the functionality described by feature f_1 requires the functionality described by feature f_2 from the same product variant in order to operate. The input *property* captures the nature of the dependsOn dependency. Such a property can express simple dependencies such as "f_1 requires f_2 in order to compile", or more complex behavior dependencies. The latter could be given as formal specifications or as a set of tests. For our example in Fig. 6(b), the soda functionality requires the pay functionality w.r.t. the property "soda is served only after a payment is received". The operator returns a *set of witnesses*, each demonstrating the dependsOn relationship between the artifacts of f_1 and f_2 (or none if the functionalities are independent). In the example above, a *witness* is the flow between the artifacts implementing the pay and soda features: transitions 1 and 2, implementing the first one, precede transitions 3 and 4, implementing the second.

4. `same?` determines whether the functionality described by feature f_1 of *variant$_1$* is consistent with the functionality described by feature f_2 of *variant$_2$*, i.e., whether there are no *disagreements* in both the features and the implementations of the two seemingly equivalent functionalities. For the products in Fig. 6, the compartment feature, allowing one to take the ordered drink, is implemented similarly in Figs. 6(a), (b), and (c), by transitions 5–7. These three product variants are in agreement on the implementation of the feature. Although feature accessible in Fig. 6(d) implements a similar functionality, this feature is implemented only by transition 4 since the corresponding product does not need to open and close the beverage compartment. Thus, this feature implementation "disagrees" with the implementation of the compartment feature in the first three variants.

   Like `dependsOn?`, the `same?` operator uses a *property* that specifies disagreements of interest and returns a *set of witnesses* exemplifying the disagreements (or none if the features agree). A simple form of disagreement is when features have different implementations, as in the above example. In that case, a *witness* could include artifacts that distinguish between the corresponding feature implementations. Disagreements can also be semantic, e.g., when checking for behavioral properties rather than the syntax of the implementing artifacts.

Table 3. Analyzed companies.

	Company #1	Company #2	Company #3
Domain	Aerospace	Electric motor controllers	Aerospace and Defense
Process	– V model (strictly waterfall) – Model-centric, with full requirements-to-code traceability – DO-178B certified	– Iterative –Code-centric	– Iterative – Code-centric – Requirements managed by a requirements management tool but no traceability to code is maintained – Requirements-based testing
Artifacts	– System and software requirements – Executable design models (code is generated) – Tests	– C/C++ code – Tests	– Textual requirements – C/C++ code – Tests

5. **interact?** determines whether combining functionalities described by a set of features would alter the behavior of one or more of those functionalities. The input *property* specifies the form of interactions to be checked and the output *set of witnesses* exemplifies them. For example, a composition of functionalities described by features pay and free from the transition systems in Figs. 6(a) and (d) might result in a transition system where the transition pay follows free: one has to pay after requesting a free drink, clearly violating the main behavioral property of the free feature.

6. **merge** puts together functionalities of the n input systems. It can be used for combining individual features (systems with a single feature each) or adding a feature to an existing product (systems with a single feature combined with a system representing a well-formed product). The *matches* parameter specifies artifacts that are considered similar and should be unified in the combined representation (see Sect. 4 for a more detailed discussion on matching). In addition, the *resolution* parameter declaratively specifies how to resolve disagreements and interactions between the input functionalities, e.g., by *overriding* one feature implementation with another, *integrating* the implementations together (thus producing a "merged" implementation), or *keeping both* as separate functionalities (with distinct feature declarations). For example, when borrowing features from transition systems in Figs. 6(a) and using them in the system in Fig. 6(d), one might choose to override the behavior of the accessible feature in Fig. 6(d) with the behavior of the compartment feature in Fig. 6(a), or keep both behaviors as *alternatives*.

5.2 Composition of the Operators

The clone-based management operators stem from interactions with numerous companies that use cloning to realize product lines and from reports published in the literature. In this section, we describe typical activities related to maintenance and evolution of existing clones and show that these activities can be mapped to instances of the conceptual operators. We thus demonstrate the applicability of the operators to improve the cloning experience and to support the clone-based SPLE approach. Our discussion is based on the detailed analysis of clone-related activities performed in three industrial companies [55,56]. Table 3 gives a high-level description of these companies.

Activity 1: Propagate changes between variants
Changes made in one cloned variant might be useful in another. To locate such changes, correspondences between features of a variant (detected using `findFeatures`) and the artifacts that implement them (detected using `findFeatureImplementation`) are established. Differences between distinct implementations of the same feature (detected using `same?` and represented by a set of *witnesses*) are inspected and propagated between variants. In the simplest form, the differences can be detected using a textual difference tool. Detecting more sophisticated behavioral differences is also possible, e.g., using the technique proposed by Jackson and Ladd [24].

Activity 2: Share features between variants
Like individual changes, complete features can be shared between distinct product variants. Here, again, a list of features, together with traces to implementation-level artifacts, is identified and maintained (instances of `findFeatures` and `findFeature- Implementation`). See the work of Li et al. on History Slicing [41,42] for some steps in that direction.

Different implementations of the chosen feature of interest are compared to each other (using `same?`), selecting the one found most appropriate. Further, the set of other features it requires (detected using `dependsOn?`) is inspected. If those features are not part of the target product, some of their artifacts have to be transferred to the target product together with the selected feature, to ensure its correct operation [57].

Next, the `interact?` operator verifies whether the new feature interferes with the functionality of the existing ones in the target product variant. Following that, `merge` integrates the selected feature and those that it requires in the target system, resolving the conflicts identified by `interact?`.

Activity 3: Retire features
While new features are added, some of the existing features might no longer be needed. Like in the previous activities, the set of features and their corresponding implementations is detected (using `findFeatures` and `findFeatureImplementation`) and features that depend on the one being removed are identified (using `dependsOn?`). Since the functionality of such features should not be affected by the feature retirement, artifacts that these features use are not removed.

Activity 4: Establish new variants
When creating a new product, the feature portfolio of all existing variants (detected using `findFeatures`) is inspected, and the variant with the most similar functionality is used as a starting point for cloning. Then, features that are not required in this variant are removed, as described in Activity 3, while additional features are either developed from scratch or "borrowed" from other

variants, as described in Activity 2. Instead of removing features, one could also mark them as optional, to start introducing variability that eventually leads to a single copy SPL representation.

5.3   Implementing the Operators

At the time of writing, we are not aware of a complete solution that implements most of the operators and/or can be used to manage clone-based SPLs. In this section, we outline individual approaches for implementing the operators and identify obvious gaps. This discussion aims at helping researchers and practitioners to scope and structure the required automation, reuse existing work, and identify research opportunities. It also allows companies to estimate the investment they need to make in order to improve their reuse practices, as they can reason about the management of clones in terms of existing and missing operator support.

findFeatureImplementation (a.k.a. feature location) and interact? (a.k.a. feature interaction) are by far the most studied operators. Over 20 different feature location techniques for source code have been developed [52]. Recently, a number of feature location techniques were designed explicitly for the product line context [43,50,68]. These techniques leverage information available when considering multiple product variants together.

Yet, it is often unclear how to compare techniques based on the features they detect, what the exact properties of the located feature implementations are, and how to extend these approaches to allow users to specify the desired properties of the location process. Also, feature location techniques for artifacts other than code, e.g., models, are poorly studied. Model slicing approaches can be seen as initial steps towards addressing this problem [1,38,39,63], but further investment in these techniques is still needed.

Feature interaction techniques (interact?) have also received significant attention, especially in the telecommunications domain [70]. Most of the existing approaches, however, deal with *pairwise* feature interactions. They have to be extended to consider interactions between sets of features that are part of real-life products: such sets can introduce interactions that are not detectable in a pairwise manner. Also, the applicability of many techniques for analyzing feature interactions is limited because they are designed to work on special-purpose models rather than unstructured slices of product artifacts that correspond to feature implementations.

Compare and *merge* techniques, for both code and models [17,45,61], as well as aspect weaving [33] and feature-oriented composition approaches [2], can be used to realize merge. Such techniques need to be extended to allow specifying the desired *resolutions*. Also, the techniques should be able to deal with unstructured product slices rather than complete, well-formed products or features declared in a specific manner.

Syntactic and semantic comparison techniques [23] can be used to implement the operator same?. The implementation of the operator for textual documents can be based on analyzing lexical similarities, e.g., using the Levenshtein distance

findFeatures	findFeatureImpl.	dependsOn?	same?	interact?	merge
Input	**Assumptions**	**Existing Implementations**	**Usage Examples**		
Textual documents	Short textual documents, e.g., requirements.	Levenshtein distance	Case study #1		
UML class diagrams	Compared models have common ancestors. Elements are compared based on their unique ids.	IBM Rational Software Architect	...		
UML class diagrams	Elements with similar names are likely to be similar.	UMLDiff	...		

Fig. 8. An initial sketch of the knowledge-based library.

metric [40] or textual diff tools [44]. For model-level artifacts, various model comparison and matching techniques can be used [61]. Comparison of code-level artifacts can also rely on tools that attempt to detect semantic differences, e.g., [24], or on more sophisticated implementations based on code clone detection [4]. Yet, like in the previous cases, additional work is required to adapt these works for analyzing unstructured feature implementations and declaratively obtaining the desired properties of the analysis.

Code analysis techniques, e.g., *program slicing* [64], can be used to implement dependsOn?. However, to the best of our knowledge, there are no dedicated works focusing on detecting semantic dependencies between model- or code-level functionalities. Such works, when developed, should clearly specify the nature of the detected dependencies and even be parameterizable to make it possible retrieving dependencies of a desired type.

findFeatures is yet another operator largely unstudied so far. Chen et al. [8], Weston et al. [66] and Davril et al. [14] describe techniques for extracting a feature model from informal specifications or publicly available product descriptions found online. These can be seen as initial implementations of findFeatures. However, the constructed feature model only includes features described in the documentation of the existing products rather than features implemented "in reality". Such approaches could be augmented with techniques that decouple product code [21], and then concisely summarize each part individually [48].

Organization-Specific Implementation of the Operators. The operator-based view provides a systematic approach for understanding the required, existing, and missing functionality. However, the specific implementation of the operators can differ between organizations and domains as no "generic" solution can work for all cases. Organizing existing implementations in an operator-based manner while explicating the exact assumptions made by these implementations, as sketched in Fig. 8, can assist both researchers and practitioners interested in improving reuse practices in families of related products. Exposing organizations to existing implementations of the operators and helping understand their applicability can enable reuse of implementations across organizations with similar needs. Researchers and tool developers can use this body of knowledge to focus their effort on functionality that is missing. As such, "crowdsourcing" of existing support can eventually lead to an increased quality and a larger spectrum of available solutions.

6   Future Research Directions

In this section, we outline future research directions that, according to our experience, can facilitate the transition from ad-hoc cloning to mature SPL management, promoting adoption of SPLE approaches in practice.

6.1   Economic Effectiveness of SPLE

Very little quantitative data is available to back up the claimed benefits of SPLE approaches – improved time-to-market and product quality, better market penetration and more. The majority of existing reports on the successful adoption of SPLE practices, including those published in the SPLC Hall of Fame[5], present mostly qualitative data that indicates or hints towards possible improvements. There are also no reports comparing the effort involved in maintaining a managed SPL versus an ad-hoc (e.g., cloned) one. It is of little surprise then that "convincing" industrial organizations to convert their development practices to follow SPLE is a challenging task. Furthermore, there is usually no way to compare the situational context in which product line approaches have been introduced, making it difficult to know if the approaches being touted are even relevant to a specific organization. All these factors impede adoption of SPLE in industry and also prevent a realistic comparison of numerous existing approaches to each other.

As part of future work, it is essential to engage the community in a more rigorous measurement and reporting system for quantifying business benefits associated with the introduction of SPLE approaches and measuring the effort of a transition from ad-hoc to well-managed reuse. Approaches and financial models for tackling technical debt can serve as an inspiration here [12,37]. Comparing different transition strategies, e.g., a bottom-up one that starts from analyzing and re-engineering code artifacts to a top-down strategy that starts from documentation and product requirements, would be beneficial. Furthermore, quantifying business benefits (or losses) associated with SPLE adoption and the context in which SPLE was applied will also make it possible to compare different SPLE technique to each other, assisting practitioners in making educated decisions when choosing an approach that best fits their goals and requirements. Such efforts are expected to benefit researchers, solution developers, and industrial organizations by allowing them to understand, measure, and report on the return on investment when shifting to SPLE.

---

[5] http://splc.net/fame.html.

6.2 Clone-Based SPLE Approaches

This paper highlighted several qualities of cloning that are appealing to practitioners, such as availability and independence of developers. Leveraging these qualities and developing structured SPLE approaches that are based on cloning (rather than trying to eliminate cloning) appears to be a direction that is worth further investigation. Initial work on exploring the space of clone-based SPLE approaches and defining the set of operators required for their management [51,55–57] is likely still incomplete; a more focused view on clone-based SPLE practices is required.

In addition, in practice, most clone variants are maintained as branches/ streams in Software Configuration Management (SCM) systems. Integrating SPLE management mechanisms on top of existing SCM systems appears to be a promising direction, which we only started to explore [41,42,57]. SCM-based approaches will let the user reason about the developed product line in terms of features rather than individual code changes made in distinct branches, will detect and maintain semantic dependencies and inconsistencies in implementations of features, and will contain feature provenance information.

Earlier works that focused on improving the maintenance of SCM branches might become relevant for this task. For example, Sarma et al. [20,59] suggest promoting team awareness by sharing information about changes and potential conflicts across branches of an SCM system. Both Gulla et al. [19] and Zeller et al. [71] propose to capture composition constraints between different versions of software components that are stored in an SCM system; these approaches allow the user to assemble a configuration containing just those component versions that satisfy the composition constraints. It might be beneficial to explore the applicability of these works to the SPLE context.

6.3 Improvements of the Cloned Product Line Management Framework

The clone-based management framework stems from interactions with numerous companies that use cloning to realize product lines and from reports published in the literature. Even though it was shown that the current set of operators is reasonable for expressing development activities related to clone management in the studied organizations [55,56], additional effort is required to refine the set of operators and their interfaces based on a larger set of case studies. Identifying and classifying contexts in which the operators are automatable, as well as quantifying the cost of providing such automation, is also still needed. Future studies addressing these questions will be of value.

A substantial amount of work also remains in devising techniques that realize the operators, in cases where such realizations are missing. The realization of some operators, such as *findFeatures* and *dependsOn?*, was, to the best of our knowledge, never attempted. "Smart" implementations of the operators that can work incrementally, to help address incremental changes in the development artifacts, as well as implementations that are able to simultaneously consider artifacts of several types, would also be highly useful.

7 Summary and Conclusions

Numerous Software Product Line Engineering (SPLE) approaches promise to ease the product line development and maintenance effort, reduce costs and improve quality of the developed products. Yet, the adoption of such approaches in industry is still limited. Instead, products are often established ad-hoc, e.g., by copying existing variants and modifying them to fit the requirements of a new customer or market. In this paper, we focused on exploring causes for this lack of adoption and suggesting approaches for improving the development experience in organizations that employ cloning to realize their product lines. We invite the readers to join our effort of helping industrial practitioners to deal with existing cloned variants by investigating approaches for an automated transition from ad-hoc to well-managed SPL development practices. In particular, we believe that building an efficient management infrastructure on top of existing clones (the clone-based SPLE approach) is a productive future research direction.

References

1. Androutsopoulos, K., Clark, D., Harman, M., Krinke, J., Tratt, L.: State-based model slicing: a survey. ACM Comput. Surv. **45**(4), 53:1–53:36 (2013)
2. Batory, D.S., Sarvela, J.N., Rauschmaye, A.: Scaling step-wise refinement. IEEE Trans. Softw. Eng. **30**(6), 355–371 (2004)
3. Bayer, J., Girard, J.-F., Würthner, M., DeBaud, J.-M., Apel, M.: Transitioning legacy assets to a product line architecture. In: Nierstrasz, O., Lemoine, M. (eds.) ESEC/SIGSOFT FSE -1999. LNCS, vol. 1687, pp. 446–463. Springer, Heidelberg (1999). doi:10.1007/3-540-48166-4_27
4. Bellon, S., Koschke, R., Antoniol, G., Krinke, J., Merlo, E.: Comparison and evaluation of clone detection tools. IEEE Trans. Softw. Eng. **33**, 577–591 (2007)
5. Berger, T., Lettner, D., Rubin, J., Grünbacher, P., Silva, A., Becker, M., Chechik, M., Czarnecki, K.: What is a Feature? A qualitative study of features in industrial software product lines. In: Proceedings of the 19th International Conference on Software Product Line (SPLC 2015), pp. 16–25 (2015)
6. Borba, P., Teixeira, L., Gheyi, R.: A theory of software product line refinement. Theor. Comput. Sci. **455**, 2–30 (2012)
7. Boucher, Q., Classen, A., Heymans, P., Bourdoux, A., Demonceau, L.: Tag and prune: a pragmatic approach to software product line implementation. In: Proceedings of the IEEE/ACM International Conference on Automated Software Engineering (ASE 2010), pp. 333–336 (2010)
8. Chen, K., Zhang, W., Zhao, H., Mei, H.: An approach to constructing feature models based on requirements clustering. In: Proceedings of the IEEE International Requirements Engineering Conference (RE 2005), pp. 31–40 (2005)
9. Chen, K., Rajlich, V.: Case study of feature location using dependence graph. In: Proceedings of the International Workshop on Program Comprehension (IWPC 2000), pp. 241–249 (2000)
10. Classen, A., Heymans, P., Schobbens, P.-Y., Legay, A., Raskin, J.-F.: Model checking lots of systems: efficient verification of temporal properties in software product lines. In: Proceedings of the International Conference on Software Engineering (ICSE 2010), pp. 335–344 (2010)

11. Clements, P.C., Northrop, L.: Software Product Lines: Practices and Patterns. Addison-Wesley, Reading (2001)

12. Cunningham, W.: The WyCash portfolio management system. In: Addendum to the Proceedings of the ACM SIGPLAN Conference on Object-Oriented Programming Systems, Languages, and Applications (OOPSLA 1992), pp. 29–30 (1992)

13. Czarnecki, K., Antkiewicz, M.: Mapping Features to models: a template approach based on superimposed variants. In: Glück, R., Lowry, M. (eds.) GPCE 2005. LNCS, vol. 3676, pp. 422–437. Springer, Heidelberg (2005). doi:10.1007/11561347_28

14. Davril, J.-M., Delfosse, E., Hariri, N., Acher, M., Cleland-Huang, J., Heymans, P.: Feature model extraction from large collections of informal product descriptions. In: Proceedings of the European Software Engineering Conference and the ACM SIGSOFT Symposium on the Foundations of Software Engineering (ESEC/FSE 2013), pp. 290–300 (2013)

15. Dubinsky, Y., Rubin, J., Berger, T., Duszynski, S., Becker, M., Czarnecki, K.: An exploratory study of cloning in industrial software product lines. In: Proceedings of the European Conference on Software Maintenance and Reengineering (CSMR 2013), pp. 25–34 (2013)

16. Ferber, S., Haag, J., Savolainen, J.: Feature interaction and dependencies: modeling features for reengineering a legacy product line. In: Chastek, G.J. (ed.) SPLC 2002. LNCS, vol. 2379, pp. 235–256. Springer, Heidelberg (2002). doi:10.1007/3-540-45652-X_15

17. Fluri, B., Wuersch, M., Pinzger, M., Gall, H.: Change distilling: tree differencing for fine-grained source code change extraction. IEEE Trans. Softw. Eng. **33**(11), 725–743 (2007)

18. Gomaa, H.: Designing Software Product Lines with UML: From Use Cases to Pattern-Based Software Architectures. Addison-Wesley, Boston (2004)

19. Gulla, B., Karlsson, E.-A., Yeh, D.: Change-oriented version descriptions in EPOS. Softw. Eng. J. **6**(6), 378–386 (1991)

20. Hattori, L., Lanza, M.: Syde: a tool for collaborative software development. In: Proceedings of the International Conference on Software Engineering (ICSE 2010), Companion Volume, pp. 235–238 (2010)

21. Herzig, K., Zeller, A.: Untangling changes. Manuscript, September 2011

22. Hetrick, W.A., Krueger, C.W., Moore, J.G.: Incremental return on incremental investment: Engenio's transition to software product line practice. In: Proceedings of the ACM SIGPLAN Conference on Object-Oriented Programming, Systems, Languages and Applications (OOPSLA 2006), Companion Volume, pp. 798–804 (2006)

23. Horwitz, S.: Identifying the semantic and textual differences between two versions of a program. In: Proceeding of the ACM SIGPLAN Conference on Programming Language Design and Implementation (PLDI 1990), pp. 234–245 (1990)

24. Jackson, D., Ladd, D.A.: Semantic Diff: a tool for summarizing the effects of modifications. In: Proceedings of the IEEE International Conference on Software Maintenance (ICSM 1994), pp. 243–252 (1994)

25. Jepsen, H.P., Beuche, D.: Running a software product line: standing still is going backwards. In: Proceedings of the International Software Product Line Conference (SPLC 2009), pp. 101–110 (2009)

26. Jepsen, H.P., Dall, J.G., Beuche, D.: Minimally invasive migration to software product lines. In: Proceedings of the International Software Product Line Conference (SPLC 2007), pp. 203–211 (2007)

27. Kang, K.C., Cohen, S.G., Hess, J.A., Novak, W.E., Peterson, A.S.: Feature-Oriented Domain Analysis (FODA) Feasibility Study. Technical report, Software Engineering Institute, Carnegie Mellon University, CMU/SEI-90TR-21 (1990)

28. Kang, K.C., Kim, M., Lee, J., Kim, B.: Feature-oriented re-engineering of legacy systems into product line assets – a *Case Study*. In: Obbink, H., Pohl, K. (eds.) SPLC 2005. LNCS, vol. 3714, pp. 45–56. Springer, Heidelberg (2005). doi:10.1007/11554844_6

29. Kang, K.C., Kim, S., Lee, J., Kim, K., Shin, E., Huh, M.: FORM: a feature-oriented reuse method with domain-specific reference architectures. Ann. Softw. Eng. **5**, 143–168 (1998)

30. Kästner, C., Apel, S.: Integrating compositional and annotative approaches for product line engineering. In: Proceedings of the Workshop on Modularization, Composition and Generative Techniques for Product Line Engineering (McGPLE) at the International Conference on Generative Programming: Concepts and Experiences (GPCE 2008), pp. 35–40 (2008)

31. Kästner, C., Apel, S., Kuhlemann, M.: Granularity in software product lines. In: Proceedings of the International Conference on Software Engineering (ICSE 2008), pp. 311–320 (2008)

32. Kelter, U., Wehren, J., Niere, J.: A generic difference algorithm for UML models. In: Proceedings of Software Engineering (SE 2005), pp. 105–116 (2005)

33. Kiczales, G., Hilsdale, E., Hugunin, J., Kersten, M., Palm, J., Griswold, W.G.: An overview of AspectJ. In: Knudsen, J.L. (ed.) ECOOP 2001. LNCS, vol. 2072, pp. 327–354. Springer, Heidelberg (2001). doi:10.1007/3-540-45337-7_18

34. Kim, K., Kim, H., Kim, W.: Building software product line from the legacy systems: experience in the digital audio and video domain. In: Proceedings of the International Software Product Line Conference (SPLC 2007), pp. 171–180 (2007)

35. Kolb, R., Muthig, D., Patzke, T., Yamauchi, K.: Refactoring a legacy component for reuse in a software product line: a case study: practice articles. J. Softw. Maint. Evol. Res. Pract. **18**(2), 109–132 (2006)

36. Koschke, R., Frenzel, P., Breu, A.P., Angstmann, K.: Extending the reflexion method for consolidating software variants into product lines. J. Softw. Qual. Control **17**(4), 331–366 (2009)

37. Kruchten, P., Nord, R.L., Ozkaya, I.: Guest Editors' introduction. Technical debt: from metaphor to theory and practice. IEEE Softw. **29**(6), 18–21 (2012)

38. Lai, X.: FormlSlicer: a model slicing tool for feature-rich state-machine models. Master's thesis, School of Computer Science, University of Waterloo, Canada (2015)

39. Lano, K., Kolahdouz Rahimi, S.: Slicing techniques for UML models. J. Object Technol. **10**(11), 1–49 (2011)

40. Levenshtein, V.I.: Binary codes capable of correcting deletions, insertions and reversals. Sov. Phys. Dokl. **10**(8), 707–710 (1966)

41. Li, Y., Rubin, J., Chechik, M.: Semantic slicing of software version histories (T). In: Proceedings of the International Conference on Automated Software Engineering (ASE 2015), pp. 686–696 (2015)

42. Li, Y., Zhu, C., Rubin, J., Chechik, M.: Precise semantic history slicing through dynamic delta refinement. In: Proceedings of the International Conference on Automated Software Engineering (ASE 2016) (2016)

43. Linsbauer, L., Lopez-Herrejon, E.R., Egyed, A.: Recovering traceability between features and code in product variants. In: Proceedings of the International Software Product Line Conference (SPLC 2013), pp. 131–140 (2013)

44. MacKenzie, D., Eggert, P., Stallman, R.: Comparing and Merging Files with GNU diff and patch. Network Theory Ltd., Bristol (2003)
45. Nejati, S., Sabetzadeh, M., Chechik, M., Easterbrook, S., Zave, P.: Matching and merging of statecharts specifications. In: Proceedings of the International Conference on Software Engineering (ICSE 2007), pp. 54–64 (2007)
46. Northrop, L.: Software product lines reuse that makes business sense. In: Proceedings of the Australasian Software Engineering Conference (ASWEC 2006) (2006)
47. Pohl, K., Boeckle, G., van der Linden, F.J.: Software Product Line Engineering: Foundations, Principles, and Techniques. Springer, New York (2005)
48. Rastkar, S., Murphy, G.C., Bradley, A.W.J.: Generating natural language summaries for crosscutting source code concerns. In: Proceedings of the IEEE International Conference on Software Maintenance (ICSM 2011), pp. 103–112 (2011)
49. Rubin, J., Chechik, M.: Combining related products into product lines. In: Lara, J., Zisman, A. (eds.) FASE 2012. LNCS, vol. 7212, pp. 285–300. Springer, Heidelberg (2012). doi:10.1007/978-3-642-28872-2_20
50. Rubin, J., Chechik, M.: Locating distinguishing features using diff sets. In: Proceedings of the IEEE/ACM International Conference on Automated Software Engineering (ASE 2012), pp. 242–245 (2012)
51. Rubin, J., Chechik, M.: A framework for managing cloned product variants. In: Proceedings of the International Conference on Software Engineering (ICSE 2013), pp. 1233–1236 (2013)
52. Rubin, J., Chechik, M.: A survey of feature location techniques. In: Reinhartz-Berger, I., et al. (eds.) Domain Engineering: Product Lines, Conceptual Models, and Languages, pp. 29–58. Springer, Heidelberg (2013)
53. Rubin, J., Chechik, M.: N-way model merging. In: Proceedings of the European Software Engineering Conference and the ACM SIGSOFT Symposium on the Foundations of Software Engineering (ESEC/FSE 2013), pp. 301–311 (2013)
54. Rubin, J., Chechik, M.: Quality of merge-refactorings for product lines. In: Cortellessa, V., Varró, D. (eds.) FASE 2013. LNCS, vol. 7793, pp. 83–98. Springer, Heidelberg (2013). doi:10.1007/978-3-642-37057-1_7
55. Rubin, J., Czarnecki, K., Chechik, M.: Managing cloned variants: a framework and experience. In: Proceedings of the International Software Product Line Conference (SPLC 2013), pp. 101–110 (2013)
56. Rubin, J., Czarnecki, K., Chechik, M.: Cloned product variants: from ad-hoc to managed software product lines. J. Softw. Tools Technol. Trans. 17(5), 627–646 (2015). http://dl.acm.org/citation.cfm?id=2822233
57. Rubin, J., Kirshin, A., Botterweck, G., Chechik, M.: Managing forked product variants. In: Proceedings of the International Software Product Line Conference (SPLC 2012), pp. 156–160 (2012)
58. Ryssel, U., Ploennigs, J., Kabitzsch, K.: Automatic variation-point identification in function-block-based models. In: Proceedings of the International Conference on Generative Programming: Concepts and Experiences (GPCE 2010), pp. 23–32 (2010)
59. Sarma, A., Noroozi, Z., Van Der Hoek, A.: Palantir: raising awareness among configuration management workspaces. In: Proceedings of the International Conference on Software Engineering (ICSE 2003), pp. 444–454 (2003)
60. She, S., Lotufo, R., Berger, T., Wasowski, A., Czarnecki, K.: Reverse engineering feature models. In: Proceedings of the International Conference on Software Engineering (ICSE 2011) (2011)
61. Stephan, M., Cordy, J.R.: A survey of methods and applications of model comparison. Technical report, Queen's University, Canada (2011)

62. Strüber, D., Rubin, J., Arendt, T., Chechik, M., Taentzer, G., Plöger, J.: Rule-merger: automatic construction of variability-based model transformation rules. In: Stevens, P., Wąsowski, A. (eds.) FASE 2016. LNCS, vol. 9633, pp. 122–140. Springer, Heidelberg (2016). doi:10.1007/978-3-662-49665-7_8

63. Struber, D., Rubin, J., Taentzer, G., Chechik, M.: Splitting models using information retrieval and model crawling techniques. In: Gnesi, S., Rensink, A. (eds.) FASE 2014. LNCS, vol. 8411, pp. 47–62. Springer, Heidelberg (2014). doi:10.1007/978-3-642-54804-8_4

64. Tip, F.: A survey of program slicing techniques. J. Program. Lang. **3**(3), 121–189 (1995)

65. Weiss, D.M., Lai, C.T.R.: Software Product Line Engineering: A Family-Based Software Development Process. Addison-Wesley, Reading (1999)

66. Weston, N., Chitchyan, R., Rashid, A.: A framework for constructing semantically composable feature models from natural language requirements. In: Proceedings of the International Software Product Line Conference (SPLC 2009), pp. 211–220 (2009)

67. Xing, Z., Stroulia, E.: UMLDiff: an algorithm for object-oriented design differencing. In: Proceedings of the IEEE/ACM International Conference on Automated Software Engineering (ASE 2005), pp. 54–65 (2005)

68. Xue, Y., Xing, Z., Jarzabek, S.: Feature location in a collection of product variants. In: Proceedings of the Working Conference on Reverse Engineering (WCRE 2012), pp. 145–154 (2012)

69. Yoshimura, K., Narisawa, F., Hashimoto, K., Kikuno, T.: FAVE: Factor analysis based approach for detecting product line variability from change history. In: Proceedings of the Working Conference on Mining Software Repositories (MSR 2008), pp. 11–18 (2008)

70. Zave, P.: FAQ Sheet on Feature Interaction (2004). http://www2.research.att.com/~pamela/faq.html

71. Zeller, A., Snelting, G.: Unified versioning through feature logic. ACM Trans. Softw. Eng. Methodol. **6**(4), 398–441 (1997)

DSLs in Robotics: A Case Study in Programming Self-reconfigurable Robots

Ulrik Pagh Schultz[1]([⊠]), Mirko Bordignon[2], Kasper Stoy[3], Arne Nordmann[4],
Nico Hochgeschwender[5], and Sebastian Wrede[6,7]

[1] Maersk Institute, University of Southern Denmark, Odense, Denmark
`ups@mmmi.sdu.ek`
[2] Frauenhofer IPA, Stuttgart, Germany
[3] IT University of Copenhagen, Copenhagen, Denmark
[4] Robert Bosch Gmbh, Stuttgart, Germany
[5] Department of Computer Science, Bonn-Rhein-Sieg University,
Sankt Augustin, Germany
[6] Cognitive Interaction Technology Excellence Cluster (CITEC),
Bielefeld University, Bielefeld, Germany
[7] Institute for Robotics and Cognition (CoR-Lab),
Bielefeld University, Bielefeld, Germany

Abstract. Robotic systems blend hardware and software in a holistic
way that intrinsically raises many crosscutting concerns such as concurrency, uncertainty, and time constraints. These concerns make programming robotic systems challenging as expertise from multiple domains
needs to be integrated conceptually and technically. Programming languages play a central role in providing a higher level of abstraction. This
briefing presents a case study on the evolution of domain-specific languages based on modular robotics. The case study on the evolution of
domain-specific languages is based on a series of DSL prototypes developed over five years for the domain of modular, self-reconfigurable robots.

1 Introduction

Model-driven and domain specific development methods are recognized approaches for coping with the challenges of building complex heterogeneous systems
in domains such as aerospace, telecommunication and automotive [12]. Robotic
systems face similar challenges, due to the need for blending hardware and software in a holistic way intrinsically raising many crosscutting concerns such as
concurrency, uncertainty, and time constraints [16]. By experience, traditional
general-purpose languages often lead to a poor fit between the language features
and the implementation requirements.

Domain-specific languages (DSLs) and models offer a powerful, systematic
way to overcome the challenges of developing software for robotics. A domain-
specific language (DSL) is a programming language dedicated to a particular
problem domain that offers specific notations and abstractions, which, at the

© Springer International Publishing AG 2017
J. Cunha et al. (Eds.): GTTSE 2015, LNCS 10223, pp. 98–123, 2017.
DOI: 10.1007/978-3-319-60074-1_5

same time, decrease the coding complexity and increase programmer productivity within that domain. Models offer a high-level way for domain users to specify the functionality of their system at the right level of abstraction.

This briefing concerns a case study on the evolution of domain-specific languages based on modular robotics. Modular, self-reconfigurable robots are distributed robotic systems that can change their own shape by autonomously rearranging the physical modules from which they are built [48]. Key issues in programming modular robotics are illustrated using a programming exercise, which is used to motivate a set of requirements for domain-specific languages for this area of robotics. The case study is based on a series of DSL prototypes for the domain of modular, self-reconfigurable robots developed over five years [4–6,36–39]. In the case study we are interested in how to program distributed behaviors that implement specific robot functionality such as locomotion or self-reconfiguration.

The rest of this document is organized as follows. First Sect. 2 introduces the concept of domain-specific languages with a particular focus on concerns relevant to robotics. Then Sect. 3 provides an overview of the use of DSLs in the robotics domain. Sections 4, 5 and 6 present the case study on language evolution for modular robots. Last, Sect. 7 concludes the paper.

2   Background: Domain-Specific Languages

Surveys with a wide scope on DSLs have been conducted both by Van Deursen et al. [12] and later by Mernik et al. [27]. According to van Deursen et al. [12], a DSL is defined as a *"programming language or executable specification language that offers, through appropriate notations and abstractions, expressive power focused on, and usually restricted to, a particular problem domain"*. The abstractions and notations must be *"natural/suitable for the stakeholders who specify that particular concern"* [46]. These definitions highlight two fundamental characteristics of well-designed DSLs: their expressive power is concentrated around a specific domain and their syntax is intuitively understandable for domain experts while being machine processable.

Model-driven software development with DSLs aims to extract agreed-upon syntax and semantics from the problem domain, e.g., by reviewing existing code examples and APIs, through the analysis of formal descriptions found in the literature or the application of further analysis patterns [27]. Based on the results of these domain analysis steps, the identified abstractions and desired notations can be realized as a DSL. Instead of hiding the domain concepts in a compilation unit implemented with traditional programming techniques, the DSL approach provides the specific abstractions at the model level. In contrast to *General Purpose Languages* (GPL) such as C++, Java, or Python, DSLs usually contain only a restricted set of notations and abstractions. Compared to *external* DSLs that define their own syntax and semantics, so-called *internal* DSLs are embedded in extensible general purpose languages such as Lua, Racket or Ruby [14]. They extend the syntax and potentially the semantics of the host language with domain-specific notations and abstractions. This adds the expressive power of the DSL to the GPL. While internal DSLs typically rely on (and are bound to) the execution semantics of their host language, external DSLs are transformed to a format that directly allows execution on a target platform or interpretation, e.g., through a virtual machine.

Similar to DSLs, *Domain-specific Modeling Languages* (DSML) are languages that are focused on expressing model instances, often using a graphical notation. DSMLs should however be considered different from general-purpose modeling languages such as UML or SysML: While it is still possible to add domain-specific abstractions to these languages, e.g., using UML Profiles (cf. MARTE [15] to describe and analyze real-time systems), adding domain-specific notation to graphical modeling languages is much harder.

In order to efficiently implement and apply a DSL approach for the development of robotics systems and to fully exploit its benefits, DS(M)Ls are typically realized in toolchains tailored to model-driven development such as the Eclipse Modeling Project [18]. These so-called *language workbenches* such as xtext [13], spoofax [22] and MPS [20] offer extensive support for the development of the DSLs themselves and for the actual system modeling tasks performed by a language user. DSLs developed in these environments facilitate the users modeling tasks typically with textual and/or graphical editors with rich code completion and dynamic constraint checking. Furthermore, these environments provide extension points to plug-in required model-to-model (M2M) and model-to-text (M2T) transformations in order to generate code from system models that integrates with the overall environment used for the development of a robotics application.

3   Programming Languages in Robotics

Surveys on programming approaches for robots in general have been conducted by Biggs et al. [3] and later with a specific focus on DSLs by Nordmann et al. [29]. Following Biggs et al. [3] robot programming systems can be divided into three categories: automatic programming, manual programming, and software architectures. In the context of this briefing, we are only interested in the manual programming category, and will furthermore focus exclusively on DSLs. To exemplify the challenges in programming distributed robot systems the area of swarm robots will furthermore be introduced and used to motivate requirements for DSLs for domain of modular robotics.

3.1   The Use of DSLs in Robotics

According to Nordmann et al., the main use-case for DS(M)Ls in robotics is to generate executable code at design time to control the robot or provide supporting routines [29]. They observe that the majority of published DSLs concern *Architectures and Programming*, which refers to the way a robotic system is designed on the software level, abstracting over the underlying computational concepts. Platform-independence is often a motivation for the development and use of DS(M)L approaches, but this is not always the case, for example to provide tool support for a specific platform.

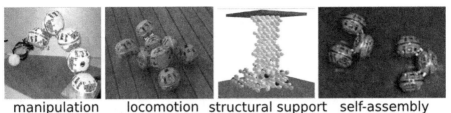

manipulation   locomotion structural support self-assembly

Fig. 1. Examples of several tasks performed by robots built from ATRON modules [21, 26]

3.2   Challenges in Programming Modular Robots

Modular robotics is an approach to the design, construction and operation of robotic devices aiming to achieve flexibility and reliability by using a reconfigurable assembly of simple subsystems [48]. Robots built from modular components can potentially overcome the limitations of traditional fixed-morphology systems because they are able to rearrange modules automatically on a need basis, a process known as self-reconfiguration, and are able to replace unserviceable modules without disrupting the system's operations significantly. The same set of modules can be used for many different purposes, as illustrated in Fig. 1 with the ATRON robot.

Naturally, since modular robots in principle can be used to build any kind of robot, many traditional concerns in robotics are relevant for modular robots. Nevertheless, some concerns are particularly important for modular robots: representations of the robot structure and specifications of coordinate representations and transformations must model a reconfigurable structure and the mappings between the individual modules, and are thereby key to many of the other subdomains (e.g., the control of the modules depends on their position in the structure). For self-reconfigurable robots the sequence of operations needed to modify the module configuration can be derived using reasoning and planning [9, 28, 34, 45, 49, 52].

Control of a modular robot as a whole requires coordination of all of the modules of the robotic ensemble. For example when programming locomotion gaits for chain-type modular robots, functional configurations within the robot ensemble can be identified and assigned controllers specified as phase automata, so as to achieve the desired group behavior [53]. In general coordination in a modular robot requires some degree of abstraction over distribution. An extreme example is ensembles composed of spherical microrobots [17] assumed to exist in massive numbers several order of magnitudes higher than macroscale modular robots. Such microscale robots could be programmed using declarative high-level programming languages specifically developed to support the operation of such million-module ensembles by abstracting over the individual modules and specifying behaviors for the ensemble as a whole [1, 11]. In this case the language can afford to overlook specific reliability issues, since failure of individual modules is often not significant in a highly-redundant context.

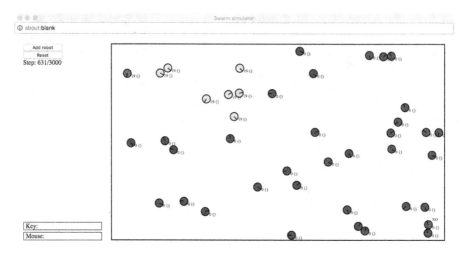

Fig. 2. Python-based simulation of robot swarm, information from red robot picked up by blue robots that have transitioned to yellow and are carrying the information to the green robot. (Color figure online)

3.3   Concrete Example: Swarm Robots

Swarm robots are a special kind of mobile robots where many smaller robots cooperate to achieve goals beyond the capability of any of the robots operating by itself [35]. Swarm robots are similar to modular robots, in the sense that many (smaller) robots collaborate towards a common goal. Similar solutions can to some extent be used across both these kinds of robots, modular robots are however normally physically interlocked, which requires a much higher degree of coordination compared to swarm robots. Nevertheless the challenges in programming modular robots can to some extent be understood by studying examples of swarm robot programming.

We use swarm robots as a concrete example to address the issue of reliable distributed programming on unreliable robot hardware by means of a programming exercise used at GTTSE'15. The problem posed and the corresponding solution serves to motivate the case study on DSLs for modular robots presented later in this briefing. We only address the challenges in programming swarm robotics briefly, for a general overview we refer to the SWARM-BOTS overview [35].

Context. The swarm-bots programming exercise is based on a minimal simulation implemented in Python using the on-line *CodeSkulptor* programming environment. The sourcecode is available online [24]. The simulator provides a rectangular two-dimensional arena environment in which a number of round robots can move around. Each robot is controlled by a Python function, and can move around in the arena, but stops if it hits the edges of the arena or bumps into other robots. Robots can sense other nearby robots and communicate with them. The simulator provides a number of parameters for tuning the behavior, including adding random noise to movement and simulating an unstable power supply that when the robot moves randomly resets the state of a robot to its initial state. A screenshot from the simulator is shown in Fig. 2. The simulation is programmed with a classical swarm robots scenario: reliably communicating information from one part of the system to another, using only ad-hoc communication between neighboring robots. The simulation uses colors to indicate the state of the robot controller: the immobile red robot represents an information source and the immobile green robot an information sink (i.e., the location that the information must be carried to). The blue robots move around looking for information, and transition to yellow when they are carrying the information.

Programming exercise. The information communication scenario formed the basis for an exercise, which was conducted as a student programming competition at GTTSE'15. The simulation as provided to the students came with a controller implementation that solved the problem within the time limit in a reliable environment scenario (precise robot movement, no risk of reset). The initial implementation could easily be improved with the given simulation parameters, for example by precisely moving the robots in a pattern that maximizes coverage or that forms a straight line between the information source and sink. The problem to solve was however expressed as *Devise [a] robot controller that exhibits the highest degree of robustness to "spurious resets" and still solves the problem [within the time limit].* When the movement randomization and reset risk are increased, the controller implementation that was provided completely fails to solve the problem. The movement randomization makes it difficult to position robots precisely, just as it would be the case in a real-world physical scenario. The reset risk is exaggerated compared to the capabilities of most real-world robots, but a solution that works in spite of many of the robots spontaneously resetting is by experience robust and likely to work in the presence of unreliable hardware [38].

Elements of a solution. A number of solutions were provided by different groups of GTTSE'15 participants, in general the recurring idea was to focus on reactive behaviors where the robot constantly adjusts its current movement pattern to the state of the immediately surrounding environment. The winning solution was programmed by Patrick Monslaup (University of Bergen), and is shown running in the simulator in Fig. 3. The solution does not rely on mobile robots being able to retain any state, but eventually builds a network of immobile robots along the edge of the arena that are within communication range of each other. The solution moreover relies on the random noise in the movement to avoid deadlock situations where robots might otherwise get stuck, due to a very simply searching behavior where the mobile robots move along the sides of the arena and stop when they find an unoccupied spot.

3.4   Key Requirements on DSLs for Modular Robotics

The main concerns in programming modular robots are *Adapting* behavior to physical shape, shape-independent *Control* and *Communication*. *Adaptation* is

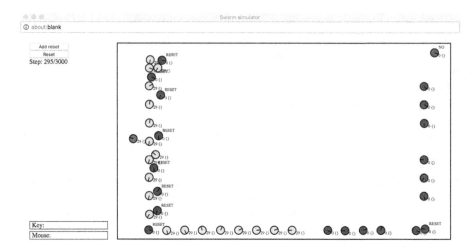

Fig. 3. Solution to the Python-based simulation problem from Fig. 2, highly tolerant to random resets and noise.

required since, unlike most other kinds of robots, a control program running on a modular robot must adapt to the current physical shape of the robot. This holds true even as a self-reconfigurable robot changes its shape, as this requires a continuous adaptation of the controller to the robot shape. Control programs will therefore often tend to make assumptions about the shape of the robot, but critically these assumptions should only concern selected properties of the robot (such as whether the robot has wheels), ideally allowing the program to abstract over uninteresting morphological details (such as the underlying symmetry of the wheel modules). *Control* of a modular robot should allow the robot to be controlled as a whole. Since centralized approaches do not scale well and are fragile in the context of unreliable hardware, this typically requires distributed and fault-tolerant control which in general is considered difficult to program manually. *Communication* is required given the distributed nature of modular robotics, but unreliable hardware complicates the implementation of reliable approaches to communication. Moreover scalability to larger numbers of modules is normally considered essential, which requires (most) communication to be local even when global coordination is needed.

4   Case Study: Modular Robots

We now present the basis for our case study in the development of DSLs for robotics: a DSL designed for programming the ATRON modular robot for locomotion tasks [6]. As described in the previous section, modular robot programming spans a number of issues ranging from algorithms for high-level coordination to dealing with programming distributed hardware modules, issues that

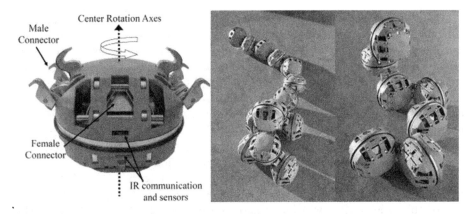

Fig. 4. The ATRON modular robot: a single module together with snake and car configurations

Fig. 5. Left: Small ATRON car. Rest: Various simulated ATRON car configurations: basic 4-wheels, long 6-wheels, and parallel 12-wheels.

must be dealt with at multiple levels in the software environments that we develop for this domain.[1]

4.1 Analysis: Hardware and Software

Our experimental platform is the ATRON self-reconfigurable robot, a 3D lattice-type robot [21,26] shown in Fig. 4. An ATRON module is spherical, is composed of two hemispheres, and can actively rotate the two hemispheres relative to each other. Each module is equipped with an Atmel 128 CPU with 4 Kb of RAM and 128 Kb of program memory. A module may connect to neighbor modules using its four actuated male and four passive female connectors. The connectors are positioned at 90° intervals on each hemisphere. Eight infrared ports, one below each connector, are used by the modules to communicate with neighboring modules and sense distance to nearby obstacles or modules. A module weighs 0.850 kg and has a diameter of 110 mm. Currently 100 hardware prototypes of the ATRON modules exist. Motion constraints on the modules affect their ability to self-reconfigure. The single rotational degree of freedom of a module makes

---

[1] This section is partially based on the paper *A Virtual Machine-based Approach for Fast and Flexible Reprogramming of Modular Robots* published at the IEEE International Conference on Robotics and Automation [6].

its ability to move very limited: in fact a module is unable to move by itself. The help of another module is always needed to achieve movement. All modules must also always stay connected to prevent modules from being disconnected from the robot. They must avoid collisions and respect their limited actuator strength: one module can lift two others against gravity. As a concrete example, consider the car robots shown in Figs. 4 and 5, which are different configurations for car-like robots, physical and simulated. These robots have a number of "wheels": modules that are in contact with the floor, that can turn freely, and that are aligned in the same direction. The two-wheeled car uses differential steering, whereas the others use one of the modules as a steering column.

General approaches to programming the self-reconfigurable ATRON robot include gradients, metamodules, and rule-based control [8,10,30,31]. In the context of this briefing, we will investigate the use of role-based control, which is a generalization of rule-based control. Role-based control is an approach to behavior-based control for modular robots where the behavior of a module is derived from its context [41,42]. The behavior of the robot at any given time is driven by a combination of sensor inputs and internally generated events. Roles allow modules to interpret sensors and events in a specific way, thus differentiating the behavior of the module according to the concrete needs of the robot. Roles have been demonstrated as a highly useful abstraction when programming locomotion for modular robots, for which reason we will investigate the development of a role-based language.

4.2   The DynaRole Language

Following the approach of role-based control [42], we propose the DynaRole DSL inspired by concepts role-oriented programming: we assign a behavioral *role* to each module depending on the properties of the module, including its physical position, current behavior, and connectivity to other modules [41]. The role assignment aspect of DynaRole is purely declarative, allowing roles to be assigned to specific modules in the structure based on invariants. DynaRole is a domain-specific language targeted to the ATRON robots with very limited support for general-purpose computation; it provides primitives for simple decision-making, but all complex computations must be performed in external code.

Figure 6 shows the EBNF of the DynaRole language (non-terminals are written using italicized capitals, concrete syntax in courier font). A DynaRole program declares a number of roles. A role normally extends a super-role meaning that it inherits all the members of the super-role; the common super-role Module defines the capabilities of all modules. A role can be concrete or abstract, with the usual semantics: all abstract members must be overridden by concrete members for a role be usable at runtime. A role declares a number of members in the form of constants, invariants, and methods. There currently is no explicit notion of state, so state is represented using external C code and accessed using functions. A constant can be concrete or abstract, and always defines an 8-bit value. For a module to play a given role, all invariants required by the role must

```
PROGRAM       ::= ROLE* DEPLOYMENT
ROLE          ::= abstract? role NAME extends NAME { MEMBER* }
MEMBER        ::= CONSTANT | INVARIANT | METHOD
CONSTANT      ::= abstract NAME | NAME = VALUE
INVARIANT     ::= requires EXP ;
METHOD        ::= MODIFIER* NAME () BLOCK
BLOCK         ::= { STATEMENT* }
STATEMENT     ::= ε | if( EXP ) { STATEMENT* } else { STATEMENT* }
                  | FUNCTION ; | handle NAME* BLOCK
EXP           ::= VAR | FUNCTION | EXP BINOP EXP | BLOCK
FUNCTION      ::= self. NAME ( EXP* ) | NAME ( EXP* )
                  | NAME . NAME ( EXP* )
MODIFIER      ::= abstract | behavior | startup | command
VAR           ::= NAME
VALUE         ::= NUMBER | PREDEFINED
DEPLOYMENT    ::= deployment { NAME* }
```

Fig. 6. EBNF for DynaRole. For simplicity, commas between function arguments are omitted in the EBNF.

be true (in case of conflicts between roles, the choice of role is undefined). An invariant is simply a boolean expression over constants and functions.

Methods are used to define the behavior that is active when a module plays a given role or any of the super-roles. A method is simply a sequence of statements that either are function invocations or conditionals. For simplicity methods currently always take one argument. Function invocations are either local commands, functions, or global commands. Local commands access the physical state of the module (sensors, actuators, external code) and are prefixed with the term "`self.`" to indicate that it is a local operation. Functions are basically used to represent stateless operations such as computing the size of (i.e., number of bits in) a bit set. Global commands are of the form "`Role.command`" and cause the command to be asynchronously invoked on all modules currently playing that role or any of its sub-roles. Arguments to functions are expressions, either constants, compound expressions, or code blocks; a code block allows code to be stored for later use (e.g., an event handler). Note that since the code is stateless no closure representation is required. The function invocation syntax for primitive functionality from the role `Module` (such as turning the main actuator) is the same as that of user-defined functions. A method declaration can be prefixed by a modifier, as follows. The method modifier "`abstract`" works in the usual way (forces the enclosing role to be declared abstract). The method modifier "`behavior`" causes the method to execute repeatedly so long as the role is active, whereas the method modifier "`startup`" causes the method to execute once when the role is activated. Last, the method modifier "`command`" causes the method to become exported for invocation as a global command.

The datatypes manipulated by DynaRole programs are all represented using single bytes, as follows: signed and unsigned 8-bit integers; sets of connectors represented as bit sets, which conveniently can be done using a single byte since there are only 8 connectors; and role identifiers corresponding to the runtime representation of a type. The single-byte limitation is naturally a severe limitation, but in practice many scenarios can nonetheless be programmed using these datatypes.

4.3   Deployment and Execution

We propose a deployment and execution model based on mobile code executing on a virtual machine designed around the DynaRole core concepts: the context of a module and its role in the ensemble, the reactive nature of robot controllers, and control programs decomposable into subparts that can be dynamically and separately redefined. By incorporating those concepts into the design we are able to achieve conciseness of compiled programs (thus providing fast and efficient code distribution) while retaining expressiveness. Compiling DynaRole to the virtual machine is fairly a straightforward process, since most concepts in the language are supported directly by the virtual machine. The role hierarchy is however not represented as a runtime model, but is rather used to generate code that can access the current role from the virtual machine.

We note that the issue of updating the software in the modules of a robot has received little attention from the research community, though in our experience it is one of the main factors hindering agile development and experimentation with physical robots: reprogramming tens or hundreds of modules can be a major overhead in the development process and cannot be done with traditional approaches without restarting the robot, which impedes updating a running system.

Our developed virtual machine enables efficient distribution of small byte-code programs throughout a structure of ATRON modules and supports dynamic live update of running programs within each module. Its design is centered on a concept we refer to as *distributed control diffusion:* controller code is selectively deployed to those modules where a specific behavior is needed to fulfill a given role, so as to efficiently use the constrained network resources. The virtual machine, named DCD-VM, has a domain-specific instruction set that is dedicated to the ATRON hardware and includes operations that are typically required in ATRON controllers. For example, it maintains an awareness of the compass direction of each module and the roles of its neighbors, and specific instructions allow this information to be queried. Moreover, it provides a lightweight and scalable broadcast protocol for distributing code throughout a structure of ATRON modules, making the task of programming controllers that adapt to their immediate surroundings significantly easier.

4.4   Example: Obstacle Avoidance

As an example, we use DynaRole to implement locomotion and obstacle avoidance for the mini 3-module car of Fig. 5. The program is shown in Fig. 7. The Head role (line 2) requires the central axis of the module to be "north-south"

```
1   // Head: react to obstacle events by triggering evasion
2   role Head extends Module {
3    require (self.center == $NORTH_SOUTH);
4    startup initialize(_) { // install evasion behavior
5     handle $EVENT_HANDLER_1 $EVENT_HANDLER_3 {
6      Wheel.evade(0)
7      (self.sleepcs(25));
8     };
9     (self.enable($EVENT_HANDLER_1));
10    (self.enable($EVENT_HANDLER_3));
11   }
12  }
13
14  // Wheel: rotate in the right direction
15  abstract role Wheel extends Module {
16   connected_direction; // constants defined
17   turn_direction;      // in subclasses
18   evasion_direction;
19   require (self.center == $EAST_WEST);
20   require (sizeof(self.connected(
21           connected_direction)) == 1);
22   behavior move(_) {
23    self.$TURN_CONTINUOUSLY(turn_direction);
24   }
25   command evade(_) {
26    self.$TURN_CONTINUOUSLY(evasion_direction);
27    (self.sleepcs(25));
28   }
29  }
30
31  // Concrete wheel definitions: left and right
32  role RightWheel extends Wheel {
33   turn_direction = 150;
34   evasion_direction = -100;
35   connected_direction = $EAST;
36  }
37
38  role LeftWheel extends Wheel {
39   turn_direction = -150;
40   evasion_direction = 100;
41   connected_direction = $WEST;
42  }
43
44  deployment { Head LeftWheel RightWheel }
```

Fig. 7. Obstacle avoidance for the mini car of Fig. 5

(the direction the robot is facing, line 3), whereas the wheels require the central axis to be "east-west" (line 19). The left and right wheels are distinguished by requiring the number of connections to be equals to one to the "west" and "east" sides respectively (lines 35 and 41). The method on the head sets up an event handler that invokes the method evade on wheel modules (lines 4–11); this method causes the car to back up for a short while before continuing forwards. The code compiles to 8 program fragments comprising 148 bytes of code in total (not all of which needs to be distributed to all modules).

4.5   Assessment

The DCD-VM and the DynaRole language demonstrated the possibility of using virtual machines and high-level domain-specific languages on a resource-constrained robotic platforms such as the ATRON. Practical experiments however demonstrated that the reliability of the underlying hardware was an issue. The modules would sometimes lock up requiring a hard reset to continue, but resetting looses the state of the individual module, often requiring the entire distributed program to be restarted. Even worse, communication via infrared was shown to be unreliable for some combinations of modules, in some extreme cases only one-way communication was physically possible between some pairs of modules. In terms of expressiveness, DynaRole could express an obstacle evasion behavior in terms of roles, but the behavior of the robot as a whole becomes an emergent behavior that arises from the collaboration of the individual roles, making programs both hard to write and difficult to understand. Last, the key feature of a robot like the ATRON is the ability to self-reconfigure, something which is not easily programmed in DynaRole.

5   Evolution: Distributed Sequences

Experimentation with the DynaRole language revealed that it was insufficient for programming key operations such as self-reconfiguration, and moreover did not help to abstract over critical issues such as distribution and unreliability in a useful way. To address these problems, the language and runtime model were evolved to better support robust execution of distributed sequences of operations [38], as described in this section.[2]

5.1   Analysis: Self-reconfiguration

Robots built from modular components can potentially overcome the limitations of traditional fixed morphology systems because they are able to rearrange modules automatically on a need basis, a process known as self-reconfiguration, and are able to replace unserviceable modules without disrupting the system's operations significantly. The generation of a centralized representation

---

[2] This section is partially based on the paper *Robust and reversible execution of self-reconfiguration sequences* published in Robotica [38].

of a self-reconfiguration sequence has been the focus of many papers in robotics [7,9,23,32–34,44,45,47,51,52]. From the point of view of programming, we are interested in the transformation of such a representation into a distributed controller. This transformation is in principle easy to do, but in practice many difficulties arise: real-world modules may have partial failures in their neighbor-to-neighbor communication abilities and may spuriously fail during the self-reconfiguration sequence. In essence, our goal must be to enable a programmer to easily describe a specific self-reconfiguration sequence and have it reliably executed by unreliable hardware.

This section presents an extension to DynaRole (as described in the previous section) that can execute self-reconfiguration sequences on the ATRON modular robot distributedly. This extension, in this briefing referred to as DynaRole++, provides a number of significant improvements. First, self-reconfiguration sequences are compiled to a robust and efficient implementation based on a distributed state machine. Second, dependencies between operations are explicitly stated to allow independent operations to be performed in parallel while enforcing sequential ordering between actions that are physically dependent on each other. Third, the language is *reversible* meaning that for any self-reconfiguration sequence the reverse one is automatically generated. Any self-reconfiguration process described in the language is reversible, subject to physical constraints.

5.2   Distributed Execution

We implement robust self-reconfiguration using a distributed state machine where each module contains a complete implementation of the state machine but only executes those states that are associated with the address of the module. The address is simply an integer that for example can be assigned using the preprogrammed internal address of the module or more generally can be assigned based on a number of predicates like we do in this work. The state machine transfers control between modules by globally sharing the active state and the address of the module that should execute the state; the state sharing is done between neighboring modules using a robust communication protocol based on continuous diffusion of state between neighboring modules, described later.

Parallel operations and global synchronization. Given a protocol for globally sharing the state, a distributed state machine that uses a single state can trivially be used to implement a sequential self-reconfiguration process. To implement parallel operations we use the concept of a *pending state* which is a state that is still actively executing an operation while the global active state advances. The set of pending states is globally shared and maintained, so that when a module starts or completes a pending state this information is propagated to the other modules of the robot. Thus, to implement a sequential operation that executes after all parallel operations have completed, a given state can wait for the set of pending operations to be empty. Our approach does not generally support dependencies between independently executing sequences of actions, e.g. execute $S_1; S_2$ sequentially but in parallel with $S_3; S_4$ that also execute sequentially. In practice this restriction is not a problem for the self-reconfiguration scenarios we are studying as they involve a fairly small number of physical modules, but for larger-scale scenarios involving tens of modules or more, the lack of nesting would seriously limit scalability. We address this issue using a notion of distributed scope, as explained in Sect. 6.

5.3 Communication Protocol

Global sharing of state is central to the robustness properties of our approach to self-reconfiguration. First, global sharing of state circumvents partial communication failure, since if there is a communication path between two modules information will eventually propagate between the two modules. Second, global sharing of state helps to tolerate reset of individual modules since the state of the individual module can be restored from the neighbors; a more detailed analysis of tolerating module reset can be found below. All communication between modules is performed using idempotent messages, meaning that they can simply be transmitted repeatedly throughout the self-reconfiguration process, which increases tolerance towards unstable communication where only a small percentage of messages get through. We refer to this approach as *state diffusion*, since any local state advancement is eventually propagated throughout the structure until it reaches an equilibrium (all modules having the same state). In addition to robustness, the protocol is oblivious to network topology, asynchronous, and scalable[3]: The protocol is oblivious to network topology in the sense that state will be propagated so long as there at some point in time is at least a one-way connection between the parts of the robot. The protocol is asynchronous since advancements to the global state and pending states can propagate independently throughout the structure while operation are being performed. The protocol is scalable since the number of packets sent per second per active connector is constant, the specific number of packets can even be tuned to the physical constraints of the system which enables developers to balance fast state propagation and computational load due to communication.

Our communication protocol is designed to share the active state, the address of the active module, and the set of pending states using idempotent messages. The set of pending states grows and shrinks as pending operations are added and completed. Each module continuously diffuses (i.e., locally broadcasts) packets that contain the local copy of the global state and is responsible for merging copies of the global state received over the network. Updates are always made to the local copy: after completing an operation a module can update the local copy of the active state and active module address (according to the state machine transition) and update the local set of pending states by adding or removing elements. An update is propagated throughout the module structure by the

---

[3] These properties are due to Shen et al. [40], in addition we note directed diffusion in sensor networks as a source of inspiration [19] for the diffusion concept.

$$\left.\begin{array}{l} \text{Local state} \quad G_0 = (s_0, a_0, P_0) \\ \text{Incoming state} \ G_1 = (s_1, a_1, P_1) \end{array}\right\} \text{Resulting state } G_2$$

$$G_2 = \begin{cases} (s_0, a_0, \{p \in P_0 | p > s_1 \vee p \in P_1\}, & s_0 > s_1 \\ (s_0, a_0, P_0 \cap P_1), & s_0 = s_1 \\ (s_1, a_1, \{p \in P_1 | p > s_0 \vee p \in P_0\}, & s_0 < s_1 \end{cases}$$

Fig. 8. Global state merge function. Let $G_i = (s_i, a_i, P_i)$ denote a copy of the global state where s_i is the currently active state, a_i is the address of the active module, and P_i is the set of pending states. Let G_0 be the local copy of the global state on a module, G_1 be the incoming global state being received over the network, and G_2 be the resulting global state which will be propagated to all neighbors of the module.

continuous transmission of local state to neighboring modules that in turn merge their local state with the incoming updated state. The merge function is shown in Fig. 8. The two key properties that we exploit are (1) that a pending state p_0 added to an active module M_0 in active state s_0 is *always* added before the active state is propagated to some other module M_1, and (2) the active state s_1 propagated to the other module M_1 is greater than p_0. This implies that when merging "older" incoming global states which have a lower active state, removal of pending states should only be taken into account for those pending states that the incoming global state could have known about, that is, those pending states that are lower than the active state of the incoming global state. The inverse relation holds for merging "newer" incoming global states which have a higher active state. A key property of this merge function is that removal of pending states can propagate along the same path as the active state is being transferred, improving tolerance towards partial failure of communication in comparison to, for example, an algorithm based on first reaching consensus over the global active state. Such an algorithm would require the newer state to be propagated back for the resolved pending states to be appended and then taken into account.

5.4   Module Reset

Numerous kinds of hardware and software faults can occur during a self-reconfiguration sequence; we are concerned with a specific fault, namely spurious reset of a module either due to hardware faults or induced by e.g. a watchdog timer firing because of a software error. Using our shared state approach, a module that is not currently performing an operation can trivially tolerate a reset in the middle of a self-reconfiguration sequence. The state will be restored from the neighbors, and if the module was to perform the next action the global state will simply not be advanced until the module is ready and starts to execute this state. A more critical case is reset of a module that is in the middle of performing an operation. Such a module can in many cases be reset, but only when all API operations are idempotent, which is the case for e.g. ATRON. Specifically, we use idempotent operations such as "extend connector" or "rotate to position 324" and such operations will under normal circumstances simply complete when power is restored and the global state is propagated to the module. Reset of a module that is performing a pending operation requires special support: the state of the module will after restarting be reset to the global state which is higher than the pending state. Each module locally keeps track of the pending states that it has started; this information will be erased after a reset which can be used to reenter the pending state when required. By combining the local set of pending states that have been started with the information of what states are globally pending and what pending states a given module is responsible for completing, a module can detect the situation where it is responsible for a pending state but has not removed it from the global state because it was stopped in the middle of the operation. Simply reentering the pending state will normally cause the pending operation to complete and hence provide the desired robustness.

5.5   Language Design

We have designed and implemented DynaRole++, a DSL that extends the Dyna-Role language as described in the previous section. In the DynaRole language, roles are used to encapsulate sets of behaviors that should be activated on specific modules in a structure. The assignment of roles is declarative and is used as a basis for dynamically updating behaviors in a running system using a virtual machine approach. Self-reconfiguration however concerns multiple tightly coordinated modules performing a number of operations, which is difficult to encapsulate using the concept of a role. As an alternative, in DynaRole++ we have implemented a new construct, the *sequence* which is a number of operations that are executed across a number of modules. The concept of a role is still used to identify which modules perform what operation.

As a concrete example, consider the sequence shown in Fig. 9 which describes the complete "8 to car" self-reconfiguration process. Each statement is prefixed with a label indicating what module is executing the statement, e.g. M0 is used to indicate a specific module in line 6. Following the label is a call to the ATRON API, for example controlling the connectors or the main joint; see Table 1 for details. Note that the rotation call has been augmented with an extra argument to facilitate reversing the program, as described later.

Table 1. The DynaRole++ ATRON API, selected operations

`M.Connector[n].retract()`
    retracts connector number n (releasing a connected module, if any).
`M.Connector[n].extend()`
    extends connector number n (connecting to an appropriately positioned module, if any).
`M.rotateFromToBy(f,t,d,s)`
    rotates the main joint from f degrees to t degrees in direction t at speed s (behavior is undefined if the joint is not at f when starting).

```
 1  role M0 { require ... }
 2  //...
 3  role M6 { require ... }
 4
 5  sequence eight2car {
 6    M0.Connector[$CONNECTOR_0].retract() &
 7    M3.Connector[$CONNECTOR_4].retract();
 8    M3.rotateFromToBy(0,324,false,150) ;
 9    M4.rotateFromToBy(0,108,true,150);
10    M4.Connector[$CONNECTOR_0].extend() &
11    M1.rotateFromToBy(0,324,false,150) &
12    M6.Connector[$CONNECTOR_2].retract();
13    M4.rotateFromToBy(108,216,true,150) &
14    M6.rotateFromToBy(0,108,true,150);
15    M0.Connector[$CONNECTOR_0].extend();
16    M6.Connector[$CONNECTOR_6].retract();
17    M0.rotateFromToBy(0,324,false,150) &
18    M1.rotateFromToBy(324,0,true,150);
19    M0.rotateFromToBy(324,0,true,150);
20    M5.Connector[$CONNECTOR_0].extend() &
21    M2.Connector[$CONNECTOR_4].extend() &
22    M1.Connector[$CONNECTOR_4].extend();
23    M4.Connector[$CONNECTOR_0].retract();
24    M3.Connector[$CONNECTOR_6].retract();
25    M1.rotateFromToBy(0,108,true,150) &
26    M3.rotateFromToBy(324,0,true,150);
27    M1.Connector[$CONNECTOR_6].extend();
28    M3.Connector[$CONNECTOR_0].retract() &
29    M3.Connector[$CONNECTOR_2].retract();
30    M1.rotateFromToBy(108,216,true,150);
31  }
```

Fig. 9. DynaRole++ sequence describing the "8 to car" self-reconfiguration sequence

Each statement is terminated either with a semicolon ";" meaning sequential execution (the next statement is dependent on this operation) or an ampersand "&" meaning parallel execution (the next statement is independent of this operation), similarly to e.g. UrbiScript [2]. A sequence of parallel statements are considered independent, that is, physically unconstrained, and may be executed in any order but must all be completed before the next sequential execution point. As an example, consider the first lines of the "8 to car" sequence, lines 6–9, which indicate that modules M0 and M3 can open their connectors in parallel whereas the rotation of modules M3 and M4 must be done sequentially and must only take place after both connectors have opened. We note that nesting of sequential statements inside parallel statements across multiple modules is not currently supported (as described earlier this feature is not supported by the current state machine design). The presented sequence completely implements the rather complex "8 to car" self-reconfiguration process; the individual steps are unimportant from the point of view of language design, whereas the readability and conciseness of the program as a whole is considered critical for the usability of the language.

The labels that indicate what module should execute a given statement are defined using roles, as outlined in lines 1–3, which as before are defined using logical predicates on the local state and the context of each module. (The context is defined as the state of the immediate neighbors.) Here we for simplicity only use a local predicate on the internal ID of the module which is programmed when flashing the module.

5.6   Reversibility

Given a distributed sequence written in DynaRole++ it is straightforward to generate the reverse sequence: the ordering of statements must be reversed while retaining dependence relations between statements, and each statement must in itself be reversed. Reversal is thus a simple syntactic transformation, similarly to (and inspired from) Janus [50]. Reversal of the ordering of the statements must preserve the semantics that a sequential dependence between two statements requires all parallel statements to have completed before the next sequential statement can execute. This implies that the statements can be ordered in reverse while retaining the same separator between each given pair of statements. For example, a sequence of statements $S_1 \& S_2; S_3;$ reverses to $S_3; S_2 \& S_1;$. Reversal of an operation is straightforward due to the design of the API operations supported in DynaRole++ sequences: `retract` becomes `extend` and vice versa, whereas `rotateFromToBy` simply swaps the from and to angles and reverses direction.

The programmer explicitly defines and invokes reversed sequences, for example the sequence shown in Fig. 9 is reversed using the following declaration:

```
sequence car2eight = reverse eight2car;
```

After this declaration the name `car2eight` can be used like any other sequence name.

5.7   Assessment

The effectiveness of DynaRole++ has been demonstrated with relatively long-running, reversible self-reconfiguration experiments using physical ATRON modules, comprehensive self-reconfiguration experiments using simulated ATRON modules, and a reversible self-reconfiguration experiment using simulated M-TRAN modules [52]. For details we refer to Schultz et al. [38]. Moreover, the DynaRole++ language was the first robotic control language to support reversible execution, a principle that we have recently applied to industrial robots to improve robustness and to automatically transform programs that assemble products into reverse programs that disassemble the same products [25].

6 Work-in-Progress: Distributed Scope

The DynaRole++ languages provides massive advantages compared to the original version of DynaRole. DynaRole++ is however very narrow in scope and is most effective for describing self-reconfiguration sequences. To address this problem, the language and runtime model should be extended to provide a richer model, ideally without compromising the robustness and reversibility features of DynaRole++. This section describes initial ideas for such an extension, based on a notion of distributed scope.[4]

6.1 Analysis: Generality and Scalability

The DynaRole++ language and runtime mechanisms for programming and execution of distributed sequences presented in the previous section improves robustness of the self-reconfiguration process by at least an order of magnitude [38]. The distributed execution aspect of DynaRole++ is however very simple and does not provide control structures or even a means to manipulate the program state. To enable robust execution to be used for more general scenarios, the language must be extended to provide such features, but without compromising the robustness of the system.

Moreover, distributed execution assumes global sharing of state, which obviously does not scale to larger hundred- or million-module ensembles. As exemplified by the metamodule control strategy [10], in such scenarios smaller groups of modules typically work together and would need to share state, but the state would be private to these strongly coupled modules and not shared with the rest of the ensemble.

6.2 Language Design

We propose the RoCE (Robust Collaborative Ensembles, pronounced "rose") language for robust, general-purpose control of modular robots. The language has two primary abstractions: ensembles and roles. An *ensemble* is a dynamic, distributed scope that covers a number of modules and introduces shared state and proactive, distributed behaviors into these modules. A *role* applies to a single module, and introduces local state and reactive behaviors into the module, in the form of a statemachine. A module can be a member of any number of ensembles at a given time. Ensembles and roles together are referred to as *entities*. Declarative rules are used to control the activation of entities based on spatial constraints, the active entities of neighboring modules, local state from roles, and shared state from ensembles. Entities can be specialized with a semantics resembling standard object-oriented inheritance: members can be added and existing members can be overridden.

---

[4] This section is based on work presented in a preliminary form at workshops and as a poster [36,37,39].

```
 1  // Shared state and behavior
 2  ensemble Car {
 3   // Enum state shared in the car ensemble
 4   state obstacle { None, Left, Right, Center } = None;
 5   // Behavior of car ensemble as a whole
 6   when (obstacle==None) Wheel.drive.Forward
 7   else { Wheel.drive.Evade; sleep(3); }
 8  }
 9
10  // Behavior local to center module
11  role Front within Car {
12   require connected(COMPASS_ANY)==2;
13   // check sensors and update shared state
14   when (isProximity(FRONT_LEFT) &&
15       isProximity(FRONT_RIGHT)) obstacle.Center;
16   when (isProximity(FRONT_LEFT)) obstacle.Left;
17   when (isProximity(FRONT_RIGHT)) obstacle.Right;
18   else obstacle.None;
19  }
20
21  // Behavior local to wheel modules
22  role Wheel within Car {
23   require connected(COMPASS_ANY)==1;
24   int MY_SIDE, FWD;
25   when connected(COMPASS_EAST==1) {
26    MY_SIDE = Left; FWD = 1;
27   }
28   when connected(COMPASS_WEST==1) {
29    MY_SIDE = Right; FWD = 0;
30   }
31   // state machine
32   state drive {
33    // rotate in appropriate direction
34    Forward {
35     rotateContinuous(100,FWD);
36    }
37    // turn while reversing
38    Evade {
39     if(obstacle==MY_SIDE)
40      rotateContinuous(50,!FWD);
41     else
42      rotateContinuous(100,!FWD);
43    }
44   }
45  }
```

Fig. 10. Obstacle evasion program in RoCE

6.3 Example

One of the primary design goals of RoCE is to allow modular robots to be controlled in a robust manner based on a global description of the behavior. As an example, consider obstacle avoidance for the small 3-module ATRON car from Fig. 5 implemented by the program shown in Fig. 10. The ensemble Car (line 2) encapsulates the overall behavior of the robot, and consists of a shared state variable obstacle (line 4) and a conditional behavior that executes continuously (lines 6 and 7). Depending on the value of the shared state, the behavior is to either drive forwards or perform an evasive behavior for 3 seconds. Roles are assigned to modules that satisfy the require clauses (such clauses can also be used to activate ensembles), and can similarly introduce states and behaviors but only locally to the given module. The role Front (line 11) applies to modules *within* the Car ensemble that have the required two connections (uniquely identifying the front module, line 12). The role checks the front sensor and updates the shared state obstacle correspondingly (lines 14 to 18, the shared state is visible here due to the within declaration). The role Wheel (line 22) acts differently depending on its connections (the left and right wheel must rotate in opposite directions), and the state drive (line 32) expresses the actions to take when driving forwards or evading (the wheel closest to the obstacle rotates slower to turn away from the obstacle).

6.4 Assessment

The RoCE language as described here has only been implemented as a number of preliminary prototypes that have been tested in simulation and in early prototype on the physical ATRON modules [36,37,39]. These initial experiments were promising in terms of testing the language concepts and their implementation. Compiling a program still produces a number of robust distributed state machines that execute in parallel on the modules of the robot (an approach which was experimentally demonstrated to work well in practice [38]). Each state machine continuously diffuses state (describing shared variables and behavior execution) to neighboring modules which are then responsible for merging this state with their own; this approach decouples communication from execution and enables modules to automatically route around failing communication paths and recover from spontaneous loss of state.

7 Conclusion

This briefing has presented three stages of an evolution of a DSL for modular robots. The key requirements outlined earlier in Sect. 3.4 concerned adapting to the physical shape, shape-independent robust control, and scalable communication and coordination. The first version of DynaRole (Sect. 4) relied on the notion of roles to provide both shape adaptation through the declarative require clauses and shape-independent control using role inheritance. The extended version DynaRole++ (Sect. 5) added support for the central self-reconfiguration scenario and massively improved the robustness properties of the language. Last, the RoCE work-in-progress language (Sect. 6) added the notion of a distributed scope as a means to providing robust and scalable communication and coordination.

The case study DSLs have not been used extensively enough to provide comparative metrics, but we note that orders-of-magnitude improvements have been demonstrated in terms of time required to reprogram physical modules [6], the number of lines of code required to implement a self-reconfiguration sequence [38], and the robustness of executing a self-reconfiguration sequence [38].

In terms of future work, we are generally interested in exploring the use of DSLs to address concerns in robotics. We refer to the recently published survey on DSLs for an overview [29], noting that some key areas such as security and safety for robots only have received limited attention in the research community. Moreover, we observe that the community is largely driven by a focus on robotic capabilities, leaving more exotic programming language features such as reversible [25] and probabilistic programming [43] largely unexplored.

References

1. Ashley-Rollman, M.P., Goldstein, S.C., Lee, P., Mowry, T.C., Pillai, P.: Meld: A declarative approach to programming ensembles. In: Proceedings of the 2007 IEEE/RSJ International Conference on Intelligent Robots and Systems (IROS 2007), pp. 2794–2800. San Diego, CA, USA, 29 October–2 November 2007
2. Baillie, J.C., Demaille, A., Hocquet, Q., Nottale, M., Tardieu, S.: The Urbi Universal Platform for Robotics. In: Proceedings of the SIMPAR 2008 Workshop on Standards and Common Platform for Robotics, Venice, Italy, 3 November 2008
3. Biggs, G., MacDonald, B.: A survey of robot programming systems. In: Australasian Conference on Robotics and Automation (2003)
4. Bordignon, M., Stoy, K., Schultz, U.: Generalized programming of modular robots through kinematic configurations. In: Proceedings of the 2011 IEEE/RSJ International Conference on Intelligent Robots and Systems (IROS), pp. 3659–3666 (2011)
5. Bordignon, M., Schultz, U., Stoy, K.: Model-based kinematics generation for modular mechatronic toolkits. In: Proceedings of the 9th ACM SIGPLAN/SIGSOFT International Conference on Generative Programming and Component Engineering (GPCE 2010), Eindhoven, The Netherlands, 10–13 October 2010
6. Bordignon, M., Stoy, K., Schultz, U.P.: A virtual machine-based approach for fast and flexible reprogramming of modular robots. In: Proceedings of the IEEE International Conference on Robotics and Automation (ICRA 2009), Kobe, Japan, pp. 4273–4280, 12–17 May 2009
7. Brandt, D., Christensen, D.J.: A new meta-module for controlling large sheets of atron modules. In: Proceedings of IEEE/RSJ International Conference on Intelligent Robots and Systems, San Diego, California, November 2007
8. Brandt, D., Ostergaard, E.: Behaviour subdivision and generalization of rules in rule based control of the ATRON self-reconfigurable robot. In: Proceeding of the International Symposium on Robotics and Automation (ISRA), Queretaro, Mexico, pp. 67–74, September 2004

9. Butler, Z., Rus, D.: Distributed planning and control for modular robots with unit-compressible modules. Int. J. Robot. Res. **22**, 699–715 (2003)
10. Christensen, D., Støy, K.: Selecting a meta-module to shape-change the ATRON self-reconfigurable robot. In: Proceedings of IEEE International Conference on Robotics and Automations (ICRA), Orlando, USA, pp. 2532–2538, May 2006
11. De Rosa, M., Goldstein, S.C., Lee, P., Campbell, J.D., Pillai, P.: Programming modular robots with locally distributed predicates. In: Proceedings of the 2008 IEEE International Conference on Robotics and Automation (ICRA 2008), pp. 3156–3162, Pasadena, CA, USA, 19–23 May 2008
12. van Deursen, A., Klint, P., Visser, J.: Domain-specific languages: An annotated bibliography. ACM SIGPLAN Not. (2000). http://www.st.ewi.tudelft.nl/arie/papers/dslbib.pd
13. Efftinge, S., Eysholdt, M., Köhnlein, J., Zarnekow, S., von Massow, R., Hasselbring, W., Hanus, M.: Xbase: Implementing domain-specific languages for java. In: Proceedings of the 11th International Conference on Generative Programming and Component Engineering, GPCE 2012, pp. 112–121. ACM (2012)
14. Fowler, M.: Domain-Specific Languages. Addison-Wesley, Reading (2010)
15. Gérard, S., Selic, B.: The UML - MARTE standardized profile. In: The International Federation of Automatic Control, Seoul, Korea, pp. 6909–6913 (2008)
16. Gherardi, L., Hochgeschwender, N., Schlegel, C., Schultz, U.P., Stinckwich, S.: Proceedings of the Fifth International Workshop on Domain-specific Languages and Models for Robotic Systems (DSLROB 2014) (2014). CoRR abs/1411.7148, http://arxiv.org/abs/1411.7148
17. Goldstein, S.C., Campbell, J.D., Mowry, T.C.: Programmable matter. IEEE Comput. **38**(6), 99–101 (2005)
18. Gronback, R.C.: Eclipse Modeling Project: A Domain-Specific Language (DSL) Toolkit. Addison-Wesley Professional, Boston (2009)
19. Intanagonwiwat, C., Govindan, R., Estrin, D.: Directed diffusion: a scalable and robust communication paradigm for sensor networks. In: Proceedings of the 6th Annual International Conference on Mobile Computing and Networking, MobiCom 2000, pp. 56–67. ACM, New York (2000)
20. JetBrains: Meta Programming System. http://www.jetbrains.com/mps/
21. Jorgensen, M.W., Ostergaard, E.H., Lund, H.H.: Modular ATRON: Modules for a self-reconfigurable robot. In: Proceedings of IEEE/RSJ International Conference on Robots and Systems (IROS), Sendai, Japan, pp. 2068–2073, September 2004
22. Kats, L.C., Visser, E.: The spoofax language workbench: rules for declarative specification of languages and IDEs, vol. 45. ACM (2010)
23. Kotay, K., Rus, D.: Algorithms for self-reconfiguring molecule motion planning. In: Proceedings of the International Conference on Intelligent Robots and Systems (IROS 2000) (2000)
24. Larsen, L.B., Schultz, U.P.: Simple simulator for robots not completely unlike the Harvard kilobots. http://www.codeskulptor.org/#user40_gEFncqmVDBkvVIF_11.py
25. Laursen, J.S., Schultz, U.P., Ellekilde, L.P.: Automatic error recovery in robot assembly operations using reverse execution. In: 2015 IEEE/RSJ International Conference on Intelligent Robots and Systems (2015)
26. Lund, H., Beck, R., Dalgaard, L.: Self-reconfigurable robots with ATRON modules. In: Murase, K., Sekiyama, K., Naniwa, T., Kubota, N., Sitte, J. (eds.) Proceedings of 3rd International Symposium on Autonomous Minirobots for Research and Edutainment (AMiRE 2005). Springer, Heidelberg (2005)

27. Mernik, M., Heering, J., Sloane, A.: When and how to develop domain-specific languages. ACM Comput. Surv. **37**(4), 316–344 (2005). http://portal.acm.org/citation.cfm?doid=1118890.1118892
28. Murata, S., Kurokawa, H., Kokaji, S.: Self-assembling machine, pp. 441–448 (1994)
29. Nordmann, A., Hochgeschwender, N., Wigand, D., Wrede, S.: A survey on domain-specific modeling and languages in robotics. J. Softw. Eng. Robot. **7**(1), 75–99 (2016)
30. Ostergaard, E.H.: Efficient distributed "hormone" graph gradients. In: Proceedings of Nineteenth International Joint Conference on Artificial Intelligence (IJCAI), Edinburgh, Scotland, pp. 1489–1495, July 2005
31. Ostergaard, E.H., Lund, H.H.: Distributed cluster walk for the ATRON self-reconfigurable robot. In: Proceedings of the The 8th Conference on Intelligent Autonomous Systems (IAS-8), Amsterdam, Holland, pp. 291–298, March 2004
32. Pamecha, A., Ebert-Uphoff, I., Chirikjian, G.S.: Useful metrics for modular robot motion planning. IEEE Trans. Robot. Autom. **13**, 531–545 (1997)
33. Prevas, K., Unsal, C., Efe, M., Khosla, P.: A hierarchical motion planning strategy for a uniform self-reconfigurable modular robotic system. In: Proceedings of the IEEE International Conference on Robotics and Automation, Washington DC, vol. 1, pp. 787–792, October 2002
34. Rosa, M.D., Goldstein, S., Lee, P., Campbell, J., Pillai, P.: Scalable shape sculpting via hole motion: Motion planning in lattice-constrained modular robots. In: Proceedings of the 2006 IEEE International Conference on Robotics and Automation (ICRA 2006) (2006)
35. Şahin, E.: Swarm robotics: From sources of inspiration to domains of application. In: Şahin, E., Spears, W.M. (eds.) SR 2004. LNCS, vol. 3342, pp. 10–20. Springer, Heidelberg (2005). doi:10.1007/978-3-540-30552-1_2
36. Schultz, U.P.: Towards a general-purpose, reversible language for controlling self-reconfigurable robots. In: Glück, R., Yokoyama, T. (eds.) RC 2012. LNCS, vol. 7581, pp. 97–111. Springer, Heidelberg (2013). doi:10.1007/978-3-642-36315-3_8
37. Schultz, U.P.: Programming language abstractions for self-reconfigurable robots. In: Proceedings of the 3rd Annual Conference on Systems, Programming, and Applications: Software for Humanity, SPLASH 2012, pp. 69–70. ACM, New York (2012). http://doi.acm.org/10.1145/2384716.2384743
38. Schultz, U.P., Bordignon, M., Stoy, K.: Robust and reversible execution of self-reconfiguration sequences. Robotica 29, 35–57 (2011), accompanying video available at. http://www.youtube.com/watch?v=SYizuooEs7s
39. Schultz, U.: Towards a robust spatial computing language for modular robots. In: Proceedings of the 2012 Workshop on Spatial Computing (AAMAS), Spain, June 2012
40. Shen, W.M., Salemi, B., Will, P.: Hormone-inspired adaptive communication and distributed control for conro self-reconfigurable robots. IEEE Trans. Robot. Autom. **18**, 700–712 (2002)
41. Stoy, K., Shen, W.M., Will, P.: Using Role Based Control to Produce Locomotion in Chain-Type Self-Reconfigurable Robots. IEEE/ASME Trans. Mechatron. **7**(4), 410–417 (2002). Special issue on Self-reconfigurable Robots
42. Støy, K., Shen, W.M., Will, P.: Implementing configuration dependent gaits in a self-reconfigurable robot. In: Proceedings of the 2003 IEEE International Conference on Robotics and Automation (ICRA 2003), Tai-Pei, Taiwan, pp. 3828–3833, September 2003

43. Thrun, S.: Towards programming tools for robots that integrate probabilistic computation and learning. In: Proceedings of the IEEE International Conference on Robotics and Automation (ICRA). IEEE, San Francisco, CA (2000)
44. Ünsal, C., Khosla, P.: A multi-layered planner for self-reconfiguration of a uniform group of I-cube modules. In: Proceedings of the IEEE/RSJ International Conference on Intelligent Robots and Systems, Maoui, Hawaii vol. 1, pp. 598–605 (2002)
45. Ünsal, C., Kiliccöte, H., Khosla, P.K.: A modular self-reconfigurable bipartite robotic system: Implementation and motion planning. Auton. Robots **10**, 23–40 (2001)
46. Völter, M., Benz, S., Dietrich, C., Engelmann, B., Helander, M., Kats, L., Visser, E., Wachsmuth, G.: DSL Engineering Designing, Implementing and Using Domain-Specific Languages (2013). http://dslbook.org
47. Yim, M., Goldberg, D., Casal, A.: Connectivity planning for closed-chain reconfiguration. In: Proceedings of Sensor Fusion and Decentralized Control in Robotics Systems III, SPIE, Bellingham, vol. 4196, pp. 402–412 (2000)
48. Yim, M., Shen, W.M., Salemi, B., Rus, D., Moll, M., Lipson, H., Klavins, E., Chirikjian, G.S.: Modular Self-Reconfigurable Robot Systems [Grand Challenges of Robotics]. IEEE Robot. Automat. Mag, March 2007
49. Yim, M., Zhang, Y., Lamping, J., Mao, E.: Distributed control for 3D metamorphosis. Auton. Robots **10**(1), 41–56 (2001)
50. Yokoyama, T., Axelsen, H.B., Glück, R.: Principles of a reversible programming language. In: Proceedings of the Computing Frontiers, pp. 43–54. ACM (2008)
51. Yoshida, E., Murata, S., Kamimura, A., Tomita, K., Kurokawa, H., Kokaji, S.: Motion planning of self-reconfigurable modular robot. In: Proceedings of the International Symposium on Experimental Robotics (2000)
52. Yoshida, E., Murata, S., Kurokawa, H., Tomita, K., Kokaji, S.: A distributed method for reconfiguration of a three-dimensional homogeneous structure. Adv. Robot. **13**, 363–379 (1999)
53. Zhang, Y., Golovinsky, A., Yim, M., Eldershaw, C.: An XML-based scripting language for chain-type modular robotic systems. In: Proceedings of the Conference on Intelligent Automous Systems (IAS-8), Amsterdam, Netherlands (2004)

People Analytics in Software Development

Leif Singer[1]([✉]), Margaret-Anne Storey[1], Fernando Figueira Filho[2],
Alexey Zagalsky[1], and Daniel M. German[1]

[1] University of Victoria, Victoria, BC, Canada
{lsinger,mstorey,alexeyza,dmg}@uvic.ca
[2] Universidade Federal Do Rio Grande Do Norte, Natal, Brazil
fernando@dimap.ufrn.br

Abstract. Developers are using more and more different channels and
tools to collaborate, and integrations between these tools are becoming
more prevalent. In turn, more data about developers' interactions at
work will become available. These developments will likely make People
Analytics — using data to show and improve how people collaborate —
more accessible and in turn more important for software developers. Even
though developer collaboration has been the focus of several research
groups and studies, we believe these changes will qualitatively change
how some developers work. We provide an introduction to existing work
in this field and outline where it could be headed.

Keywords: People analytics · Developer analytics · Social network
analysis · Feedback · Collaboration · Computer-supported collaborative
work

1 Introduction

How people behave at work is becoming more and more measurable. For example,
some companies are exploring the use of *sociometric badges* [25] that track the
location and meta data about the interactions employees have during the day.
But even without such devices, knowledge workers use more and more services
that collect usage data about their activities.

Developers are an extreme case of this — the center of their work is their
computer on which they write code, create and close tickets, and initiate text-
based chats or calls that are all recorded in some way or another. Changes to a
source code repository are recorded in full, task management applications have
an API that makes changes available to API clients, and calendar systems track
whom people have appointments with and when.

These changes in software development practice are paralleled by academic
research: there are new insights into how developers collaborate, established
and new methods in social network analysis, ongoing research in visualizing
collaboration, recent attempts to measure developer affect, and research on giving (developers) feedback. We discuss these areas and how they are relevant to
changes in how software developers work in Sect. 2.

© Springer International Publishing AG 2017
J. Cunha et al. (Eds.): GTTSE 2015, LNCS 10223, pp. 124–153, 2017.
DOI: 10.1007/978-3-319-60074-1_6

While one option would be to discuss this development as an issue of increasing potential surveillance, we consider it an opportunity to make work itself better. The rise of distributed and remote work also means that developers need better support to improve how they collaborate.

An analytics system could track unusual events in source code repositories, project management tools, calendaring applications, or video conferencing. This would help monitoring whether some team members are isolated or disengaged — and thus might need assistance — or whether employees working on the same or related artifacts are communicating enough. Contrarily, visualizing and providing feedback about the steady progress that a team of developers makes could be introduced, e.g., as motivational support.

What is People Analytics? This opportunity to improve work is called *People Analytics* by some. There are multiple, but fuzzy definitions of the term. Even the book that helped coin the term, "People Analytics" by Waber [57], does not provide a definition of what is actually meant.

We therefore provide a definition by relying on our interpretation of People Analytics literature and a previous definition of generic analytics by Liberatore et al. [28]:

Definition 1. *People Analytics is the use of data, quantitative and qualitative analysis methods, and domain knowledge to discover insights about how people work together with the goal of improving collaboration.*

As such, People Analytics shares some similarities with the *Quantified Self* movement[1] — but in this case, it is applied to groups of professionals instead of private individuals.

Similar to the recently popularized areas of *Big Data* or *Data Science*, the specific technical methods are not necessarily new. However, their deliberate application within the context of the goal of improving how people work has, as far as we know, not been embraced by the software engineering research community. We believe that it could be a useful umbrella term to bring disparate research groups closer together.

We distinguish People Analytics from code analytics and from the mining software repositories lines of research. Instead of focusing on the artifacts that people create and modify, we now concentrate on how they work together to achieve their goals. The central element we are interested in is not the source code file or the commit, but the developer.

Phases in People Analytics. Again leaning on previous work on general analytics [28] and Singer's work [46], we divide the application of People Analytics into six activities: *goal setting, data collection,* two parallel phases of *analysis* and *intervention, change,* and *reflection* (cf. Fig. 1).

---

[1] *"individuals engaged in the self-tracking of any kind of biological, physical, behavioral, or environmental information"* [55].

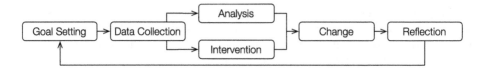

Fig. 1. The phases in People Analytics.

Goal Setting. In this first phase, those implementing a People Analytics project define what the project's subject of interest is, what it is supposed to discover more about, and what it is supposed to change or improve.

Data Collection. Now, the data needed for achieving the goal is chosen. A collection strategy is formulated and systems are being set up for cleaning, aggregating, and otherwise manipulating the collected data.

Analysis and Intervention. While or after the data is being collected, the analyst will either run one or multiple analyses of the data, deploy an intervention — such as a feedback system based on the collected data (cf. Sect. 3) — or both.

Change. Depending on the project, an analysis could provide proof or hints for required changes in how developers work together, or an intervention could provoke these changes to occur without further actions. For example, an analysis could show that all communication between two groups goes through a single developer, posing a risky bottleneck. A pure analysis-based management intervention could then consist of assigning individuals to similar bridging roles. An intervention in our sense would give the affected developers automatic feedback about this bottleneck and potentially trigger them to reorganize around it themselves.

Reflection. Finally, those implementing the People Analytics project will want to reflect on whether the project reached its stated goal, why it worked, or possibly why it did not work. Often novelty in reconfigurations or feedback systems can wear off, making them less effective over time. Therefore, whether the change will last needs to be considered and perhaps a strategy to evolve the manual or automatic intervention will need to be put in place. In this phase, further data collection to gather insights about the successes and failures that occurred in the project can be helpful in understanding the second-order effects of an intervention — including, but not limited to qualitative post-mortem interviews with the affected developers (cf., e.g., Sect. 3).

People Analytics has a lot of potential for improving how developers collaborate. At the same time, there are multiple challenges that need to be overcome to be able to implement a successful People Analytics project. Mistrust, fear of surveillance, or choosing metrics for feedback that make matters worse are only a few examples from the problems that can arise.

Those implementing a People Analytics project need to be fluent in diverse methods of data collection and analysis, but also need expertise in creating interventions by using insights from human-computer interaction as well as organizational studies and management science.

We contribute our views on these challenges, possible solutions, and promising paths to be taken that could help fulfill the promise of this emerging field.

This paper is structured as follows: after this introduction, we review existing literature that could help those trying to drive People Analytics in software engineering forward. Section 3 presents a simple application of People Analytics in which we nudged student developers towards a certain behavior when committing to a version control system. We then conclude the paper with an outlook.

2   Background and Related Work

This section gives an overview of existing literature that we consider to be relevant and interesting when applying People Analytics to software engineering. It is not a complete list, but rather a collection of research that we believe could be inspiring when conducting research on or implementing People Analytics projects in practice. At the same time, we use it to roughly define what our view of People Analytics in software development entails.

We see five major areas that are especially relevant for People Analytics research in software engineering: general insights on how developers collaborate, social network analysis to discern interaction patterns and relationships between developers, visualizing collaboration to support developer understanding, measuring developer affect to enable adaptable development tools, and giving developers feedback to help them understand and act upon their own behaviors. We now discuss each in turn.

In their discussion of groupware [13], Ellis, Gibbs, and Rein emphasized the importance of communication, collaboration, and coordination for group-based activities. Since a few decades, software development is usually performed in groups that work together. We therefore start with a discussion of how developers collaborate and what challenges they meet. We then turn to how communication, collaboration, and coordination of developers can be measured. We close with a brief discussion of how to use such metrics for giving developers and their managers feedback.

2.1   Insights on Communication, Collaboration, and Coordination

To understand what the customs and challenges are in developer collaboration, we discuss some relevant studies.

Organizational Factors: Lavallée and Robillard [26] report on a study in which they observed a team of developers in a large organization. Over a period of ten months, they attended weekly status meetings and noted interactions and the topics that were discussed. The researchers condensed their observations into a list of ten organizational factors that hurt the overall quality of the software produced in the project under study. Several of them are related to communication between developers themselves or between developers and business stakeholders — such as undue pressure from management delivered through informal channels, differences between the formal and the actual processes, or needing the right social capital to be able to get work done.

Pair Programming: Stapel et al. [50] study how student developers communicate during pair programming: they find that many conversations between developers are about concrete code, but when considering conversation length they spend the most time discussing software design. When considering how conversations change over time, discussions about code becomes less and less — possibly because developers learn syntax and project-specific conventions. Plonka et al. [38] found that pair programming as a method that influences developer communication can help diffuse knowledge within teams and organizations.

Team Mood and Interaction Intensity: Schneider et al. [44] investigate the relationships between media, mood, and communication in teams of student developers. Amongst other findings, the authors report that excessive positive mood around a project's midpoint could actually be detrimental, as it would often signal too much optimism that could easily derail the project in its later stages. To this end, the authors recommend providing developers with technical milestones such as objective quality gates to provide feedback to developers regularly, improving their self-evaluation. They also find that having early indicators for isolated team members or high variance in a developer's participation can be helpful tools for project managers. Since they find a relationship between developer affect and project success, the authors recommend that the mood in developer teams be regularly measured to serve as a heuristic to alert managers about potentially problematic projects. At the same time, both data about mood and interaction intensity between team members should be made available to the developers themselves to make them aware of things that might be going wrong in their project.

The Role of Social Software: In previous work, we and others have studied how developers use signals in social media to collaborate [53]. These signals could, e.g., be text and visuals that convey someone's status in a community or their experience with a particular technology. We found that these signals influence how developers collaborate with others, how recruiters evaluate them, what and from whom they learn, and even whether and how they test their open source contributions.

Singer et al. [47] report on a qualitative study involving both developers with active social media profiles and software development recruiters. The authors find that public profiles, aggregated activity traces, as well as the detailed activity data and artifacts developer create are useful for both assessment between developers and also the assessment of developers by external parties, such as recruiters. Capiluppi et al. [8] argue that these activity signals could help recruiters find suitable candidates even if these do not have a traditional degree, helping non-traditional candidates start their career in software development.

Pham et al. [37] conducted a qualitative study with users of GitHub, finding that the affordances of the site — several of them reflecting information about people and groups, not artifacts — are helpful in nudging inexperienced developers towards the expected behavior and norms of an open source project they want to contribute to. In part, this was due to normative behavior — such as what a good pull request should contain — being published and discussed in the open.

Finally, Singer et al. [48] conducted a study on how and why software developers use the microblogging service Twitter. Two of the more prominent findings were that (a) microblogging helps developers connect with one another and participate in cultures they are geographically not a part of and (b) that access to such a diverse network of other developers can provide developers with rich opportunities for learning new technologies and practices.

Take-away: There has been quite some research on issues such as how developers work, why they behave the way they do, why they use the tools they use, what challenges they really face, and how they currently cope with these challenges. We should use these studies to learn from and to better understand what problems we should attempt to solve.

2.2   Methods: Social Network Analysis

Now that we have provided an impression of recent research in how developers collaborate, we turn to research that attempts to measure it. We begin with the fundamentals of social network analysis and then discuss its relevance to team work.

Fundamentals: A social network is a structure that is composed of actors and the ties between them. Actors — the nodes — and ties — the edges between the nodes — form a graph. Depending on the application, ties can be weighted or unweighted, directed or undirected. The weight of an edge can, e.g., represent the strength of a relationship or the number of interactions between two actors. The social networks of development teams can, for example, be derived from organizational data [33], commit histories [10,30], or email exchanges [2].

Parts of this graph can be considered their own sub-networks and can follow distinct patterns. Some typical sub-networks to consider in analyses are, for example, the *singleton* (an unconnected node), the dyad (a connection between two nodes), or the triad (with all possible edges between three nodes). Another important sub-network is the clique: a number of nodes where every node is connected to every other node.

Network science has invented many different metrics and properties that can be helpful when trying to understand how and why a social network functions:

- *Connectedness:* two nodes are connected if there is a path in the graph that leads from one node to the other.
- *Centrality:* this describes a few different measures that determine how *central* a node is in a graph. Examples are *degree centrality* (a node's number of

edges) or *betweenness centrality* (measures the importance of a node to the shortest paths through the graph).

– *Density:* the number of edges in a graph divided by the numbers of *possible* edges in the graph. Intuitively, this measures how well connected a social network is.
– *Centralization:* measures how evenly distributed *centrality* is across all the nodes of a graph.

Discovering Roles: Such properties can be useful, e.g., in automatically finding *bridges* — nodes that form the only connection between two separate groups — or for discovering equivalent roles in a social network. Golbeck [16] provides an accessible introduction to these and many more analyses.

For example, Burt [5] provides a note on discovering equivalent roles in a social network by categorizing every actor by the triad types they have. Practically, this allows clustering of actors by the role they occupy in an organization. Comparing the result of such an analysis with the officially assigned roles could help uncover discrepancies — enabling organization to, e.g., become aware of what its employees actually do or to bring official roles more in line what is really happening.

Relationship Intensity: Weak ties [17] between people within different parts of an organization can speed up projects by providing a project team with knowledge not available within its own ranks [22]. However, this is only true if the needed knowledge is simple enough — needing to transfer complex knowledge via weak ties can slow projects down. Strong ties across organizational boundaries might be preferable in this case, however these are usually not numerous enough to ensure access to the relevant knowledge. The weight of an edge between actors in a social network can also be important when measuring the decay [6] between relationships that naturally happens over time. Organizations could use this information to improve employee retention.

Nagappan et al. [33] calculated eight different *organizational* measures about the Microsoft developers who worked on Windows Vista. Examples are *number of engineers* having edited a binary, *number of ex-engineers*, the position of a binary's owner in the *hierarchy*, or the *number of different organizations* making changes to a binary. They found that their measures were more reliable and accurate at predicting failure-proneness than any of the code-based metrics they compared them against.

Social Networks over Time: Apart from the relatively static metrics discussed so far, social networks and the events happening to them can also be analyzed with a temporal dimension added. Xuan et al. [58] use both data on communication (exchanged messages) and collaboration (artifacts edited) over time to reveal the structure of development teams and model individual and team productivity. In this case, actors in the network can be either developers or edited artifacts.

Composing Teams: Finally, Reagans et al. [39] show that for organizations, it might be easier and more effective to compose teams based on employees' social networks instead of their demographics. There is no doubt that social networks within organizations can have a significant impact on the organization's productivity, speed, and success — and that being able to analyze these social networks is a necessary step to improvement.

Take-away: By combining methods and insights from classic social network analysis with organizational studies, we can gain valuable insights that neither discipline would have discovered on its own.

2.3   Methods: Visualizing Collaboration

While an analysis may often require only data and an algorithm, visualizing data can aid exploration — we therefore briefly discuss some approaches to visualizing the collaboration between software developers.

Repository Evolution: Both Gource [9] and Code Swarm [34] produce high-level video visualizations of a source repository's history. Software evolution story lines [35] attempt to show more detail than the aforementioned, but in consequence do not scale as well to larger projects.

Visualizing Information Flows: Stapel et al. [51,52] present *FLOW Mapping*, a visualization of both formal and informal information flows through diverse communication channels. Their approach is both for planning and monitoring the media and indirections through which developers communicate during a project. It is meant to improve communication in distributed software projects. In an evaluation within a distributed student project, the authors monitored meta data about communication through channels such as instant messaging, audio and video calls, as well as source code repositories. The project manager in the evaluation reported that the technique helped plan and measure compliance with a communications strategy, and also to become aware of the different developers' locations and connections.

Related to the *FLOW Mapping* visualizations, Schneider and Liskin [43] define the *FLOW Distance* to measure the degree of indirection in communication between developers. Their metrics takes into account indirections created through other people, documents, and processes. The authors believe this to provide an objective metrics to measure how *remote* developers might feel from each other.

Meeting Profiles: Liskin et al. [29] measured meeting frequency and length in a project with student developers. The authors visualize the *meeting profiles* of different teams and assign them to different categories. By comparing meeting profiles with the actual projects, they find that high project pressure seems to correlate with more frequent meetings. The authors argue that such a visualization could be a significant help for managers who want to assess the stress level in the projects they're responsible for. Extreme meeting profiles or sudden changes in meeting intensity could be sufficient heuristics for evaluating a project's problems more closely. At the same time, the data to produce meeting profiles can be measured easily.

Take-away: Visualizing activity in code repositories is an interesting field of study. But crucial insights can be gained using simpler visualizations and instead focusing more effort on figuring out how to measure things that have previously been too hard to measure.

2.4 Methods: Measuring Developer Affect

Having discussed the measuring of interactions between developers, we now turn to the individual — specifically, developers' emotions, moods, or affects. Graziotin et al. [19] provide a comprehensive overview of the involved psychological concepts and challenges in conducting experiments that measure affect.

Affect and Productivity: Previous research suggests this is an important topic. Meyer et al. [31] report on a study about the perceptions developers have about their own productivity. Their participants report that completing big tasks results in feelings of happiness and satisfaction. Relatedly, Graziotin et al. [18] found that the attractiveness of a task and perceiving to have the skills required to complete it correlate with developers' self-assessed productivity. Khan et al. [24] found that developer mood affects debugging tasks. Finally, in a study on the reasons for developer frustrations, Ford and Parnin found that the majority of developers is able to recall recent experiences of severe frustration [14]. Being able to measure the affective state of a developer therefore seems potentially valuable.

Measuring Emotions: Fritz et al. [15] provide a method based on biometric measures to estimate task difficulty. The authors argue that this will enable them to stop developers to let them reconsider the task when it seems too difficult. Relatedly, Müller et al. [1] use biometric sensors to detect when a developer is "stuck." Shaw [45] provides a method to assess developer emotions purely based on psychological questionnaires — which is likely more cost-effective, but also similarly distracting and likely less reliable than biometric sensors. Cheaper and less intrusive methods, such as the mouse- and keyboard-based approach proposed by Khan et al. [23], could prove to be more applicable, even though they seem to be much less reliable.

Guzman et al. [20] report on a sentiment analysis of commit messages from a set of open source projects. The authors find that developers in more distributed teams tend to write more positive messages, that commit messages in Java-based projects tend be more negative, and that code committed on Mondays also comes with more negative messages. However, Murgia et al. [32] show that emotions expressed within software development are often more nuanced than expected, and that an automatic analysis will likely not be precise enough.

Summarizing the above, we note that it would be valuable to be able to assess developers' moods and emotions, but sufficiently reliable solutions are currently costly, inconvenient, or both. Light-weight solutions do not yet seem to achieve a suitable level of reliability.

Emotionally Adaptive Tools: However, assuming a light-weight, but reliable method to measure developer affect would exist, interesting possibilities would open up in supporting collaborative work. Dewan [12] proposes a collaboration system that tailors messages, tasks, and notifications between colleagues to their current level of frustration and interruptibility.

Take-away: Measuring developer affect is an interesting and challenging topic, but we need to keep in mind that results so far have been mixed. Future improvements in methods will likely bring new ethical challenges.

2.5   Feedback Interventions

The previous sections have described what data could be interesting to gather and how it could be manipulated to make insights more obvious. We now focus on delivering feedback and insights to developers to support them and positively influence their behavior.

Workspace Awareness: Several existing interventions fall into the sub-class of workspace awareness tools. These use data on developer activity and display them to developers — usually in a continuous and unobtrusive manner. Palantír by Sarma et al. [41] is one of the more prominent examples. Notably, it uses a change severity metric to decide how prominently a change should be displayed to a developer.

What Developers Want: Treude et al. [56] recently reported on a qualitative study in which they investigated how developers believe activity should be measured, summarized, and presented. Among other findings, they report that unexpected events such as changes in estimates, new dependencies, or API changes could be highly valuable for developers to be notified of. With *UEDashboard* [27], they have recently shown a tool that supports detecting and displaying such unusual events.

Finding Expertise: Guzzi and Begel [21] present *CARES*, a Visual Studio extension. When opening a file under version control, *CARES* displays a list of developers who had previously committed changes to that file. The authors report that developers in an evaluation successfully used CARES to find relevant colleagues to talk to.

Establishing and Changing Habits: Pham et al. [36] augment the Eclipse IDE with a testing-specific dashboard that presents developers with a set of signals inspired by the social transparency framework [54]. The authors' aim is to nudge novice or newly hired developers towards the testing culture implemented by existing developers.

Finally, *Teamfeed* [49] is a Web application that uses a very simple metric — the number of commits made by a developer in a project — to create a project-internal developer ranking. The first author conducted a quasi-experiment on this intervention with student developers, which we report on in detail in the following section.

Take-away: Often, the problems of software engineering are being worked on from the perspective of software engineers. Adding a more design-oriented lens to the process can lead to more interesting results in both practice and research. In our opinion this specific combination of fields still contains much unrealized potential for interdisciplinary collaboration.

3   Making Analytics Feedback Useful: Gamification of Version Control

The preceding section has discussed a range of different ideas on measuring and giving feedback on developer collaboration — yet it has merely scratched the surface of each of the few areas it addresses. We suspect that choosing the right things to measure and giving appropriate feedback could be one of the more challenging aspects in People Analytics.

In the following, we show how a very simple metric — the number of commits a developer makes to a repository — can be used to influence the commit behavior of a cohort of student developers. This illustrates that *what is measured potentially matters less than how it is presented* to developers.

The quasi-experiment we are about to describe evaluated the *Practice Adoption Improvement Process (PAIP)*. PAIP is a systematic process for improving the adoption of software engineering practices, and includes a catalog of patterns that can be applied during that process.

The process, the catalog, as well as the quasi-experiment are part of Singer's thesis [46]. They are an example for a specific application of People Analytics — namely affecting behavior change in how developers collaborate.

3.1   Introduction

Together with Stapel and Schneider [49], the first author conducted the following quasi-experiment while in Hannover, Germany. In a student project lasting a full semester, we attempted to improve the adoption of version control practices in small teams of student developers. We used early versions of both PAIP and the catalog of adoption patterns and used the experience from this evaluation to refine both.

A quasi-experiment is an experiment in which the assignment of subjects to the control vs. treatment conditions is non-random. In our case, the control group was comprised of data from the version control repositories of previous years in which our group organized this project. The treatment group was the cohort of students taking the project in the fall term of 2011.

Developers do not always strictly follow software development processes and software engineering practices [46]. Even though individuals may be aware of a practice and its advantages, as well as capable of implementing it, they do not always adopt it — a situation called the *Knowledge-Attitude-Practice-gap* (or *KAP-gap*) in the innovation-decision process by Rogers [40].

In centralized version control systems such as Subversion[2], developers should commit early and often to decouple changes from each other and to spot conflicts with the work of other developers earlier [4]. To make browsing historical data easier, each change should include a description of its contents — the commit message. Even though many developers know of these or similar guidelines, they do not always follow them. This can influence the maintainability — and therefore quality and costs — of a software project negatively.

In our experience, student projects can be problematic in this regard: developers include several different features and fixes in a single commit. They leave commit messages empty. These problems occur regularly, even though the organizers of the project emphasize every year that they want students to commit regularly, since the version control repository is the only way for our group to continue work on the students' projects later — for which a meaningful commit history would be useful. The organizers also emphasize that other students — peers of the student developers — might need to access the repository in the future, e.g., to improve on one of the student projects for a thesis.

However, the problem persists. We suspect the reason to be a combination of missing knowledge regarding best practices and a lack of motivation for spending the additional effort needed for thoughtful commits. We therefore decided to apply an early version of PAIP in the fall 2011 term's project and used a selection of adoption patterns to create a persuasive intervention to alleviate this problem. Before documenting our application of PAIP, the following section introduces the experiment context.

3.2 Experiment Context

Each fall semester, our research group organizes the *software project* (SWP) course, a mandatory course for computer science undergraduates. The course has roughly 35 to 70 participants every time, most of them in their fifth semester. The students form teams of four to six members, and elect a project leader as well as a quality agent. The project starts at the beginning of October and lasts until the end of January.

The members of our research group act as customers, proposing software projects that we would like to have developed. That way, we are able to provide projects with real requirements while keeping control of their size and technological demands. This is beneficial for the comparability of projects in experiments

---

[2] http://subversion.apache.org.

such as the one presented here. Usually, each student team will work on a different project with a different customer, however some projects may be given to multiple teams to work on independently.

Each project is divided into three main phases: requirements elicitation, software design, and implementation. After that, customers get to try out the produced software and assess their compliance with requirements in a short acceptance phase.

After each phase, the teams have to pass a quality gate (QG) to proceed to the next phase. This ensures a minimum quality of the artifacts developed in each phase. If a team fails a quality gate, they are allowed to refine their artifacts once. Failing the quality gate for a single phase repeatedly would lead to failing the course. However, this has not happened yet.

So far, we have conducted this course every year since 2004. For this experiment, we only consider the years starting with 2007, as this was the first year we had the students use Subversion for version control. The process we use and the size of the projects have not changed significantly since then. The duration has constantly been the whole fall semester. While each project is different, we take care to always provide projects with similar requirements regarding effort and proficiency in software development. This is to ensure fairness between the teams with the added benefit of better comparability.

The preconditions regarding the participants have been very stable. Our group teaches all the basic courses on software engineering, software quality, and version control. The contents of these courses have remained similar over the years.

In the first phase, students make appointments with their customers and interview them about their requirements. They produce a requirements specification that they need to get signed by their respective customer to proceed to the next phase. In the second phase, the teams can choose between preparing an architecture or creating exploratory prototypes. In both variants, they are required to produce a software design document. They implement the actual applications in the third and final phase.

During the project, a member of our group will act as coach, answering questions about technical subjects and the development process. To create time scarcity, each team receives six vouchers for customer appointments of 15 min each and six vouchers for coach appointments of 30 min each.

At the end of the project, the customer executes the acceptance tests from the requirements specification and decides whether rework is needed. Once the customer has finally accepted or rejected the software product, the role-play ends.

Finally, we conduct an *LID* session with each team. LID — short for *Lightweight Documentation of Experiences* — is a technique for the elicitation of project experiences [42]. A typical LID session for the course takes about two hours during which the team members and a moderator jointly fill in a template for experience elicitation. An LID session inquires students about impressions, feelings, conflicts, and advice, and has them review the whole project from beginning to end. In the sessions, we emphasize that their passing of the course will not be affected anymore and encourage them to honestly describe the negative experiences as well.

For each team, we provide a Subversion repository, a Trac[3] instance for issue tracking, and a web-based quality gate system that is used to progress the teams through the project phases. The Trac instance is linked to the team's version control repository, so students are able to see their team's commits using either Trac or any Subversion client.

3.3   Experiment Design

This section documents how we applied PAIP and deployed a persuasive intervention — with a Web application called *Teamfeed* as its treatment — to a student population of 37 participants. The section's organization is based on PAIP's first five steps: *Characterize Context, Define Adoption Goal & Metrics, Choose Adoption Patterns, Design Treatment,* and *Deploy Intervention.* The succeeding section implements the sixth step: *Analyze Results.*

Characterize Context. In the first step of PAIP, the change agent determines the current context in which PAIP is to be applied. This entails the practice for which adoption should be improved and its properties, as well as the characteristics of the developer population.

The Software Engineering Practice. To apply PAIP, the change agent decides whether the practice for which adoption is to be influenced is comprised of primarily routine or creative tasks. This experiment is concerned with practices for committing to version control, which involves deciding when to commit, what to commit, and how to describe it in the commit message. Based on the rough guidelines given in PAIP's description [46], we determine that our practice entails *creative* tasks.

The Developer Population. Regarding the developer population, the change agent determines whether there are any existing adopters of the practice that could act as role models. As we have seen *some* student developers adhering to good committing practices in previous years, we decide that we can indeed assume existing adopters in our population.

Define Adoption Goal & Metrics. In this second step, we define the adoption goal that the intervention should be optimized for. To measure success in the last step, we define metrics.

Defining a Goal. As advised by PAIP, we first choose simple goals that will improve the performance of those developers with less experience. Further improvements would be possible in future iterations. Therefore, we want students to commit at all, to commit more often, to commit more regularly, to write commit messages for their commits, and to write longer commit messages overall.

---

[3] http://trac.edgewall.org.

When defining the goal, PAIP requires the change agent to choose either one or both of "Start Adopting a New Practice" or "Improve Adoption of a Known Practice"; for our experiment, we choose both. In every previous instance of the software project course, there have been some students who never committed to version control, while most did commit at least once. Some of those committed only in bursts, some committed more regularly; some wrote commit messages, and some others did not. For the goals above, we therefore want to both *increase* adoption and *increase* frequency.

Research Questions. For the context of this evaluation, we formulate our goals into research questions that we will investigate in the succeeding section, documenting PAIP's sixth step:

- *RQ 1:* Does our intervention influence student developers to make more commits and space them out more evenly over time?
- *RQ 2:* Does our intervention influence student developers to write more and longer commit messages?

Defining the Metrics. To measure our previously defined goals, we choose the metrics listed in Table 1. The table also assigns metrics to research questions. Most metrics are self-explanatory, except possibly the time between consecutive commits. We use this metric to measure whether developers commit more *regularly* — that is, more evenly spread out over time, with fewer *bursts* of commits. Assuming a constant number of commits, a more regular committing behavior would then result in the median time between commits to *increase*.

Table 1. Summary of the defined metrics, assigned to their respective research questions.

RQ	Metric	Counting rule
RQ 1	c	Number of commits per user
	$\Delta t_{C,avg}$ $\Delta t_{C,med}$	Average and median time between two consecutive commits of a user in seconds
RQ 2	c_M	Number of commits with message per user
	c_M/c	Message-to-commit-ratio per user
	$l_{M,avg}$ $l_{M,med}$	Average and median number of characters of the commit messages of a user

We follow the *playful metric* recommendation [46] in that we never connected the committing behavior of students with actual consequences, such as passing or failing the course. We made this clear to students in person and via email, emphasizing that we provided the Teamfeed tool purely for the students' own benefit.

Finally, PAIP requires us to define when to take measurements and to record a baseline measurement. For this quasi-experiment, our baseline — i.e., the control group — consists of the Subversion repositories collected during previous instances of the course from 2007 to 2010. These repositories contain the commits of 214 students. The results are measured after the course has ended.

Hypotheses. For our experiment, we derive the alternative hypotheses for our research questions. We assume that a positive influence on the commit behavior of developers can be exerted by deploying our persuasive intervention. This influence should lead to more commits per developer, to temporally more evenly spaced commits, to more commits with messages per developer, and to longer commit messages. Accordingly, our respective null hypotheses are that the deployment of the intervention has no influence on these phenomena.

Choose Adoption Patterns. The previous two steps of applying PAIP reveal that we want to either start or improve the adoption of a practice that is comprised of relatively creative tasks. We assume to have some existing adopters. Based on this information, we choose the following adoption patterns for our intervention in the third step of PAIP. For each pattern, we also repeat its *solution* below.

- *Normative Behavior:* "Make explicit what normative behavior should be by continuously publishing the behavior of developers, positively emphasizing desirable behavior."
- *Triggers:* "Use notifications to cue developers to applying a practice by directing their attention to a task related to the practice. To support motivation, associate triggers with positive feedback or a goal to be reached. Do not overload developers with triggers."
- *Points & Levels:* "Award points and levels for the activity that is to be started or intensified. Provide a space for users to display their points and levels, e.g., on a user profile. Give clear instructions on how to attain different levels."
  Note that the recommendation for *clear instructions* was added only after the completion of this experiment, and therefore was not taken into account.
- *Leaderboard:* "Use a metric that measures compliance with the software engineering practice to rank developers against each other, creating explicit competition. If possible, have groups compete against each other instead of individual developers against each other."
  Note that the recommendation for *groups competing against each other* was added only after the completion of this experiment, and therefore was not taken into account.
- *Challenge:* "Provide developers with explicit, attainable, and challenging goals. Make sure developers understand what the conditions for attaining the goal are and give explicit feedback on results. Prefer challenges that require

the developer to learn something new over those that merely require reaching a certain performance as measured by a metric."
Note that the recommendation for *learning goals* was added only after the completion of this experiment, and therefore was not taken into account.
- ***Progress Feedback:*** "Provide developers with positive feedback on the progress they are making in their application of the practice."

Except for the knowledge stage — which was not addressed by the early version of PAIP —, this selection of adoption patterns covers all stages of the innovation-decision process that are relevant to PAIP. Three of the patterns are from the *motivation* category: as mentioned before, we suspect missing motivation to be a reason for the adoption issues.

3.4   Designing a Treatment

Using the adoption patterns chosen in the previous step, we now create a treatment that implements the patterns. This design is in part informed by the examples listed for each adoption pattern.

Newsfeed. A newsfeed displaying the version control commits for each team implements the *Normative Behavior* adoption pattern. When no commit message is given, the application displays a highlighted text stating that a message is missing.

Leaderboard. A list of a team's members, ordered by their respective number of commits so far, implements the *Leaderboard* adoption pattern. Next to the name of each team member, the member's current number of commits is given. Below, the total number of commits for the team is displayed.

Milestones. At predefined thresholds for numbers of commits, the application congratulates users and teams on reaching a milestone. This implements the *Points & Levels* pattern. By slowly increasing the distance between the thresholds, this also implements the *Challenge* pattern: by committing, developers are able to recognize that there will be another milestone at an even higher number of commits, providing them with a goal. The congratulatory messages implement the *Progress Feedback* pattern.

Notifications. For positive events, such as reaching an individual or team milestone, the application sends out email notifications — this implements the *Triggers* adoption pattern. The congratulatory messages in the emails implement the *Progress Feedback* pattern.

Weekly Digest. Every Sunday, the application emails a weekly digest to each developer. It shows the current leaderboard, as well as any milestones reached in that week. This implements the *Triggers* adoption pattern. The congratulatory messages that were given when a milestone was reached implement the *Progress Feedback* pattern.

Teamfeed. We now present Teamfeed, a Web application that uses email for notifications. It periodically reads the commits to each team's repository and saves them to a database. These are then displayed in a newsfeed for each team. Every student in the project can log in to Teamfeed using their Subversion account and is then presented with their respective team's newsfeed. The newsfeeds of other teams are not accessible to the students. Figure 2 shows an anonymized screenshot of the application in which the names of students and their team have been altered.

Fig. 2. A screenshot of Teamfeed's newsfeed and leaderboard.

Reaching a milestone generates a special post to the newsfeed. For the milestones, we defined thresholds of 1, 10, 25, 50, 100, 250, 500, 750, 1000, 1500, 2000, 2500, 3000, 4000, 5000, 7500, and 10000 commits. These generate posts such as *"Congratulations! Jane Doe has reached her 200th commit!"* or *"Wonderful! Your team has just reached the 1000th commit!"* We based the thresholds on previous semesters' commit counts and added a buffer.

On the right, the leaderboard lists the team members and the counts of their respective commits so far. For higher ranks, name and commit count are displayed in a larger font.

Each Sunday at around 3pm, Teamfeed sent out the weekly email digest to each student. The digest summarizes how many commits the individual student has made in the past week, but also provides this information about their teammates. It also mentions milestones that were reached during the week and shows the current state of the leaderboard.

Deploy Intervention. Once the treatments have been created, the change agent deploys them as a persuasive intervention in the organization. We deployed *Teamfeed* at the start of the software project course in the fall term of 2011. The students were told that the purpose of Teamfeed was to support their collaboration.

3.5   Results and Analysis

The final stage of PAIP involves taking a measurement and comparing it to the baseline to assess the effectiveness of the intervention. This informs the next iteration of the process.

Table 2 shows the data sources we used for data collection in our experiment. It includes the data from five years of the software project course, i.e., the data accumulated in the fall terms of the years 2007 through 2011. The first four years were used as the control group. In 2011, we introduced the Teamfeed application and therefore used it as our treatment group.

Table 2. Overview of data sources and their values for number of subjects (n), number of subjects who committed (n_C), number of subjects who never committed ($n - n_C$), percentage of committing subjects (n_C/n), number of total commits (c_{total}), and average commits per subject (c_{total}/n).

Group	Control					Teamfeed
Term	**2007**	**2008**	**2009**	**2010**	**Σ**	**2011**
n	40	40	76	58	214	37
n_C	31	36	73	55	195	37
$n - n_C$	9	4	3	3	19	0
n_C/n	78%	90%	96%	95%	91%	100%
c_{total}	3973	3680	6993	7223	21869	4842
c_{total}/n	99	92	92	125	102	131

In total, there were 26,711 commits in the five years (c_{total}). In the first four years, each participant made 102 commits on average (c_{total}/n). In 2011, this value was at 131 commits. 251 students took the course over the five years, which can be seen as n in Table 2. The treatment group consisted of 37 participants.

n_C documents the number of students that did commit at all in the respective year. As the values for n_C/n show, all students in the treatment group committed at least once to version control (100%). In the previous years, however, some participants never made a single commit (i.e., on average, 91% committed at least once).

Descriptive Statistics. We now present the data we collected for the metrics we defined, aggregated in Table 3 and visualized as box plots in Fig. 3. Each set of data is declared for the control group (C) and the treatment group (T), respectively. For each value, we provide the minimum, the median, and the maximum value.

For example, Table 3 shows a 76% increase in median commits per participant (c) for the treatment group. The ratio of commits with messages to commits overall (c_M/c) increased by 75%. We now discuss whether these and other differences are statistically significant.

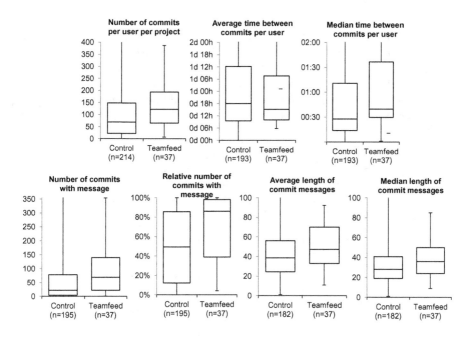

Fig. 3. Box plots of the data collected for the metrics.

Table 3. Minimum, median, and maximum values for the collected metrics: number of commits per subject (c), average ($\Delta t_{C,avg}$) as well as median ($\Delta t_{C,med}$) time between commits, number of commits with a message per subject (c_M), percentage of commits with a message (c_M/c), and average ($l_{M,avg}$) as well as median ($l_{M,med}$) lengths of commit messages.

Metric	Group	Min	Median	Max
c	Control (n=214)	0	69	683
	Treatment (n=37)	7	122	387
$\Delta t_{C,avg}$	C (n=193)	00:00	17:55	>17d
hh:mm	T (n=37)	05:51	15:09	>8d
$\Delta t_{C,med}$	C (n=193)	00:00	00:27	>6d
hh:mm	T (n=37)	00:00	00:39	>1d
c_M	C (n=195)	0	22	587
	T (n=37)	1	69	354
c_M/c	C (n=195)	0%	49%	100%
	T (n=37)	4%	86%	100%
$l_{M,avg}$	C (n=182)	1	39	211
	T (n=37)	11	47	92
$l_{M,med}$	C (n=182)	1	28	165
	T (n=37)	9	36	85

Hypothesis Testing. For most metrics, we were able to determine a statistically significant difference between the values for the control group and the values for the treatment group. We performed a Kolmogorov-Smirnov normality test for all the metrics. These tests showed that the data do not follow a normal distribution. Therefore, we had to use the non-parametric two-tailed Mann-Whitney U test to test for the significances of differences. Table 4 presents the results of our tests for statistical significance.

Table 4. Overview of statistical test results.

RQ	Metric	Control	Treatment	Difference	Confidence
RQ 1	c	69	122	+76%	$p < 0.01$
	$\Delta t_{C,avg}$	17:55	15:09	-15%	$p > 0.1$
	$\Delta t_{C,med}$	00:27	00:39	+44%	$p < 0.05$
RQ 2	c_M	22	69	+213%	$p < 0.01$
	c_M/c	49%	86%	+75%	$p < 0.01$
	$l_{M,avg}$	39	47	+20%	$p < 0.1$
	$l_{M,med}$	28	36	+28%	$p < 0.05$

For research question 1, there is a significant difference between the number of commits per student for the two groups: an increase in 76% ($c; p < 0.01$). The average time between commits does not differ significantly ($\Delta t_{C,avg}$). However, the median time between commits exhibits a significant ($\Delta t_{C,med}; p < 0.05$) difference: an increase in 44%. We therefore reject the null hypotheses for the first and the third metrics of research question 1.

The measurements for research question 2 show significant differences. The number of commits with messages per developer increased by 213% ($c_M; p < 0.01$); the ratio of commits with messages to overall commits increased by 75% ($c_M/c; p < 0.01$).

The difference for the average length of commit messages is not significant, with a 20% increase ($l_{M,avg}; p < 0.1$). The difference for the median length of commit messages is significant with a 28% increase ($l_{M,med}; p < 0.05$). We therefore reject three of the four null hypotheses for research question 2.

Qualitative Analysis. To better understand the effects of our intervention, we now provide an additional qualitative discussion based on the *LID sessions* conducted at the end of the project. At the end of the sessions, we inquired about each team's impressions of Teamfeed. This provided us with some notable insights:

- More experienced developers often ignored Teamfeed and the emails it sent. Some even had setup a filter in their email clients for this purpose. However, only few seemed to be annoyed by the emails. In an industry setting, one might want to give developers a way to opt out of such email. Yet, none asked us about such an option during the course.

– Several of the more novice developers reported that they felt motivated by the milestones. The only team which reached the *1000 commits* milestone was comprised of such members.

– No developer reported any manipulative attempts by themselves or by team mates. To help ensure this, we performed regular sanity checks of commits and commit messages, finding no indication for manipulation (such as empty commits). Overall, we estimate to have sampled about 5% of commits in this manner.

– One developer explicitly said that Teamfeed's milestones made him commit in smaller batches. Instead of putting several bug fixes into a single commit, he committed his changes after every single fix. In our view, this is desirable behavior for centralized version control systems.

Research Questions. In our research question 1 we asked: *Does our intervention influence student developers to make more commits and space them out more evenly over time?*

To answer this question, we defined three metrics: the number of commits per student, the average time between commits, and the median time between commits. Based on our measurements, we were able to reject the null hypothesis for the first and the third metrics. Therefore, we conclude that our treatment was indeed able to influence student developers to make more commits and space them out more evenly over time. Not only did it lead to a significantly higher number of commits per developer, but also resulted in a more evenly distributed time between commits.

Research question 2 asked: *Does our intervention influence student developers to write more and longer commit messages?*

For this question, we defined four metrics: the number of commits with messages, the ratio of commits with messages to overall commits, the average length of commit messages, and the median length of commit messages. For three of these metrics, we were able to reject the null hypothesis. We conclude that the introduction of our application did indeed influence student developers to write more and longer commit messages. More commits contained commit messages at all, and those that did contained longer messages.

3.6   Threats to Validity

This section discusses threats to the validity of our quasi-experiment. We show how we tried to minimize them through the experiment design and mention remaining limitations.

Internal Validity. A significant difference between the control group and the treatment group does not in itself represent a causal relationship between our intervention and the differences in measurement. Other confounding factors might have had an influence. The population itself, the students' education, details in the execution of the course, and our behavior towards the students might all have been different.

The advantage of using different populations for the control and treatment groups, however, is that there should have been no confounding effects with regard to learning or maturation. In addition, we took care to execute the course the same as in previous years. As our group also provides the basic software engineering courses, we feel qualified to say that we did not notice any notable differences in the students from the control group compared to the students in the treatment group. Additionally, our courses provide the basic education on version control, which was the same for both groups.

It is conceivable that general trends in software development and general computer use changed how students adopt version control practices.

Through the qualitative interviews conducted at the end of the study, we might have noticed such trends, as we also inquired about how students used version control — not merely how they used Teamfeed. In these interviews, we did notice one change in computer use: to exchange files, students had started using Dropbox, a service that makes it easy to share folders between different users and synchronizes them over the Internet. In previous cohorts, students had used version control for exchanging files.

This change in computer use might have influenced the measured impact of our intervention, as there would have been fewer commits in the treatment cohort. Those would have been commits made solely for the quick and ephemeral exchange of project files, however — something that we wouldn't necessarily consider the intended use of version control.

Construct Validity. Whether the practices we chose for version control are preferable in a given software engineering situation is debatable. However, we consider them an important step for the population we investigated. Populations at other levels of version control proficiency may require different interventions. Even though the use of metrics in software development can be problematic [3], our research questions and the metrics we derived address the adoption of these practices as directly as possible. We therefore consider them appropriate.

In a future investigation, we plan to examine any quality differences in the commits and commit messages of the control and treatment groups. A preliminary investigation of 100 commit messages showed indications for a decrease of nonsense messages ("hahaha!"), a decrease of purely technical messages that do not mention a change's utility ("add getter getUser()"), and an increase in mentions of functional changes ("fix incompatibility with framework version 1.2.5").

One possible effect of public, competitive metrics is that people try to "game the system" — i.e., they try to increase their value for the metric using the easiest strategies, which might often not be what the creators of the system intended. In our case, these would be empty commits or nonsense commits. To rule this effect out, we randomly sampled some of the commits from our treatment group. We found no indications for invalid or manipulative commits.

Conclusion Validity. To mitigate threats to conclusion validity, we used the data collected over several years of the software project course for our control group. These 214 participants, combined with 37 participants in the treatment group, were suitable to provide statistically significant results. To decrease the risk of manual errors, all data were collected automatically.

External Validity. The participants of our experiment were mostly students of computer science in their 5th semester. As the German Bachelor of Science degree lasts 6 semesters, most students were almost finished with their studies. As our treatment was directed at issues with version control practices we had experienced from similar populations, we cannot generalize this concrete intervention to different populations. Another application of PAIP, while more elaborate than a simple transfer of the intervention, would be more sensible.

It is questionable how many metrics and additional interventions can be introduced before software developers start ignoring such measures. The tolerable amount of such treatments might be very low. Further research regarding such scenarios is warranted.

Similarly, our software projects are restricted to a single semester, i.e., about four months. We do not think that our experiment can be generalized to much longer runtimes, as potential numbing effects seem plausible. Again, further research is needed in this regard.

3.7   Summary

Our quasi-experiment demonstrated that PAIP and the catalog of adoption patterns can be used to improve the adoption of software engineering practices — in this case, the commit behavior of student developers. While we tried to design our experiment to minimize threats to validity, some of them were beyond our control. It is therefore still possible that the effects we measured were created or influenced by other, confounding factors. However, the qualitative data from the LID sessions back our interpretation.

This specific intervention worked for less experienced software developers in a university setting. As we argued in section on validity, the intervention itself might not generalize. However, this is exactly what PAIP intends: it provides a way to create interventions that are tailored to a practice, an adoption problem, a population, and adoption goals.

Our quasi-experiment has shown that the application of PAIP is feasible and can be effective. While this need not be true for every possible adoption problem or situation, this data point serves as a good indicator. More evaluations in different contexts would be needed to improve confidence in this regard.

The metrics we chose to feed back to the students were relatively simple — a commit count per team member and a newsfeed of commit messages. All this information was available to previous teams via Subversion clients such as the one included in the Eclipse IDE. Still, the different presentation of this data made a difference in observed developer behavior.

We believe that this suggests that People Analytics projects do not need to measure especially interesting behavior or even do so in a necessarily exact manner. Instead, we believe that the presentation and the context of the chosen metrics matters most.

4   Outlook

We have discussed many options and opportunities for implementing People Analytics projects, and have hinted at the benefits. There are many different analyses and metrics available, originating from diverse fields. We hope that these can be useful as starting points for future research.

In the previous section, we have shown that complicated metrics possibly are not that important, after all. Maybe the most important research that is still to conduct lies more in the field of HCI and psychology — our conception of what it takes to create a tool that supports collaborative work still seems more diffuse than we are comfortable with. This feeling is likely related to the fact that collaboration is mostly about people, and the path towards gathering reliable knowledge about people and the processes between them seems much less clear than algorithmic endeavors.

So far, we have ignored the more severe challenges present in People Analytics. We conclude this paper by discussing some of the challenges we believe will have the most impact on implementing People Analytics, and what we consider to be likely good practices to handle them.

4.1   Gaming the System

We have discussed how metrics are likely less important than their presentation. Using a systematic process that aligns one's goals with metrics seems sensible and helpful.

But at the same time, how metrics are used must be informed and systematic, which can be challenging as there are many unknowns about the possible side effects or second-order effects of using a certain metric.

Considering the quasi-experiment discussed in the previous section — what would have happened if the number of commits by a student would have been tied to their course grade?

It seems very likely that students would have been more motivated to commit more. However, it seems similarly likely that the barrier to trying to cheat the system would have been lower, as the potential reward would have been much higher. Campbell [7] gives an insightful overview of how metrics — in his case, for public policy — can have the opposite effect of what was intended.

Using metrics to influence behavior is a double-edged sword: it can have positive results, but can also backfire. To lessen this risk, metrics should be kept playful. That is, they should not be tied to a person's income, their grades, or their career options. But at the same time, for a metric to have any effect, it needs to be meaningful to those involved. Leaning on Deci's and Ryan's self-determination theory [11], relatedness — relationships to others — could help create meaning.

4.2   Surveillance

Tracking activity data from potentially many services that developers use throughout the day also elicits thoughts about surveillance. If an employer uses People Analytics to improve internal collaboration, employees could easily feel monitored.

We believe that this would especially be the case if employees are not sufficiently informed about what is being tracked about their behavior, what happens to the data, and what the goal of the tracking is. After all, some employers could indeed think that the number of commits per day that a developer pushes to the repository should have a direct influence on salaries or promotions.

The only somewhat reliable solution to not tracking too many details about developers' behaviors would be to aggregate personally identifying data. Simply anonymizing such data has been shown to be easily reversible, especially when social networks are involved.

4.3   Public Data vs. Accessible Data

At the same time, we acknowledge that many things are already public, at least *within a team* — commit data and calendar data being two of the more obvious examples. That colleagues can look up these activity traces if they so wish we consider as accepted as normal today.

In our experiment, we did not make more data public — we merely presented it differently. All the data we used was available to every student all the time, e.g., through a Subversion client. The same goes for GitHub's newsfeed — it is also just making existing, accessible data more visible and accessible with fewer barriers.

This illustrates that the mere availability of data is usually not sufficient to make it have an impact on behavior. In order to do that, data needs to be presented in an accessible and goal-oriented manner.

4.4   Transparency

The most sensible strategy likely is to make transparent what is being measured and to what end. This will help developers understand what their activity data is being used for and, ideally, they will see a worthy cause in their employer's intentions. At the same time, employees can also act as an ethical canary for their employer, notifying management of instances where a line has been crossed. However, this will require a workplace culture that permits this. Part of such a culture would be attempts from the organization to actually get any honest feedback on their People Analytics projects from employees.

Ethical standards regarding these things will surely change with time. Yet organizations should err on the side of standards that are too high.

4.5   Conclusions

Despite the challenges mention above, the potential upsides of People Analytics for software development are enticing. Collaboration is one of the hardest problems in software engineering, and any improvement would likely be welcome by developers, organizations, and researchers alike.

More and more Internet-based services are becoming available and being used. Data about employee behavior will likely become more rather than less. Both researchers and practitioners need to be prepared so we handle it appropriately. To do so, we need open discussions about ethical standards, best practices on which metrics to use, and on appropriate delivery of feedback.

There are many more open challenges in People Analytics than we could possibly have discussed, and even for those we have touched upon, we barely scratched the surface. With this in mind, we hope our contribution can help continue the discussion within the software engineering research community. We would feel honored if you took us up on that — our email addresses are listed at the top of the paper for a reason.

References

1. Müller, S.C., Fritz, T.: Stuck and frustrated or in flow and happy: sensing developers' emotions and progress. In: Proceedings International Conference on Software Engineering, ICSE 2015 (2015)
2. Bird, C., Gourley, A., Devanbu, P., Gertz, M., Swaminathan, A.: Mining email social networks. In: Proceedings of the 2006 International Workshop on Mining Software Repositories, MSR 2006, pp. 137–143. ACM, New York (2006)
3. Bouwers, E., Visser, J., van Deursen, A.: Getting what you measure. Commun. ACM **55**(7), 54–59 (2012)
4. Brun, Y., Holmes, R., Ernst, M.D., Notkin, D.: Proactive detection of collaboration conflicts. In: Proceedings ESEC/FSE, pp. 168–178 (2011)
5. Burt, R.S.: Detecting role equivalence. Soc. Netw. **12**(1), 83–97 (1990)
6. Burt, R.S.: Decay functions. Soc. Netw. **22**(1), 1–28 (2000)
7. Campbell, D.T.: Assessing the impact of planned social change. Eval. Program Plann. **2**(1), 67–90 (1979)
8. Capiluppi, A., Serebrenik, A., Singer, L.: Assessing technical candidates on the social web. IEEE Softw. **30**(1), 45–51 (2013)
9. Caudwell, A.H.: Gource: visualizing software version control history. In: Proceedings of the ACM International Conference Companion on Object Oriented Programming Systems Languages and Applications Companion, OOPSLA 2010, pp. 73–74. ACM, New York (2010)
10. de Souza, C., Froehlich, J., Dourish, P.: Seeking the source: software source code as a social and technical artifact. In: Proceedings of the 2005 International ACM SIGGROUP Conference on Supporting Group Work, GROUP 2005, pp. 197–206. ACM, New York (2005)
11. Deci, E., Ryan, R.: Handbook of Self-Determination Research. The University of Rochester Press, Rochester (2002)
12. Dewan, P.: Towards emotion-based collaborative software engineering. In: 2015 IEEE/ACM 8th International Workshop on Cooperative and Human Aspects of Software Engineering (CHASE), pp. 109–112, May 2015

13. Ellis, C.A., Gibbs, S.J., Rein, G.: Groupware: some issues and experiences. ACM Commun. **34**(1), 39–58 (1991)
14. Ford, D., Parnin, C.: Exploring causes of frustration for software developers. In: 2015 IEEE/ACM 8th International Workshop on Cooperative and Human Aspects of Software Engineering (CHASE), pp. 117–118, May 2015
15. Fritz, T., Begel, A., Müller, S.C., Yigit-Elliott, S., Züger, M.: Using psycho-physiological measures to assess task difficulty in software development. In: Proceedings of the 36th International Conference on Software Engineering, ICSE 2014, pp. 402–413. ACM, New York (2014)
16. Golbeck, J.: Analyzing the Social Web. Newnes, Oxford (2013)
17. Granovetter, M.S.: The strength of weak ties. Am. J. Sociol. **78**(6), 1360–1380 (1973)
18. Graziotin, D., Wang, X., Abrahamsson, P.: Are happy developers more productive? In: Heidrich, J., Oivo, M., Jedlitschka, A., Baldassarre, M.T. (eds.) PRO-FES 2013. LNCS, vol. 7983, pp. 50–64. Springer, Heidelberg (2013). doi:10.1007/978-3-642-39259-7_7
19. Graziotin, D., Wang, X., Abrahamsson, P.: Understanding the affect of developers: theoretical background and guidelines for psychoempirical software engineering. In: Proceedings of the 7th International Workshop on Social Software Engineering, SSE 2015. ACM, New York (2015). (to appear)
20. Guzman, E., Azócar, D., Li, Y.: Sentiment analysis of commit comments in github: an empirical study. In: Proceedings of the 11th Working Conference on Mining Software Repositories, MSR 2014, pp. 352–355. ACM, New York, NY (2014)
21. Guzzi, A., Begel, A.: Facilitating communication between engineers with CARES. In: Proceedings of the 2012 International Conference on Software Engineering, ICSE 2012, pp. 1367–1370. IEEE Press, Piscataway (2012)
22. Hansen, M.T.: The search-transfer problem: the role of weak ties in sharing knowledge across organization subunits. Adm. Sci. Q. **44**(1), 82–111 (1999)
23. Khan, I.A., Brinkman, W.-P., Hierons, R.: Towards estimating computer users' mood from interaction behaviour with keyboard and mouse. Front. Comput. Sci. **7**(6), 943–954 (2013)
24. Khan, I.A., Brinkman, W.-P., Hierons, R.M.: Do moods affect programmers' debug performance? Cogn. Technol. Work **13**(4), 245–258 (2011)
25. Kim, T., McFee, E., Olguin, D.O., Waber, B., Pentland, A.S.: Sociometric badges: using sensor technology to capture new forms of collaboration. J. Organ. Behav. **33**(3), 412–427 (2012)
26. Lavallée, M., Robillard, P.N.: Why good developers write bad code: an observational case study of the impacts of organizational factors on software quality. In: Proceedings of the 2015 International Conference on Software Engineering (2015)
27. Leite, L., Treude, C., Figueira Filho, F.: UEDashboard: awareness of unusual events in commit histories. In: Proceedings of the 10th Joint Meeting of the European Software Engineering Conference and the ACM SIGSOFT Symposium on the Foundations of Software Engineering, ESEC/FSE 2015. ACM, New York (2015). (to appear)
28. Liberatore, M.J., Luo, W.: The analytics movement: implications for operations research. Interfaces **40**(4), 313–324 (2010)
29. Liskin, O., Schneider, K., Kiesling, S., Kauffeld, S.: Meeting intensity as an indicator for project pressure: exploring meeting profiles. In: 2013 6th International Workshop on Cooperative and Human Aspects of Software Engineering (CHASE), pp. 153–156, May 2013

30. Lopez-Fernandez, L., Robles, G., Gonzalez-Barahona, J.M., et al.: Applying social network analysis to the information in CVS repositories. In: International Workshop on Mining Software Repositories, pp. 101–105. IET (2004)
31. Meyer, A.N., Fritz, T., Murphy, G.C., Zimmermann, T.: Software developers' perceptions of productivity. In: Proceedings of the 22Nd ACM SIGSOFT International Symposium on Foundations of Software Engineering, FSE 2014, pp. 19–29. ACM, New York (2014)
32. Murgia, A., Tourani, P., Adams, B., Ortu, M.: Do developers feel emotions? An exploratory analysis of emotions in software artifacts. In: Proceedings of the 11th Working Conference on Mining Software Repositories, MSR 2014, pp. 262–271. ACM, New York (2014)
33. Nagappan, N., Murphy, B., Basili, V.: The influence of organizational structure on software quality: an empirical case study. In: Proceedings of the 30th International Conference on Software Engineering, ICSE 2008, pp. 521–530. ACM, New York (2008)
34. Ogawa, M., Ma, K.-L.: code_swarm: a design study in organic software visualization. IEEE Trans. Vis. Comput. Graph. **15**(6), 1097–1104 (2009)
35. Ogawa, M., Ma, K.-L.: Software evolution storylines. In: Proceedings of the 5th International Symposium on Software Visualization, SOFTVIS 2010, pp. 35–42. ACM, New York (2010)
36. Pham, R., Mörschbach, J., Schneider, K.: Communicating software testing culture through visualizing testing activity. In: Proceedings of the 7th International Workshop on Social Software Engineering, SSE 2015. ACM, New York (2015). (to appear)
37. Pham, R., Singer, L., Liskin, O., Figueira Filho, F., Schneider, K.: Creating a shared understanding of testing culture on a social coding site. In: Proceedings International Conference on Software Engineering, ICSE 2013, pp. 112–121 (2013)
38. Plonka, L., Sharp, H., Van der Linden, J., Dittrich, Y.: Knowledge transfer in pair programming: an in-depth analysis. Int. J. Hum.-Comput. Stud. **73**, 66–78 (2015)
39. Reagans, R., Zuckerman, E., McEvily, B.: How to make the team: social networks vs. demography as criteria for designing effective teams. Adm. Sci. Q. **49**(1), 101–133 (2004)
40. Rogers, E.M.: Diffusion of Innovations, 5th edn. Free Press, New York (2003)
41. Sarma, A., Noroozi, Z., van der Hoek, A.: Palantir: raising awareness among configuration management workspaces. In: 2003 Proceedings 25th International Conference on Software Engineering, pp. 444–454, May 2003
42. Schneider, K.: LIDs: a light-weight approach to experience elicitation and reuse. In: Bomarius, F., Oivo, M. (eds.) PROFES 2000. LNCS, vol. 1840, pp. 407–424. Springer, Heidelberg (2000). doi:10.1007/978-3-540-45051-1_34
43. Schneider, K., Liskin, O.: Exploring flow distance in project communication. In: 2015 IEEE/ACM 8th International Workshop on Cooperative and Human Aspects of Software Engineering (CHASE), pp. 117–118, May 2015
44. Schneider, K., Liskin, O., Paulsen, H., Kauffeld, S.: Media, mood, and meetings: related to project success? ACM Trans. Comput. Educ. (2015). (accepted–to appear(n/a): n/a)
45. Shaw, T.: The emotions of systems developers: an empirical study of affective events theory. In: Proceedings of the 2004 SIGMIS Conference on Computer Personnel Research: Careers, Culture, and Ethics in a Networked Environment, SIGMIS CPR 2004, pp. 124–126. ACM, New York (2004)

46. Singer, L.: Improving the adoption of software engineering practices through persuasive interventions. Ph.D. thesis, Gottfried Wilhelm Leibniz Universität Hannover (2013)
47. Singer, L., Figueira Filho, F., Cleary, B., Treude, C., Storey, M.-A., Schneider, K.: Mutual assessment in the social programmer ecosystem: an empirical investigation of developer profile aggregators. In: Proceedings 2013 Conference Computing Supported Cooperative Work, CSCW 2013, pp. 103–116. ACM, New York (2013)
48. Singer, L., Figueira Filho, F., Storey, M.-A.: Software engineering at the speed of light: how developers stay current using twitter. In: Proceedings of the 36th International Conference on Software Engineering, ICSE 2014, pp. 211–221. ACM, New York (2014)
49. Singer, L., Schneider, K.: It was a bit of a race: gamification of version control. In: Proceedings of the 2nd International Workshop on Games and Software Engineering (2012)
50. Stapel, K., Knauss, E., Schneider, K., Becker, M.: Towards understanding communication structure in pair programming. In: Sillitti, A., Martin, A., Wang, X., Whitworth, E. (eds.) XP 2010. LNBIP, vol. 48, pp. 117–131. Springer, Heidelberg (2010). doi:10.1007/978-3-642-13054-0_9
51. Stapel, K., Knauss, E., Schneider, K., Zazworka, N.: Flow mapping: planning and managing communication in distributed teams. In: 2011 6th IEEE International Conference on Global Software Engineering (ICGSE), pp. 190–199. IEEE (2011)
52. Stapel, K., Schneider, K.: Managing knowledge on communication and information flow in global software projects. Expert Syst. **31**, 234–252 (2012)
53. Storey, M.-A., Singer, L., Cleary, B., Figueira Filho, F., Zagalsky, A.: The (R)evolution of social media in software engineering. In: Proceedings of the on Future of Software Engineering, FOSE 2014, pp. 100–116. ACM, New York (2014)
54. Stuart, H.C., Dabbish, L., Kiesler, S., Kinnaird, P., Kang, R.: Social transparency in networked information exchange: a theoretical framework. In: Proceedings of the ACM 2012 Conference on Computer Supported Cooperative Work, CSCW 2012, pp. 451–460. ACM, New York (2012)
55. Swan, M.: The quantified self: fundamental disruption in big data science and biological discovery. Big Data **1**, 85–99 (2013)
56. Treude, C., Figueira Filho, F., Kulesza, U.: Summarizing and measuring development activity. In: Proceedings of the 10th Joint Meeting of the European Software Engineering Conference and the ACM SIGSOFT Symposium on the Foundations of Software Engineering, ESEC/FSE 2015. ACM, New York (2015). (to appear)
57. Waber, B.: People Analytics: How Social Sensing Technology Will Transform Business and What It Tells Us about the Future of Work, 1st edn. FT Press, Upper Saddle River (2013)
58. Xuan, Q., Fang, H., Fu, C., Filkov, V.: Temporal motifs reveal collaboration patterns in online task-oriented networks. Phys. Rev. E **91**(5), 052813 (2015)

Structured Program Generation Techniques

Yannis Smaragdakis$^{(\boxtimes)}$, Aggelos Biboudis, and George Fourtounis

University of Athens, Athens, Greece
{smaragd,biboudis,gfour}@di.uoa.gr

Abstract. So, you can write a program that generates other programs. Sorry, ... not impressed. You want to impress me? Make sure your program-generating program only produces well-formed programs. What is "well-formed", you ask? Well, let's start with "it parses". Then let's get to "... and type-checks". You want to really impress me? Give me an expressive language for program generators in which any program you write will only generate well-formed programs.

In this briefing, we will sample the state-of-the-art in program generation relative to the above important goal. If we want to establish program generation as a general-purpose, disciplined methodology, instead of an ad hoc hack, we should be able to check the generator once and immediately validate the well-formedness of anything it might generate. This is a modular safety property for meta-programs, much akin to static typing for regular programs.

Some of the emphasis will be on our own work on "class morphing" (or just "morphing"): the statically-safe adaptation of the contents of a class, depending on other classes supplied as parameters. Along the way, lots of other techniques will be discussed and contrasted, from different template facilities, to syntactically-safe program generation, to program staging techniques.

1 Introduction

A *program generator* (or just *generator*) is a program that generates programs expressed in a high-level language. The language in which the generator is written (commonly called the *host* or the *meta* language) and the output language (commonly called the *object* or *target* language) do not have to be the same, although they often are.[1]

Generators arise in so many practical scenarios that one may wonder whether they deserve a special name, or they are merely "programs". Generators appear as wizards or refactorings in IDEs, as template or macro libraries, as implementations (compilers) of domain-specific languages (DSL), as high-performance optimizing libraries, as modularity (e.g., *aspect-oriented*) mechanisms, as frameworks (e.g., for dependency injection), and much more.

---

[1] A closely related concept is that of a *program transformer*, which modifies an existing program, instead of generating a new one. The main principles and ideas behind generators and transformers are virtually identical. In this text, we write "generator" to mean "generator or transformer".

© Springer International Publishing AG 2017
J. Cunha et al. (Eds.): GTTSE 2015, LNCS 10223, pp. 154–178, 2017.
DOI: 10.1007/978-3-319-60074-1_7

Generators exist because of the desire, as old as programming itself, to automate, elevate, modularize or otherwise facilitate program development. In practice, generators are one of many technologies for enabling modularity and software reuse—other examples are binary or source libraries, application frameworks, component technologies, and services. However, generators are often the technique of last resort. They are used for programming automation patterns not covered by other, conventional technologies. Generators offer the potential for more advanced optimizations, syntactic convenience, or static checking than plain libraries or component technologies.

Generators are also an intellectually fascinating topic: what can be more interesting to a computer scientist than computing programs? The canonical sensationalist example is self-generating programs. For example, we can have:

```
((lambda (x) (list x (list'quote x)))
'(lambda (x) (list x (list'quote x))))
```

in Lisp or:

```
main(a){a="main(a){a=%c%s%c;printf(a,34,a,34);}";printf(a,34,a,34);}
```

in C.

The power and appeal of generators comes at a cost, however. Programmers often view program generation technology as low-level and largely ad hoc. A common complaint concerns debugging: an error in the generated program can be very hard to debug and may require full understanding of the generator itself. In more general terms, the fault is due to lack of *modular* reasoning. The generator author cannot easily consider what the generator will do for every input, only for the inputs he/she has tested. The generator user (i.e., the end programmer) should not have to reason about the code produced by the generator, only about the way he/she uses it.

This need is the focus of our briefing. We discuss *structured program generation techniques,* i.e., techniques that can offer guarantees on the correctness (w.r.t. static semantics, i.e., at most type-correctness) of generated programs *before these are generated,* i.e., for all inputs to the generator. We will refer to this property as *modular safety* of a generator.[2]

Ensuring that a generator only produces well-formed programs (typically under some assumptions on the generator input) is practically important and intuitively appealing. Viewed as a type-checking matter, this property is quite similar to static typing of regular programs. Much like in standard static typing, we want to statically check the generator and be sure that no type error arises during its *run time,* which happens to be the *compile time* of the generated program.

If the problem of structured program generation is solved, "program generation" will become mere "programming", raising the level of programming automation without sacrificing high-level, modular reasoning. Consider: if a generator that can do most useful things that current generators do can also be checked modularly, i.e., for all possible inputs, then why does it matter that

---

[2] This is also occasionally called *meta type-safety.*

it is a generator? The output program will never need to be inspected by the end programmer. Instead, we might prefer to mentally model what the generator does as program generation, while in reality we will not care whether a program is actually ever generated.

In the next sections, we present current program generation mechanisms and levels of modular safety, before focusing on state-of-the-art techniques for modular safety of generators. Our goal is not to offer an exhaustive survey of the literature but to inform of different levels of reasoning power, with selected pioneering or representative work in each one.

2   Kinds of Generation and Program Transformation

There is a large variety of mechanisms that can be used to generate or transform programs—for instance, see Reference [12] for a representative comparison. We briefly survey the general classes of such mechanisms, for reference in future sections.

Generation of programs as text. The most basic technique for program generation is that of producing character strings containing the text of a program, which is subsequently interpreted or compiled. For instance, a common approach for generating database queries (in SQL) inside an imperative language program is via string concatenation—for instance:

```
sqlProg ="SELECT name FROM" + tableName + "WHERE id =" + idVar;
```

Note the distinction between target language identifiers (`name`, `id`) and meta-variables (`tableName`, `idVar`). The latter correspond to parts of the generated program text that may vary, depending on the generator's execution. The former are fixed and need to have a meaning in the context of the generated program. (We discuss the topic of what generated names may refer to in the next section, under "Scoping and Hygiene".)

Text-based program generation is readily available in most programming settings, yet clearly low-level. There is nothing in the generator code to indicate that the string that is being assembled represents a program. Therefore, this program could have errors at any level of program processing (lexical analysis, parsing, static semantics, etc.).

Syntax tree manipulation. A more sophisticated, yet commonly used, technique is to generate the syntax tree of a program, instead of its unstructured text. This requires defining host language concepts that correspond to the syntactic structure of the target language—an idea we will revisit in the next section. For example, our SQL-generating program could be written as follows:

```
sqlProg = new SelectStmt(new Column(name), table,
                 new WhereClause(new Column(id), idVar));
```

The generated program can be produced by either pretty-printing the syntax tree and invoking a traditional language processor (e.g., a compiler for the target language) or by interfacing with the post-parsing stage of such a target language processor.

Code templates, quoting. Generating programs by assembling syntax trees can be tedious, even in languages with pattern-matching constructs [54]. Therefore, several facilities for program generation (e.g., [2,35,43,56], among many) offer the ability to generate program fragments by "quoting" the code to be generated, i.e., using code templates with constant and variable parts. This requires language constructs for generating program fragments in the target language (typically called a *quote*—e.g., "'[...]'") as well as for supplying values to fill in holes in the generated syntax tree (typically called an *unquote* or *escape*—e.g., "#[...]"). For instance, our earlier code fragment might be written as:

```
sqlProg = '[SELECT name FROM #[table] WHERE id = #[idVar]];
```

As can be seen, this approach (often termed *meta-programming with concrete syntax* [54]) approximates the syntactic simplicity of a plain evaluated program, significantly simplifying the program text of the generator.

Macros. Another meta-programming approach of widespread use is *macros*: reusable code templates with pre-set rules for parameterizing them and yielding different generated program fragments. A typical macro only allows substitution of parameters in its body, as opposed to more general program generation control flow—e.g., a loop that generates an unbounded number of statements. A reference facility for high-level macros is the Scheme macro system [46]. A swapping macro, replacing its uses by an expression that swaps two values, can be written as follows:

```
(define-syntax-rule (swap x y)
  (let ([tmp x])
    (set! x y)
    (set! y tmp)))
```

Macro languages can vary greatly in sophistication and are difficult to categorize. A common element is that they blend the distinction between generator and generated program. The generated fragment is typically not treated as a data structure (e.g., a syntax tree) but instead replaces program expressions wherever it occurs. Thus, the usual relationship between meta-program and object program is inverted: in macros, the default, undistinguished program text is as-if generated and augmented/transformed by the output of the generator (i.e., the macro), whereas in typical program generation undistinguished program text is part of the generator and generated code is clearly marked.

Generics. Common (type-)genericity mechanisms in programming languages may occasionally be powerful enough to be considered general-purpose program generation facilities. Genericity refers to the ability to parameterize a code template with different static types. Mechanisms such as C++ templates work by producing specialized code for each concrete type parameter. Furthermore, the specialization mechanism is powerful enough to allow conditional reasoning, and templates can be recursive, thus allowing full Turing-complete computation [53]. C++ templates are also explicitly able to compute over compile-time constants, using regular C++ operators. This capability is used to define a compile-time adder in the following code fragment:

```
template<int X, int Y>
struct Adder {
    enum { result = X + Y };
};
```

There are several standard techniques that have harnessed the expressiveness of C++ templates to yield arbitrary program generation capabilities, as discussed in References [12,52].

Specialized languages. Beyond the above classes of mechanisms, there are several specialized languages for program generators. For example, *aspect-oriented programming* facilities can be viewed as implicit transformations of a program [28,29]. This is most evident in features such as *inter-type declarations*:

```
aspect S {
  declare parents:
  Car implements Serializable;
}
```

The above aspect adds a supertype (`Serializable`) to an existing class `Car`. As in more overt program generation/transformation techniques, we can ask the question of what guarantees are offered on the generated program, when the aspect is generic and can apply to yet-unspecified classes.

In Sect. 4, we will see more examples of languages specifically designed for expressing meta-programs.

3   Kinds of Generator Safety

The main focus of this briefing is on *statically-safe* (or just *safe* for brevity) program generation techniques: certifying the generator as "safe" should guarantee the well-formedness of any generated program.

One can perhaps debate whether the static safety of a generator is an essential feature. After all, the generated program will be checked statically before it runs, so why try to catch the same errors before the program is even generated? The answer is that static checking is not mainly intended to detect errors in the generated program or even errors in the generator input, but errors in the generator itself. Such errors are typically mismatched assumptions: the generator fails to take into account some input case, so that, even though the generator writer has tested the generator under several inputs, other inputs result in badly-formed programs. Although these errors will be detected at compile time of the *generated program*, this is (at least as late as) the generator's *run time*. Thus, errors of program well-formedness, which a programmer would hope to have eliminated once and for all, can arise dynamically, as far as the generator is concerned.

Consider a simple scenario in a realistic generator. The generator examines an input program, and for every class containing a designated method—e.g., `register`—produces registration code that invokes the method. The generated code will fail to compile if the `register` method is private. This is an error in the generator itself! The generator writer has failed to take into account the possibility of private `register` methods. (Multiple fixes may be possible: the generator could ignore non-accessible methods, or the generated code could invoke them indirectly—e.g., via reflection.) Even worse, the generator writer could have extensively tested his/her code with large, realistic inputs, just never with private `register` methods.

As discussed in the introduction, tools that only generate well-formed programs are often called *structured* meta-programming tools. The term "structured" only captures the basic premise, however: there are several levels of well-formedness and we need to distinguish them for purposes of precise characterization.

Lexical and syntactic well-formedness. The first level of static safety for generators is safety with respect to lexical and syntax checking. That is, such safety entails employing techniques for building or checking generators so that any generated/transformed program is guaranteed to pass the lexical analysis and parsing phases of a traditional compiler. A common way to satisfy this property is by encoding the syntax of the object language using the type system of the host language. For instance, consider traditional syntax checking expressed as context-free grammar (CFG) rules. Rules for top-level syntactic categories of an imperative language (statement, declaration, expression) will typically take a form such as that below:

```
AST     ::= Stmt
        |   Expr
        |   Decl
Stmt    ::= IfStmt
IfStmt  ::="if" "(" Expr ")" Stmt
   ...
```

The above CFG specification can map to types for values that the generator manipulates, as well as constructors for these values. This yields a subtyping hierarchy[3] where types *Stmt*, *Expr*, and *Decl* are subtypes of type *AST* and

---

[3] Alternatively, one can represent a grammar as an *algebraic data type* (ADT), for equivalent functionality, with respect to our static safety guarantees.

type *IfStmt* is a subtype of *Stmt*. Furthermore, values of type *IfStmt* are created using a constructor that accepts an *Expr* value and a *Stmt* value. If the generator type checks, then the values it manipulates are guaranteed to conform to the induced type constraints, which means that they are fragments of syntactically-correct code in the target language, per the CFG rules. There is no possibility of, e.g., creating an *IfStmt* with a *Stmt* instead of an *Expr* in the condition of the generated if code fragment.

Scoping and hygiene. Programming languages typically support variables, which obey scoping rules: each variable is first declared and then used, and the rules define where the declaration starts having effect and what variables are visible at each program point. When an *identifier* (i.e., a name) is used to denote a variable, we say that the identifier is a *reference* to the variable, or that the identifier *binds* to the variable declaration.

A correctness property of great interest for generated programs concerns the appropriate binding of identifiers, i.e., ensuring that produced variable references are bound to the *intended* variable declaration. Consider an example of meta-programming with concrete syntax:

```
expr = '[ for (int i = 0; i < #[boundExpr]; i++) { #[bodyExpr] } ];
```

The generated code fragment introduces a new identifier, i, in a binding position, i.e., in a declaration. Can this declaration bind references that the generator programmer did not intend? For instance, if boundExpr holds an expression from the input program, could this expression refer to a variable i, bound to the newly declared i? Conversely, can declarations of the input program accidentally bind references in the generated code? Mistakes in binding resolution may or may not appear as static checking errors—e.g., binding to an unintended variable may not be a type error, depending on the declared types and the static semantics of the target language. Thus, the problem is a semantic one: even well-typed programs may have a different meaning than what was intended.

The absence of unintended name binding is typically called *hygiene*. Questions of hygiene have been studied in depth, over some-30 years of research in meta-programming. The same issues arise in generics (e.g., C++ templates perform hygienic renaming), in quoting/meta-programming with concrete syntax [45,51], and, most prominently, in macros [10,17,32,50].

Macros have been the first setting where the question of hygiene has been examined [32]. In macros, there is a clearly designated part of the generated program that comes from the input program, and another that comes from the macro definition. Therefore, the issue of hygiene takes a simple form: a macro system is hygienic if the familiar *lexical scoping* rules (i.e., an identifier is bound to a declaration in its lexical context) are obeyed. Hygienic macros are a fundamental feature of Scheme [17,46]. Racket, a Scheme descendant, goes even further by implementing the whole language using code generation via hygienic macros [50].

Hygienic meta-programming systems enforce their hygiene property automatically—typically by performing variable renaming to eliminate ambiguity. Therefore, hygiene is a rather orthogonal property to the rest of the mechanisms we discuss in this briefing. Most of the research in hygienic mechanisms has focused on designing and implementing the right scoping mechanisms for meta-programs, not on finding errors (with no possibility of automatic fixes) in the generator code.

Full well-formedness. Extrapolating from the above kinds of statically-safe program generation, it is reasonable to ask how easy it is to achieve full static safety. That is, to write generators in such a way that every generated program is guaranteed to pass any static check in the target language. This is a hard property to ensure: static checks beyond the syntax phase (i.e., in type checking or other semantic analysis) require context information, which is tough to maintain by merely analyzing the generator. A rich host language can express generators with arbitrarily complex structure, whose control-flow paths map to different static contexts of generated programs.

To see the problem in an example, consider a program generator that emits programs depending on two input-related conditions:

```
if (pred1())
  emit( '[int i;] );
...
if (pred2())
  emit( '[i++;] );
```

If, for some input, `pred2` does not imply `pred1` (or if the first `if` is unreachable), then the generator can emit the reference to variable `i` without having generated the definition of `i`. This is an error in the generator and it should be the responsibility of the infrastructure for generator development to prevent such errors. (Of course, it is rather easy to catch this error at generation time of the `i++` fragment, but this just shifts the blame: the generator does not produce an invalid program, but fails to produce anything.)

As the above example shows, static safety for generated programs corresponds to arbitrarily complex properties of the generator's control- or data-flow. In our example, determining the reachability of the statement emitting the declaration of variable `i` is a complex program analysis property.

4   Mechanisms for Fully Structured Generation

In order to achieve guarantees of full static safety for generators, we need to place restrictions on what generators are expressible in a language or development setting. As in any other kind of approach for establishing complex program properties, the restrictions can take many forms: we can limit the expressiveness of the host language for generators via disciplined syntactic or type-system constructs, we can permit only generators that successfully pass an analysis phase, and more. We see such mechanisms next.

4.1 Multi-stage Programming

A simple way to ensure the static safety of generated programs is to map them one-to-one to fragments of the generator's code. As a result, the generator and the generated program can be viewed as one, are type-checked by the same type system, and some parts of the program are merely evaluated later (i.e., generated). This approach is commonly called *staging* [27] and the program is called *multi-stage* or *staged*. Multi-Stage Programming (MSP) is the general paradigm for writing staged programs. MSP is a powerful and general approach, yet with significant limitations—e.g., a statement of the generator code is not allowed to produce arbitrarily many declarations in the generated program.

MSP views program generation as the addition of extra stages to regular programs. Instead of a plain execution stage (possibly internally broken into multiple stages, such as compilation and object execution) we have at least a generation stage and an execution phase. Programmers make use of a set of language constructs that introduce more stages for explicitly annotated segments of their code, so that these segments are evaluated at different times. At a later time, the previously (partially) evaluated, in earlier stages, parts of the program can be replaced by simpler constructs, such as constant values and statements with linear control flow.

The origins of staging constructs are found in languages like *MetaML* [49]: a statically-typed, multi-stage programming language, as an extension of Standard ML/NJ [1]. MetaML introduced four language constructs:

- the meta-brackets that delay a computation e.g., `<40+2>`. Evaluation cannot happen and the computation is considered *frozen*. These are *future-stage* computations, and can be thought of as generated code.
- the *escape* operator, `~x` for some variable x, can be used only inside meta-brackets—e.g., `<40+~x>`. This operator permits calculations at the current stage and splices the result inside the delayed expression for later use. This allows evaluation steps to take place during program generation, i.e., to vary the generated code.
- `run x` forces the evaluation of a meta-bracket expression. Essentially, it compiles the computation at run-time and runs it to produce the result.
- `lift x` allows the conversion of a value—the result of the evaluation of an expression that does not contain a function—into code.

Consider a function whose body contains a mix of staged and unstaged parts. What happens when we evaluate that method with an argument list consisting of some known values and some to-be-supplied at a later stage? MSP evaluates the unstaged and escaped parts of the program, utilizing information that is available at the current stage. Then it produces a residual program that is going to be evaluated at a subsequent stage, when the rest of the parameters are available. This is similar to a *partial evaluation* (PE) of the program [11,25], where the unstaged and escaped parts are evaluated, with staged parts left for later evaluation. (Staging and partial evaluation are closely related concepts [24,27]: staging can be seen as instructing a partial evaluator as to what parts of the program to partially evaluate. Conversely, automatic partial evaluation can be seen as computing the staging annotations automatically—a step called *binding-time analysis* in the PE literature [26].)

Applications of staging include the implementation of domain-specific languages [18], building compilers from interpreters [48] and the "finally tagless" approach to building efficient interpreters [6].

We next review staging in more detail via two modern staging implementations.

BER MetaOCaml. MetaOCaml [5] is a bytecode MSP compiler for OCaml and BER MetaOCaml [30] is its continuation: a heavily re-factored version of the MetaOCaml compiler that is more extensible and easier to integrate with releases of the regular OCaml compiler.[4]

We illustrate staging via the folklore example of a simple power function, which has been used for demonstrating partial evaluation (and staging) since at least 1977 [14]. The power function is defined recursively using the basic method of exponentiation by squaring. If the exponent is even we square the result of raising x to half the given power. Otherwise, we reduce the exponent by one and we multiply the result by x.

```
let even n = (n mod 2) = 0;;
let square x = x * x;;
let rec power n x =
  if n = 0 then 1
  else if even n then square (power (n/2) x)
  else x * (power (n-1) x);;
```

We can stage the above function in the MetaOCaml code below to produce power functions specialized for a certain n—e.g., 5. The staged version of the function is identical to the original, with the mere addition of staging annotations/constructs. BER MetaOCaml has three of the four MetaML constructs mentioned earlier: meta-brackets, escape and run. In this example, although n is statically known, x remains a variable: its value will only be known at a later evaluation stage.

```
open Runcode;;
let even n = (n mod 2) = 0;;
let square x = x * x;;
let rec powerS n x =
  if n = 0 then .<1>.
  else if even n
       then .<square .~(powerS (n/2) x)>.
       else .<.~x * .~(powerS (n-1) x)>.;;

let power5 = !. .<fun x -> .~(powerS 5 .<x>.)>.;;
```

---

[4] More historical details about the evolution path of MetaOCaml can be found at "A brief history of (BER) MetaOCaml", http://okmij.org/ftp/ML/MetaOCaml.html#history.

Note the structure of the above code. The return value of the `powerS` function is a staged computation, but it includes a part that can be evaluated, which is the recursive application. The result (i.e., the code/AST of the result) is spliced back into the staged computation of the final value, `power5`: a specialized function, to be available to later stages.

The operator `!.` is aliased to `Runcode.run`—the "run" functionality of MetaOCaml. This function compiles the staged lambda function, and links it back as the (specialized) code to be executed in the body of the `power5` function. Simply put, `!.` transfers our code from the world of representations of functions, (`int -> int`) `code`, to the world of functions, (`int -> int`).

BER MetaOCaml lets us inspect the code that is generated from our staged algorithm, using the `print_code` function. The result looks like the following snippet. As the reader observes, the recursive applications are performed at compile-time, partially evaluating the function. The result is the residue program below:

```
fun x -> x * (square (square (x * 1)))
```

In the example, the `square` function is referred from a future-stage computation using an identifier (`square`) bound at the present stage. This function is characterized as *cross-stage persistent*.

Lightweight Modular Staging. Rompf et al. introduced MSP support in Scala with *Lightweight Modular Staging* (LMS) [41]. In LMS, the programmer has just one staging construct available, in the form of a user-level type. To indicate that, e.g., an expression does not have a current-stage integer value but a future-stage integer value, the user changes the declared type of the expression from `Int` to `Rep[Int]`. The unary abstract type constructor `Rep[_]` indicates future-stage values. Types for other values, as well as the exact version of (overloaded, current or future stage) operators are inferred.

LMS follows a library-based approach, relying on a special and extensible version of the Scala compiler called *Scala-Virtualized* [39]. In Scala-Virtualized, a Scala program is represented in terms of function calls, e.g., the control-flow construct `do b while (c)` is represented by the `__doWhile(b, c)` function call. In this way, all interesting program statements are mapped to function calls. Even method calls are represented as infix functions—e.g., `x.a(y)` as `infix_a(x,y)`. This technique permits operations to be added to the type `Rep[T]` which also supports every method of a bare `T`. Staging `power` in LMS resembles the following code:

```
def even (n: Int) = n
def square (x: Rep[Int]) = x * x
def powerS (n : Int, x : Rep[Int]) : Rep[Int] = {
  if (n == 0) 1
  else if (even(n)) square(powerS(n/2, x))
  else x * powerS(n-1, x)
}

def powerTest(x : Rep[Int]) : Rep[Int] = powerS(5, x)
```

The input that needs to be designated as *future-stage* is the base x. This is the dynamic part of this snippet. All other is static input and will participate in compile-time evaluation. The type constructor `Rep` in, e.g., `Rep[T]` has the property that all operations on T are applicable to `Rep[T]` as well and operations on it will be generated later.

The core difference of LMS from other staging approaches is that *binding times (i.e., stages) are distinguished only by types*. The simplicity of the type-based approach to staging has been a significant boost for LMS, and owes much to the power of the Scala type system. In LMS applications, regular computations are routinely switched to staged computations with small, local changes to declared types.

Practical Notes. The two modern incarnations of staging concepts (BER MetaOCaml and LMS) integrate several practical enhancements and have seen significant applications. In both technologies, the user has multiple ways to generate code. For example, in LMS, CUDA code can be generated instead of Scala, and in BER MetaOCaml the user can compile directly to native code instead of the bytecode-generating, `Runcode.run` function. A notable recent application, with versions for both BER MetaOCaml and LMS, is the Strymonas library [31], which offers highly-optimized streaming functionality (e.g., `map`, `filter`, `zip` combinators), often over an order-of-magnitude faster than conventional libraries. More generally, staging, using LMS, has been proposed as a key part of an ambitious development methodology for high performance without sacrificing abstraction [40]. The methodology has seen several instances of successful application. It centers around the creation of domain-specific languages (DSLs) that obtain high-performance implementations via interpreters staged to become (effectively) compilers.

4.2   Class Morphing

Class morphing is a technique for writing program generators that take classes as input and generate new type-safe classes, based on the structure of the input ones. Morphing has been implemented as MorphJ [16, 19–21]: a language that adds compile-time reflection capabilities to Java. A programmer is able to capture compile-time patterns and encode them in (meta-)classes.

In MorphJ, a generator `Gen` taking as input a class `C` corresponds to a meta-class `Gen` parameterized by the input `C`, similar to Java generics (`Gen<C>`). From this perspective, morphing is a strong generalization of generics: for different values of the type parameters of a class `Gen`, radically different contents may be generated, which are the output of the generator. The body of the generator class then contains regular Java code mixed with MorphJ annotations describing the *reflection* (i.e., content-inspection) patterns that guide generation.

Each pattern is associated with a generative scenario. In the following example, the `LogMe` generator accepts as a parameter a class `X` and produces a subtype of `X` that logs the returns of calls to `X`'s (non-`void`) methods:

```
class LogMe<class X> extends X {
  <R,A*>[m] for ( public R m(A) : X.methods )
  public R m (A a) {
    R result = super.m(a);
    System.out.println(result);
    return result;
  }
}
```

The second line in the above (meta-)class is a *static for-loop* over methods of class `X` (designated `X.methods`) that match a pattern, `public R m(A)`, where `R` and `A` are type parameters (`A` can match any number of type parameters, as indicated by the `A*` syntax in its declaration) and `m` is a name parameter, as indicated by its distinct declaration syntax (`[m]`). Other facilities for inspecting the contents of type parameters (e.g., iterating over fields) are defined similarly in MorphJ.

In another example, a morphed class `Listify` may statically iterate over all the methods of another, unknown, type, `Subj`, pick those that have a single argument, and offer analogous "lifted" methods: whenever `Subj` has a method with argument `A`, `Listify` accepts a `List<A>`. (The implementation of every method in `Listify` can then, e.g., iterate over all list elements, and manipulate them using `Subj`'s methods.)

```
class Listify<Subj> {
  Subj ref;
  Listify(Subj s) {ref = s;}

  <R,A>[m] for (public R m(A): Subj.methods)
  public R m (List<A> a) {
    ... /* e.g., call m for all elements */
  }
}
```

Observe here that, in contrast to the previous example, this generator does not generate a subtype of `Subj` but an unrelated class that internally uses a `Subj` object.

In general, MorphJ offers program transformation capabilities but with modular type-safety guarantees: type-checking (via MorphJ) the code of `Listify` guarantees that all the classes it may produce (for any type `Subj`) also type-check (via the plain Java type system).

Type-checking a MorphJ program/generator to guarantee the static safety of all possible generated classes is based on determining the *uniqueness* of declarations and the *validity* of references. Uniqueness means that for each generated declaration of a variable or method in morphed code, the MorphJ type system needs to ensure that the declaration does not conflict with others in the same scope. Validity means that each reference to an identifier needs to map to an appropriate, type-correct morphed or pre-existing declaration in the morphed code. Because of static for-loops, a single identifier in morphed code (e.g., m in the LogMe class, above) maps to possibly many generated identifiers. Therefore, the checking of uniquness and validity needs to process the reflection patterns of static for-loops. This checking is done in MorphJ via the well-known concept of *unification* in patterns: for uniqueness, any two declaration-generating patterns in the same scope should never unify, while for validity, the pattern producing a reference should be a specialization (i.e., one-way unification) of a pattern producing a corresponding declaration. The pattern-based type-checking mechanism is mixed with subtyping and conventional type reasoning in the full MorphJ type checker [20]. The decidability of type-checking also hinges on expressiveness limitations placed on the MorphJ program: static for-loops cannot be nested (although a single for-loop can contain a nested, secondary pattern, with type variables bound in the primary pattern), and there is only a limited compile-time conditional statement [19].

The generator programmer has several facilities for influencing the result of MorphJ type-checking. The simplest one is that of stating subtyping constraints on type parameters (e.g., C<X extends I>), as in regular Java. Additionally, the programmer can add explicit static prefixes or suffixes to generated identifiers, to ensure their uniqueness—the $a\#b$ notation designates identifier concatenation with one of a, b being a constant.

Morphing enables great expressiveness when added to a conventional language. In fact, morphing can even simulate inheritance by offering safe delegation over classes. This requires some extra functionality, namely the addition of a single keyword (subobject) [16]. To see why such an extension might be needed, consider this example of a logger generator similar to LogMe given above:

```
class Logger<Subj> {
  Subj ref;
  Logger(Subj s) {ref = s;} // initialize

  <R,A*>[m] for (public R m(A) : Subj.methods)
  public R m (A a) {
    System.out.println("method" + m.name + "called with arg" + a);
    return ref.m(a);
  }
}
```

The morphed methods defined here report when they are called but the delegation will occur only during external-client calls to methods of Logger<C>, for some C. Any further calls happening inside the parent are not logged and thus the morphed class does not behave like a class that would override each method with a logged one. The problem is the lack of the *late binding* property. To remedy this, the object targeted by delegation must be identified using the `subobject` keyword:

```
class Logger<Subj> {
  subobject Subj ref;
  ... // as before
}
```

This small change ensures that method calls are late-bound so that a generated class, `Logger<C>` behaves like a true subclass of the original, `C`. However, the addition of `subobjects` has significant repercussions. For instance, two references to the same subobject (i.e., aliases), via different access paths can behave differently [16].

4.3   Shortcomings and More Power

Staging and morphing are broad approaches that can ensure statically-safe program generation, by focusing on specific (albeit broad) classes of program generation tasks. For more power, there have been several approaches that allow arbitrary program generation constructs, yet impose a discipline (based on type-checking or other analysis) over how these constructs are composed. We see some interesting such mechanisms next, noting the differences from staging and morphing, both in style and in expressive power.

SafeGen. SafeGen [22] is a meta-programming language for writing generators of Java code that are statically guaranteed to produce type-safe code.

The SafeGen language targets generators that can be written as transformations using reflection, i.e., inspection of the structure of existing code. SafeGen can thus be used for tasks similar to those that class morphing targets. SafeGen handles generated names and can guarantee that generated definitions have fresh names, not clashing with existing ones.

Compared to multi-stage languages and class morphing, SafeGen is more expressive in principle, as it permits the specification of a generator via arbitrary constructs. For example, it permits generators that generate and use names more freely than the scoping of multi-stage languages allows; it also enables generators that test arbitrary logic formulas over reflective properties, compared to the more constrained way of handling the same properties in morphing.

However, the type system of SafeGen is undecidable and it depends on an automated theorem prover for discharging proof goals for common cases. This means that more generators can be written and proved correct in SafeGen, but the user can also write generators that SafeGen cannot prove correct automatically and will report a "possible error".

A simple example in SafeGen (that could also be written using morphing) is that of a generator that takes a Java class as input and produces a Java interface of void methods that have the same name as the methods in the input class:

```
#defgen MakeInterface (Class c) {
  interface I { #foreach(Method m : MethodOf(m,c)) { void #[m] (); } }
}
```

In the code above, #defgen declares the generator, the #foreach syntax iterates over the methods of the input class, and #[m] uses the name of the meta-variable m in the generated code. This generator may seem too simple, but is buggy: since Java permits method overloading, two methods of the input class can have the same name and thus the generator may generate an interface with duplicate method declarations. SafeGen catches this error as it cannot prove that the generated output will always be type-safe.

A working SafeGen example is that of a generic delegator, which was also given in Sect. 4.2, using morphing:

```
#defgen MakeDelegator ( input(Class c) => !Abstract(c) ) {
  #foreach( Class c : input(c) ) {
    public class Delegator extends #[c] {
      #foreach(Method m : MethodOf(m, c) & !Private(m)) {
        #[m.Modifiers] #[m.Type] #[m] ( #[m.Formals] ) {
          return super.#[m](#[m.ArgNames]);
} } } } }
```

Although this is essentially a morphing example, the flavor of operators offers a glimpse of actual program manipulation with SafeGen. Static reflective iteration is supported, as well as arbitrary generation-time nesting of primitives (e.g., nesting of #foreach loops), compile-time conditionals, identifier manipulation, etc. The type system of the target language is fully encoded in input for the automated theorem prover that SafeGen employs as part of its checking. Part of this input is constant and encodes assumptions of the language (e.g., the single-inheritance nature of Java), while another part is custom-generated by translation of the generator specification, to encode the structure of the generated code. Finally, the generator specification is used to produce a logical sentence that establishes the generated program's well-formedness for unknown generator inputs. The automated theorem prover then attempts to prove this sentence.

In all, despite its power, the SafeGen approach suffers from lack of programmer control, due to the undecidable nature of the checking process. It is not easy to know when a generator fails to type-check due to a bug vs. due to limitations in automated formal reasoning.

Ur. Instead of translating a generator specification into a logical sentence for an automated theorem prover (as in SafeGen), one can attempt to enlist a powerful type system that can simultaneously express conventional type-level properties of a program and the logical structure of a generator under unknown inputs. This typically entails the use of *dependent types*: types that can use program expressions as terms. An advantage of this approach is that the user can improve the theorem proving ability of the system by just applying better type annotations (though these can be arbitrarily complex).

The Ur system [7] for program generation adopts this principle. Ur permits the declaration of generators that can be generic on their input while still producing only well-formed output. Ur's metaprogramming model is based on type-level computation and type-level records, following a functional programming style. The input of a generator defined in Ur can contain records of values or types and such records can be taken apart or built in the body of the generator, in a safe way, using functional programming machinery (e.g., higher-order functions such as `map` and `fold`). The type system keeps track of the origin and manipulation structure of records and values, much like the SafeGen type system, earlier, kept track of the patterns used to produce definitions and references to identifiers.

Targeting pragmatic applications and ease of use, Ur is using a restricted form of dependent types, combined with ad-hoc logic for common cases (such as special provers for the inference of intermediate proofs of a particular shape or automatic code transformations, such as `map` fusion). The safety guarantees of Ur assume that the writer of the generator dedicates some effort in writing type annotations and reasoning about output safety using the record-specific features of the language. On the other hand, the *user* of the generator can be spared this effort as Ur's heuristics fill in many holes, resulting in simple-to-use generators.

Although Ur offers type safety based on its records reasoning, the data format output by a generator may be subject to additional well-formedness constraints, such as the need for sanitization in HTML and SQL to address code injection attacks. In the case of HTML and SQL, Ur has been extended with additional functionality that guarantees this well-formedness, resulting in Ur/Web, a domain-specific language for web application development, implemented on top of Ur as a special library with extra rules for parsing and optimization [7,9]. Other generated data formats and their needs would need a similar extension of Ur.

As an example, consider a dynamic webpage that defines a generic `sum` function that sums an arbitrary list (record) of integers and then calls it to sum three lists of integers (one of them being the empty list):[5]

```
fun sum [fs ::: {Unit}] (fl : folder fs) (x : $(mapU int fs)) =
    @foldUR [int] [fn _ => int]
    (fn [nm :: Name] [rest :: {Unit}] [[nm] ~ rest] n acc => n + acc)
    0 fl x
```

```
fun main () = return <xml><body>
  {[sum {}]}<br/>
  {[sum {A = 0, B = 1}]}<br/>
  {[sum {C = 2, D = 3, E = 4}]}
</body></xml>
```

---

[5] The two pieces of code here are contained in Ur/Web distribution version 20150520 as demos `sum` and `tcSum`.

In this example, main is the entry point of the dynamic web page, which calls sum three times. (The nm and ~ syntax found in the body of sum is part of the Ur/Web support for record manipulation.) The results of sum calls are then embedded in well-formed XML. The sum function is declared using a fold, as in standard functional programming practice. The interesting part is the ability to iterate over the (unknown) fields of any record and to modularly assert that the iteration (i.e., sum) is well-defined, no matter what record is supplied as input. What sets Ur/Web apart from other Web frameworks is the amount of type information inferred: only x is explicitly given in the calls to the function; everything else is inferred. In particular, Ur/Web manages to infer the folding mechanism used (the folder). While in principle the type inference of Ur/Web is not complete, in practice it addresses many common cases encountered during Web development.

The example above was the definition of summing for integer records. The following example shows how to define a generic sum in a similar fashion:

```
fun sum [t] (_: num t) [fs ::: {Unit}] (fl: folder fs) (x: $(mapU t fs)) =
    @foldUR [t] [fn _ => t]
    (fn [nm :: Name] [rest :: {Unit}] [[nm] ~ rest] n acc => n + acc)
    zero fl x


fun main () = return <xml><body>
  {[sum {A = 0, B = 1}]}<br/>
  {[sum {C = 2.1, D = 3.2, E = 4.3}]}
</body></xml>
```

This example uses type classes, another feature of functional programming [55], to define sum on number-like data, i.e., values of types in the num type class. In this way, sum can be applied to records of integers and floats, with the same ease of development (inference) as before.

4.4 Other Techniques

There are several other techniques that are close relatives of the ones we discussed in the previous sections. We mention some of them for completeness and as starting points for further study.

The Genoupe system [13,34] allows expressing generators in an extended version of C#, using constructs similar to the static #foreach of SafeGen. Like SafeGen, the system allows arbitrary expressiveness (e.g., nesting of static for loops, static conditionals, and more) but, in contrast to SafeGen, does not encode the full complexity of the meta type-safety question in its type-checking. In SafeGen, this complexity mandated the use of a rich logic and an automated theorem prover. In contrast, the Genoupe checking is done through standard type-system techniques and is even more restrictive than MorphJ's. For instance, there is no way to generate declarations under a set of conditions and generate references to them under stricter conditions—the type system treats expressions in static constructs as opaque values that can only be compared for equality.

The compile-time reflection (CTR) facility [15] is a close relative of morphing, yet presents a different tradeoff in the design space. It introduces the concept of a self-contained transformation (instead of merging meta-programming features inside generic classes, as in MorphJ) and sacrifices some modular type safety: the system catches invalid references, though not duplicate definitions. The work has been recently extended with addition of features from morphing, and applied to several different program elements, such as pattern-based traits and reflection at the statement level [36,37].

In recent work on active libraries, Servetto and Zucca propose METAFJIG*, a rich meta-language for safe reflection with nested class support and composition operators [42]. These new features do not have a counterpart in classical morphing. In Sect. 4.5 we discuss interesting research avenues that incorporate such features.

Concepts of static safety have also arisen in the context of refactoring transformations, with work by Steimann and von Pilgrim [47]. An interesting aspect of this work is that it treats the program as a constant (i.e., does not guarantee the safety of a refactoring for all possible input programs) yet attempts to solve a hard problem—namely, to compute the constraints that need to hold in the post-transformation state of the program for the refactoring to have been semantics-preserving.

Recent work in the literature has focused on offering static safety guarantees for macro systems and other syntactic extension mechanisms. Lorenzen and Erdweg [33] propose a syntactic language extension facility that offers *type-based* syntax desugaring (allowing the desugaring specifications to employ type information) while guaranteeing automatically that desugarings only generate well-typed code. Chlipala's Bedrock system [8] is a relative of the Ur approach of Sect. 4.3. Bedrock introduces "certified low-level macros", for an assembly-level target language. These are highly expressive macros, allowing the implementation of a full C-like language stack. However, safety guarantees carry the cost of some manual verification effort by the programmer. The host language in Bedrock is the functional programming language of the Coq proof assistant [3]. In this setting, safety properties are also low level, guaranteeing the absence of invalid jumps or bad memory reads/writes in the resulting machine code.

4.5   Remarks and Future

The techniques we saw in the previous sections cover several points in the space of expressiveness/static safety tradeoffs. Perhaps the techniques with the easiest path to mainstream adoption are the ones that enforce clear, up-front expressiveness restrictions, yet support general as well as popular program generation patterns. Staging and morphing (Sects. 4.1 and 4.2) are the clearest such instances. Both of them have significant expressiveness limitations and addressing such limitations is the topic of active research.

Staging requires a one-to-one mapping between code fragments of the generator and the generated code. In multi-stage languages, one cannot escape an identifier in a binding position. For instance, it is not possible to generate the definition of a variable whose name will be determined at generator run-time, as in:

```
emit( '[ int #name; ] );
```

In a recent position paper [23], Inoue et al. argue that the "next stage of staging" will need to lift constructs to the type level. Allowing the generation of binding instances with variable names ("splicing binders") is identified as a major challenge. This is indeed the focus of morphing mechanisms: reasoning about generated declarations and their references, without knowing what the declared names will be until generator run-time. Therefore, an interesting direction for both morphing and staging are to combine forces, in language designs that enable meta type-safety for some of the most common kinds of program generation.

At the same time, morphing is evolving to acquire further functionality, for reflecting over classes. Recent work [4] presents *universal morphing*: an extension of morphing to permit patterns iterating over types. This ability captures morphing functionality at a much larger granularity than before, and enables several interesting programming abstractions. Examples include iterating over all supertypes of a class, over all its nested classes, over all classes in a given set, etc. Such static iteration can generate new classes that subclass or reference input classes, emulate a subset of their supertypes while adding new ones, morph over their members (via standard morphing patterns), etc. This enables, for instance, highly generic *mixin layers* [44]: parametric components containing classes that each inherit from a corresponding class in an unknown super-component supplied as a parameter. The ability to iterate over classes can also be used to support type constructor polymorphism and higher-kinded types, as in the work of Moors et al. [38].

In Sect. 4.4 we mentioned METAFJIG* as a source of features that are still not satisfactorily handled by other meta-programming systems. METAFJIG* defines a language that supports reflection over classes: the user can write reflective code that generates expressions of a "class" type (i.e., class definitions are seen as expressions) and there are operators over classes (such as sum). Universal morphing can also support versions of these concepts: it supports safe reflection over nested classes, and class operators can be encoded through morphing. For an example of this encoding, the sum operator can be defined as a class Sum<A,B> that contains methods of both A and B, guarantees the absence of method name clashes, and supports recursive summing.

5 Conclusions

Programming language design evolves with the invention of new kinds of abstraction. *Procedural abstraction* was introduced in the 50 s and 60 s and ushered in the era of structured programming languages. *Type abstraction* or *polymorphism*, in the 70 s and 80s, brought about modern functional and object-oriented languages. These advances were foreshadowed by program generation techniques that attempted to achieve the same expressiveness benefits with much lower-level concepts and no safety guarantees. Before there were structured procedures, there were macros that achieved similar benefits in many cases. Before there was polymorphism, there were generators that produced isomorphic code for different types, or copied one type's definitions into another. Generators are inevitable every time existing abstraction mechanisms are not enough. Conversely, getting generators to support an abstraction pattern with full static safety means that they are no longer "generators": it becomes a mere implementation detail whether a program is indeed generated as part of supporting an abstraction.

Therefore, the question of how to make generators statically type safe (i.e., statically checkable for all possible, unknown, inputs) is central to the future of programming language design. A technique from this solution space may be behind the next major evolution of programming languages. For instance, the morphing approach exemplifies *structural abstraction*: code can be agnostic of the structure of other program elements, yet interface with them correctly. This matches the widespread low-level practice of generating code via reflecting over existing classes or modules.

Given the importance and appeal of the underlying problem, it is no surprise that the field is active and diverse. This briefing gave an overview from a viewpoint that we hope illuminates rather different and typically disconnected approaches.

Acknowledgments. This work was funded by the Greek Secretariat for Research and Technology under the "MorphPL" Excellence (Aristeia) award.

References

1. Appel, A.W., MacQueen, D.B.: Standard ML of New Jersey. In: Maluszyński, J., Wirsing, M. (eds.) PLILP 1991. LNCS, vol. 528, pp. 1–13. Springer, Heidelberg (1991). doi:10.1007/3-540-54444-5_83. http://www.springerlink.com/index/YMU0P7QN06713188.pdf
2. Batory, D., Lofaso, B., Smaragdakis, Y.: JTS: tools for implementing domain-specific languages. In: Proceedings Fifth International Conference on Software Reuse, pp. 143–153. IEEE, Victoria, BC, Canada (1998). citeseer.nj.nec.com/171171.html
3. Bertot, Y., Castran, P.: Interactive Theorem Proving and Program Development: Coq'Art The Calculus of Inductive Constructions, 1st edn. Springer Publishing Company Incorporated, Heidelberg (2010)
4. Biboudis, A., Fourtounis, G., Smaragdakis, Y.: jUCM: universal class morphing (position paper). CoRR abs/1506.05270 (2015). http://arxiv.org/abs/1506.05270
5. Calcagno, C., Taha, W., Huang, L., Leroy, X.: Implementing multi-stage languages using ASTs, gensym, and reflection. In: Pfenning, F., Smaragdakis, Y. (eds.) GPCE 2003. LNCS, vol. 2830, pp. 57–76. Springer, Heidelberg (2003). doi:10.1007/978-3-540-39815-8_4

6. Carette, J., Kiselyov, O., Shan, C.C.: Finally tagless, partially evaluated: tagless staged interpreters for simpler typed languages. J. Funct. Program. **19**(5), 509–543 (2009). http://dx.doi.org/10.1017/S0956796809007205
7. Chlipala, A.: Ur: statically-typed metaprogramming with type-level record computation. In: Proceedings of the 31st ACM SIGPLAN Conference on Programming Language Design and Implementation, PLDI 2010, NY, USA, pp. 122–133 (2010). http://doi.acm.org/10.1145/1806596.1806612
8. Chlipala, A.: The Bedrock structured programming system: combining generative metaprogramming and Hoare logic in an extensible program verifier. In: Proceedings of the 18th ACM SIGPLAN International Conference on Functional Programming, ICFP 2013, NY, USA, pp. 391–402 (2013). http://doi.acm.org/10.1145/2500365.2500592
9. Chlipala, A.: The Ur/Web Manual (2015). http://www.impredicative.com/ur/manual.pdf
10. Clinger, W., Rees, J.: Macros that work. In: Proceedings of the 18th ACM SIGPLAN-SIGACT Symposium on Principles of Programming Languages, POPL 1991, NY, USA, pp. 155–162 (1991). http://doi.acm.org/10.1145/99583.99607
11. Consel, C., Danvy, O.: Tutorial notes on partial evaluation. In: Proceedings of the 20th ACM SIGPLAN-SIGACT Symposium on Principles of Programming Languages, POPL 1993, NY, USA, pp. 493–501 (1993). http://doi.acm.org/10.1145/158511.158707
12. Czarnecki, K., O'Donnell, J.T., Striegnitz, J., Taha, W.: DSL implementation in MetaOCaml, Template Haskell, and C++. In: Lengauer, C., Batory, D., Consel, C., Odersky, M. (eds.) Domain-Specific Program Generation. LNCS, vol. 3016, pp. 51–72. Springer, Heidelberg (2004). doi:10.1007/978-3-540-25935-0_4
13. Draheim, D., Lutteroth, C., Weber, G.: A type system for reflective program generators. In: Glück, R., Lowry, M. (eds.) GPCE 2005. LNCS, vol. 3676, pp. 327–341. Springer, Heidelberg (2005). doi:10.1007/11561347_22
14. Carette, J., Kiselyov, O., Shan, C.C.: Finally tagless, partially evaluated: Tagless staged interpreters for simpler typed languages. J. Funct. Program. **19**(5), 509–543 (2009). http://www.sciencedirect.com/science/article/pii/0020019077900783
15. Fähndrich, M., Carbin, M., Larus, J.R.: Reflective program generation with patterns. In: Proceedings of the 5th International Conference on Generative Programming and Component Engineering, GPCE 2006, NY, USA, pp. 275–284 (2006). http://doi.acm.org/10.1145/1173706.1173748
16. Gerakios, P., Biboudis, A., Smaragdakis, Y.: Forsaking inheritance: supercharged delegation in DelphJ. In: Proceedings of the 2013 ACM SIGPLAN International Conference on Object Oriented Programming Systems Languages & Applications, OOPSLA 2013, NY, USA, pp. 233–252 (2013). http://doi.acm.org/10.1145/2509136.2509535
17. Herman, D., Wand, M.: A theory of hygienic macros. In: Drossopoulou, S. (ed.) ESOP 2008. LNCS, vol. 4960, pp. 48–62. Springer, Heidelberg (2008). doi:10.1007/978-3-540-78739-6_4
18. Herrmann, C.A., Langhammer, T.: Combining partial evaluation and staged interpretation in the implementation of domain-specific languages. Sci. Comput. Program. **62**(1), 47–65 (2006). http://www.sciencedirect.com/science/article/pii/S0167642306000736
19. Huang, S.S., Smaragdakis, Y.: Expressive and safe static reflection with MorphJ. In: Proceedings of the 29th ACM SIGPLAN Conference on Programming Language Design and Implementation, PLDI 2008, NY, USA, pp. 79–89 (2008). http://doi.acm.org/10.1145/1375581.1375592

20. Huang, S.S., Smaragdakis, Y.: Morphing: structurally shaping a class by reflecting on others. ACM Trans. Program. Lang. Syst. **33**(2), 6:1–6:44 (2011). http://doi.acm.org/10.1145/1890028.1890029

21. Huang, S.S., Zook, D., Smaragdakis, Y.: Morphing: safely shaping a class in the image of others. In: Ernst, E. (ed.) ECOOP 2007. LNCS, vol. 4609, pp. 399–424. Springer, Heidelberg (2007). doi:10.1007/978-3-540-73589-2_19

22. Huang, S.S., Zook, D., Smaragdakis, Y.: Statically safe program generation with safegen. Sci. Comput. Program. **76**(5), 376–391 (2011). http://www.sciencedirect.com/science/article/pii/S0167642308001111

23. Inoue, J., Kiselyov, O., Kameyama, Y.: The next stage of staging. In: Proceedings of the 17th workshop on Programming and Programming Languages (PPL) (2015)

24. Jones, N.D.: An introduction to partial evaluation. ACM Comput. Surv. **28**(3), 480–503 (1996). http://doi.acm.org/10.1145/243439.243447

25. Jones, N.D., Sestoft, P., Søndergaard, H.: An experiment in partial evaluation: the generation of a compiler generator. SIGPLAN Not. **20**(8), 82–87 (1985). http://doi.acm.org/10.1145/988346.988358

26. Jones, N.D., Sestoft, P., Søndergaard, H.: Mix: a self-applicable partial evaluator for experiments in compiler generation. LISP Symb. Comput. **2**(1), 9–50 (1989). http://dx.doi.org/10.1007/BF01806312

27. Jørring, U., Scherlis, W.L.: Compilers and staging transformations. In: Proceedings of the 13th ACM SIGACT-SIGPLAN Symposium on Principles of Programming Languages, POPL 1986, NY, USA, pp. 86–96 (1986). http://doi.acm.org/10.1145/512644.512652

28. Kiczales, G., Hilsdale, E., Hugunin, J., Kersten, M., Palm, J., Griswold, W.G.: An overview of AspectJ. In: Knudsen, J.L. (ed.) ECOOP 2001. LNCS, vol. 2072, pp. 327–354. Springer, Heidelberg (2001). doi:10.1007/3-540-45337-7_18

29. Kiczales, G., Lamping, J., Mendhekar, A., Maeda, C., Lopes, C., Loingtier, J.-M., Irwin, J.: Aspect-oriented programming. In: Akşit, M., Matsuoka, S. (eds.) ECOOP 1997. LNCS, vol. 1241, pp. 220–242. Springer, Heidelberg (1997). doi:10.1007/BFb0053381

30. Kiselyov, O.: The design and implementation of BER MetaOCaml. In: Codish, M., Sumii, E. (eds.) FLOPS 2014. LNCS, vol. 8475, pp. 86–102. Springer, Cham (2014). doi:10.1007/978-3-319-07151-0_6

31. Kiselyov, O., Biboudis, A., Palladinos, N., Smaragdakis, Y.: Stream fusion, to completeness. In: Proceedings of the 44th ACM SIGPLAN-SIGACT Symposium on Principles of Programming Languages, POPL 2017, NY, USA, pp. 285–299 (2017). http://doi.acm.org/10.1145/3009837.3009880

32. Kohlbecker, E., Friedman, D.P., Felleisen, M., Duba, B.: Hygienic macro expansion. In: Proceedings of the 1986 ACM Conference on LISP and Functional Programming, LFP 1986, NY, USA, pp. 151–161 (1986). http://doi.acm.org/10.1145/319838.319859

33. Lorenzen, F., Erdweg, S.: Sound type-dependent syntactic language extension. In: Proceedings of the 43rd ACM SIGPLAN-SIGACT Symposium on Principles of Programming Languages, POPL 2016, NY, USA, pp. 204–216 (2016). http://doi.acm.org/10.1145/2837614.2837644

34. Draheim, D., Lutteroth, C., Weber, G.: A type system for reflective program generators. In: Glück, R., Lowry, M. (eds.) GPCE 2005. LNCS, vol. 3676, pp. 327–341. Springer, Heidelberg (2005). doi:10.1007/11561347_22. http://dx.doi.org/10.1016/j.scico.2010.12.002

35. Mainland, G.: Why it's nice to be quoted: quasiquoting for haskell. In: Proceedings of the ACM SIGPLAN Workshop on Haskell Workshop, Haskell 2007, NY, USA, pp. 73–82 (2007). http://doi.acm.org/10.1145/1291201.1291211

36. Miao, W., Siek, J.: Pattern-based traits. In: Proceedings of the 27th Annual ACM Symposium on Applied Computing, SAC 2012, NY, USA, pp. 1729–1736 (2012). http://doi.acm.org/10.1145/2245276.2232057

37. Miao, W., Siek, J.: Compile-time reflection and metaprogramming for Java. In: Proceedings of the ACM SIGPLAN 2014 Workshop on Partial Evaluation and Program Manipulation, PEPM 2014, NY, USA, pp. 27–37 (2014). http://doi.acm.org/10.1145/2543728.2543739

38. Moors, A., Piessens, F., Odersky, M.: Generics of a higher kind. In: Proceedings of the 23rd ACM SIGPLAN Conference on Object-oriented Programming Systems Languages and Applications, OOPSLA 2008, NY, USA, pp. 423–438 (2008). http://doi.acm.org/10.1145/1449764.1449798

39. Moors, A., Rompf, T., Haller, P., Odersky, M.: Scala-virtualized. In: Proceedings of the ACM SIGPLAN 2012 Workshop on Partial Evaluation and Program Manipulation, PEPM 2012, NY, USA, pp. 117–120 (2012). http://doi.acm.org/10.1145/2103746.2103769

40. Rompf, T., Brown, K.J., Lee, H., Sujeeth, A.K., Jonnalagedda, M., Amin, N., Ofenbeck, G., Stojanov, A., Klonatos, Y., Dashti, M., Koch, C., Püschel, M., Olukotun, K.: Go meta! a case for generative programming and DSLs in performance critical systems. In: Ball, T., Bodík, R., Krishnamurthi, S., Lerner, B.S., Morrisett, G. (eds.) 1st Summit on Advances in Programming Languages, SNAPL 3–6, 2015, Asilomar, California, USA. LIPIcs, 32, pp. 238–261. Schloss Dagstuhl - Leibniz-Zentrum fuer Informatik (2015). http://dx.doi.org/10.4230/LIPIcs.SNAPL.2015.238

41. Rompf, T., Odersky, M.: Lightweight modular staging: a pragmatic approach to runtime code generation and compiled DSLs. In: Proceedings of the Ninth International Conference on Generative Programming and Component Engineering, GPCE 2010, NY, USA, pp. 127–136 (2010). http://doi.acm.org/10.1145/1868294.1868314

42. Servetto, M., Zucca, E.: A meta-circular language for active libraries. Sci. Comput. Program. **95**(Part 2), 219–253 (2014). selectedandextendedpapersfromPartialEvaluationandProgramManipulation2013. http://www.sciencedirect.com/science/article/pii/S0167642314002317

43. Sheard, T., Jones, S.P.: Template meta-programming for haskell. In: Proceedings of the 2002 ACM SIGPLAN Workshop on Haskell, Haskell 2002, NY, USA, pp. 1–16 (2002). http://doi.acm.org/10.1145/581690.581691

44. Smaragdakis, Y., Batory, D.: Implementing layered designs with mixin layers. In: Jul, E. (ed.) ECOOP 1998. LNCS, vol. 1445, pp. 550–570. Springer, Heidelberg (1998). doi:10.1007/BFb0054107

45. Smaragdakis, Y., Batory, D.: Scoping constructs for software generators. In: Czarnecki, K., Eisenecker, U.W. (eds.) GCSE 1999. LNCS, vol. 1799, pp. 65–78. Springer, Heidelberg (2000). doi:10.1007/3-540-40048-6_6. Earlier version in Technical Report UTCS-TR-96-37 (1999)

46. Sperber, M., Dybvig, R.K., Flatt, M., van Straaten, A., Findler, R., Matthews, J.: Revised [6] Report on the Algorithmic Language Scheme, 1st edn. Cambridge University Press, New York (2010)

47. Steimann, F., Pilgrim, J.: Constraint-based refactoring with foresight. In: Noble, J. (ed.) ECOOP 2012. LNCS, vol. 7313, pp. 535–559. Springer, Heidelberg (2012). doi:10.1007/978-3-642-31057-7_24

48. Taha, W.: A gentle introduction to multi-stage programming. In: Lengauer, C., Batory, D., Consel, C., Odersky, M. (eds.) Domain-Specific Program Generation. LNCS, vol. 3016, pp. 30–50. Springer, Heidelberg (2004). doi:10.1007/978-3-540-25935-0_3

49. Taha, W., Sheard, T.: Multi-stage Programming with explicit annotations. In: Proceedings of the 1997 ACM SIGPLAN Symposium on Partial Evaluation and Semantics-based Program Manipulation, PEPM 1997, NY, USA, pp. 203–217 (1997). http://doi.acm.org/10.1145/258993.259019

50. Tobin-Hochstadt, S., St-Amour, V., Culpepper, R., Flatt, M., Felleisen, M.: Languages as libraries. In: Proceedings of the 32Nd ACM SIGPLAN Conference on Programming Language Design and Implementation, PLDI 2011, NY, USA, pp. 132–141 (2011). http://doi.acm.org/10.1145/1993498.1993514

51. Tratt, L.: Domain specific language implementation via compile-time metaprogramming. ACM Trans. Program. Lang. Syst. **30**(6), 31–40 (2008). http://doi.acm.org/10.1145/1391956.1391958

52. Veldhuizen, T.: Expression templates. C++ Rep. **7**, 26–31 (1995)

53. Veldhuizen, T.: C++ templates are Turing complete. Indiana University, Technical report (2003)

54. Visser, E.: Meta-programming with concrete object syntax. In: Batory, D., Consel, C., Taha, W. (eds.) GPCE 2002. LNCS, vol. 2487, pp. 299–315. Springer, Heidelberg (2002). doi:10.1007/3-540-45821-2_19

55. Wadler, P., Blott, S.: How to make ad-hoc polymorphism less ad hoc. In: Proceedings of the 16th ACM SIGPLAN-SIGACT Symposium on Principles of Programming Languages, POPL 1989, NY, USA, pp. 60–76 (1989). http://doi.acm.org/10.1145/75277.75283

56. Zook, D., Huang, S.S., Smaragdakis, Y.: Generating AspectJ programs with MetaAspectJ. In: Karsai, G., Visser, E. (eds.) GPCE 2004. LNCS, vol. 3286, pp. 1–18. Springer, Heidelberg (2004). doi:10.1007/978-3-540-30175-2_1

Refactoring Tools and Their Kin

Friedrich Steimann[✉]

Lehrgebiet Programmiersysteme, Fernuniversität in Hagen, Hagen, Germany
steimann@acm.org

Abstract. Refactoring is the process of changing a program in such a way that its design improves with respect to some specific goal, while its observable behaviour remains the same. Trivially, the latter includes the preservation of the program's well-formedness, since arguably, a malformed program has no behaviour to be preserved.

While the problem of refactoring is easily stated, casting it into fully functional refactoring tools for contemporary programming languages is surprisingly hard. In fact, most refactoring tools in use today cannot even guarantee to preserve well-formedness, let alone behaviour, not even for some of the most basic refactorings (such as RENAME or PULL UP MEMBER).

In Part I of this briefing, I will report on some of the most promising techniques for implementing correct refactoring tools. Common to these techniques is that they give up the notion of behaviour preservation in favour of the more basic (and less demanding) notion of invariant preservation: to be correct, a refactoring tool must not accidentally change the binding of names, the overriding of methods, the synchronization on a monitor, etc. Preservation of well-formedness is then the preservation of invariants relating to well-formedness.

With invariant preservation tackled, it is straightforward to transfer refactoring technology to other programming tools, including tools for automatic repair and completion of programs, mutation testing, and program generation. How these are related to refactoring tools, and how they can be developed in concert, I will propose in Part II of this briefing.

Part I: Refactoring Tools

The term *refactoring* refers to at least:

- a discipline (e.g., when it is used as the label of a session at a conference),
- an activity (when somebody is practicing that discipline),
- the result of such an activity (e.g., one program is said to be a refactoring of another),
- a pattern of such an activity (for instance, an element of a refactoring catalogue; e.g., RENAME FIELD),
- an instance of such a pattern (when the pattern is applied to concrete code; e.g., "after a RENAME FIELD refactoring"); and
- a programming tool (as in "Which refactorings does your IDE come with?").

© Springer International Publishing AG 2017
J. Cunha et al. (Eds.): GTTSE 2015, LNCS 10223, pp. 179–214, 2017.
DOI: 10.1007/978-3-319-60074-1_8

In Part I of this briefing, I will focus on *refactoring tools*, and will use this term throughout for disambiguation from all other meanings of *refactoring*. That said, I will start with some observations and remarks on refactoring in general.

1 Origins of Refactoring

Refactoring as a tool-supported discipline goes back to the independent works of William Griswold (with the late David Notkin; see, e.g., [19]), and of William Opdyke (with Ralph Johnson; see, e.g., [30]). Although Griswold's PhD thesis on program restructuring ([18], from 1991) pre-dates Opdyke's ([29], from 1992), the latter is usually cited as the origin of refactoring, not least because it has the term in its title (another reason may be that with C++, Opdyke addressed a more widespread language than Griswold, who addressed Scheme). Although Opdyke reports that the term was coined some time earlier, it wasn't before the implementation of the Smalltalk refactoring browser [34], the adoption of refactoring as a core practice in XP [4], and Fowler's widely recognized book [12] that it became commonplace.

Refactoring as a manual activity is probably as old as programming itself [26]. Especially in the old days, when computing resources where scarce, programs had to be restructured regularly so as to reduce memory usage (both program and data) and execution time. In these days, instruction sets and programs were small, and development environments consisted largely of brains, pens, and paper; refactoring was an inherent part of coding, which required the code to be concise enough to meet the tight space requirements of the machine.

In later years, the task of making the most out of the given hardware resources was shifted from programmers to compilers, specifically to optimizing ones. Refactoring shares with compiler optimization the goal (and problem!) of behaviour preservation. However, compiler optimizations are often local and can be switched off. The latter is a concession to the state-of-the-art, namely that guarantees of behaviour preservation are hard to give. Refactorings, on the other hand, are often non-local; in fact, while coding along, the non-local changes disrupt the workflow most, so that their automation promises to be the most rewarding.

2 The Current Refactoring Crisis

Following its original conception, refactoring is today still mostly perceived as *improving the design of a program while preserving its observable behaviour.* Naturally, this definition is challenged by two questions:

1. What does *improving the design* mean?
2. What does *preserving the observable behaviour* mean?

While both questions appear natural, if not mandatory, to ask in purely academic circles, the current mindset of the refactoring community, a sound mixture of researchers and practitioners, is perhaps best characterized by a third one:

3. Who cares?

2.1 The Elusiveness of Design Improvement

Many refactorings presented in Fowler's catalogue [12] are complemented by reverse refactorings: EXTRACT METHOD — INLINE METHOD; PULL UP FIELD — PUSH DOWN FIELD; REPLACE INHERITANCE WITH DELEGATION — REPLACE DELEGATION WITH INHERITANCE, to name a few. This fact alone suggests that improving design is not in the nature of specific refactoring patterns: what results in good design in one context can result in bad design in another. Furthermore, since refactoring tools today usually tackle only fairly small changes from which bigger refactorings can be manually composed, each application of a refactoring tool by itself may result in unimproved design: as with solving Rubik's cube, intermediate steps may let the program look dramatically worse temporarily.

A more neutral goal of refactoring is therefore to make subsequent changes easier. However, even this goal is not universal: Refactorings introducing parallelization, for instance, do not target at better changeability, but at improved utilization of the underlying hardware (see, e.g., [10]; but note that this could be considered an optimization rather than a refactoring). Also, it is conceivable that refactoring is performed for obfuscation, i.e., a design that makes (informed) code changes largely impossible (which presents an improved design if unchangeability is the goal).

2.2 The Elusiveness of Behaviour Preservation

An answer to the second above question is often given as "the program still compiles and passes the same tests the program passed before the refactoring" (see, e.g., [12]). While pragmatic, this answer merely suggests a post-hoc check of whether some concrete changes actually represent a refactoring; for refactoring tool builders, it translates to "for all possible applications to all possible programs with all possible test suites, the resulting program must still compile and pass the tests". Surely, this cannot be proven experimentally[1], but would require some abstract, formal argument, which is however hard to give. In practice, therefore, tool builders rely on testing their tools, and on users submitting bug reports.

Even with testing in place, the notion of behaviour that is to be preserved by refactoring is not unchallenged. For instance, the refactoring REPLACE CONDITIONAL WITH POLYMORPHISM [12] may adversely affect program performance (by replacing explicit branching with dynamic dispatch), and this deteriorated performance may mean an intolerable change of behaviour in certain contexts. While such a deterioration may be detected by test cases (leading to a subsequent rejection of the refactoring), it cannot lead to a general abandonment of REPLACE CONDITIONAL WITH POLYMORPHISM as a refactoring, as other

---

[1] I have gathered some first-hand experience with this, which drove me to lamenting "whenever we believed that we had made correctness of the refactoring plausible, testing it on a new project revealed a new problem we had not previously thought of" [24].

users may not conceive of slower performance as a behavioural change. On the other hand, a change of performance may be the very purpose of a refactoring: for instance, when refactoring for parallelization, a better user experience, and hence externally perceivable behaviour, may be the very goal. While one could argue again that such a change represents an optimization, this does not seem enough to expel corresponding work from the refactoring realm.

2.3   Ignoring the Unresolved Correctness Problem

Although correctness of refactoring tools has been a concern from the very beginning of the discipline (see, e.g., [18,29]), it seems that the builders of contemporary refactoring tools have surrendered to the complexity of the problems (see, e.g., [15,39,40]; Sect. 4 will give a concrete taste of the complexity of the problems one may encounter). While this has sparked off some research on how the correctness problems can be tackled (see, e.g., [3,5,13,47]; also, Sect. 6 is devoted to this entirely), I also observe that the refactoring community has some sympathy for downplaying the correctness problems (see, e.g., [7]), focusing on other topics instead. Particularly popular seem empirical investigations exploring the use of refactoring tools (mostly suggesting that the correctness problem is not one; see, e.g., [28,50]); other work focuses on increasing the utility of existing (even though buggy) refactoring tools, for instance by automatically discovering manual refactoring activities and completing them with tool support [11,14], or by automatically synthesizing larger refactorings from smaller ones [33]. Since the defectiveness of the underlying refactoring tools is not ironed out by automatically applying or combining them, the tools assembled from them are also defective. This however is almost consistently ignored.

2.4   The Easy Way Out: Liberation from Academic Chains

The more popular refactoring is becoming, the more its definition is being challenged (with arguments partly given above). Specifically, practitioners more and more suggest that refactoring amounts to automated program change, with behaviour preservation and design improvement, if at all desired, being left to the responsibility of the user. This culminates in the view that the laxer the preconditions of a refactoring tool, the higher its utility, even if this means that the tool introduces errors that then need to be fixed manually. Given this mindset, it may not be so surprising that sentences like "Even though our approach is neither sound, nor complete, it is still useful." (cited from a refactoring paper presented at a highly respected conference) make it into the academic literature.

I do not condemn this departure from the refactoring ideal — whichever tool works best for a programmer is good (although I maintain that the question, what works best for the programmer?, cannot be decided by the programmer alone, but must also be judged by the quality of the result; see [7] for a recent discussion). However, I grant myself the freedom of pursuing a more scholarly perspective here (which includes the liberty to choose my challenges independently from the purported programming practice), and to uphold the original definition of refactoring. I do however concede that whether or not design is actually improved is not a part of the definition of a refactoring (more precisely: a refactoring pattern), only of its application (an instance of the pattern).

3 The Generic Nature of Refactoring Tools

Following the school of Opdyke and Johnson [29,30], implementing a refactoring tool requires

1. implementing a check of the *preconditions* of the refactoring and
2. implementing a sequence of changes, also called the *mechanics* [12] of the refactoring.

Postconditions are usually considered dispensable by this school, unless refactorings are chained, in which case postconditions are to provide guarantees that the next refactoring's preconditions are met by the outcome of the present one [35]. Of course, this view ignores that every refactoring has a purpose, which is naturally reflected in its postcondition. A more pragmatic argument for dismissing the need for postconditions is that they follow from the preconditions and the mechanics of the refactorings and hence are redundant; this of course ignores that the mechanics could be flawed (see above), or the preconditions too weak. Both are however not uncommon for today's refactoring tools.

For this briefing, I will adopt a more fundamental viewpoint and regard refactoring tools as *metaprograms*, specifically as programs that implement source-to-source program transformations [18,21,27]. Metaprograms are programs and hence are specified using preconditions *and* postconditions. While this may seem overly academic, the reader will learn below that the pre- and postconditions of refactoring tools are, to a large extent, generic so that identifying and expressing them for a specific tool should not present too much of an effort. At the same time, the reader will (hopefully) join me in appreciating the ready availability of pre- and postconditions for refactoring tools as a (rare) occasion of being able to derive an implementation directly from its specification.

3.1 Generic Pre- and Postconditions

A *generic precondition* of all refactoring tools is that input programs must be well-formed.[2] *Generic postconditions* are that

---

[2] Practitioners may find this precondition too strong. Indeed, it seems that it could be relaxed to requiring well-formedness only for the parts of the program that are in some way connected to the intended refactoring. However, it seems difficult, if not impossible, to decide if a malformed part of a program is connected to a refactoring. For example, what if the refactoring makes the formerly malformed part well-formed, for instance by renaming a declared element so that a formerly unbound reference now binds to this element?

- the refactored program is still well-formed, that
- it behaves the same, and that
- the program either exhibits at least the changes immediately associated with the refactoring (the *refactoring intent*), or remains unchanged.

3.2   Specific Pre- and Postconditions

Beyond the generic preconditions, preconditions specific to a concrete refactoring tool are to protect the tool from input (programs to be refactored and user-supplied parameters of the refactoring) that it cannot handle, either because the refactoring is undefined for them, or because of unresolved technical challenges (including the impossibility to guarantee behaviour preservation, if this escapes the current capabilities of static program analyses). If preconditions are violated, the refactoring tool should leave the program unchanged, and report the violation to the user, who can then try to prepare the program manually (by performing required changes, arguably refactorings) for successful tool application.

The postconditions specific to a concrete refactoring assert that the changes associated with the refactoring are actually seen in the refactored program. Basically, they have the form "the refactored program shall exhibit property X", where X expresses a change (such as a change in the type hierarchy etc.). Some (if not most) refactorings require additional changes to be made, changes that complement the refactoring intent to restore the program's well-formedness or its behaviour (see Sects. 4.3 and 6 for examples). These changes are typically not part of the specific postconditions; indeed, computing them is the hard part of refactoring tool implementation. However, as we will see, the required additional changes can sometimes be derived from the (generic and specific) postconditions.

3.3   Generic Refactoring Invariants

That a program must be well-formed before and after a refactoring, and that the behaviour must remain the same (conditions included in the generic pre- and postconditions of a refactoring tool) can be viewed as *generic invariants*. If behaviour is specified in terms of a test suite, preservation of these invariants is easily checked: by running the compiler and test suite before and after the refactoring.

If however a test suite sufficient for checking behaviour preservation is unavailable, or if behaviour preservation is to be specified independently of any given program, checking invariant preservation requires the following generic procedure:

1. check well-formedness
2. extract the behaviour-critical invariants
3. perform refactoring
4. check well-formedness
5. check extracted invariants

Here, it is understood that the behaviour-critical invariants extracted from the program before the refactoring (Step 2) hold at the time of extraction. A failure of any the refactoring invariants after a refactoring can be interpreted as the violation of specific preconditions, which are however not explicitly specified (see Sect. 6.1 for a brief discussion of the pros and cons of this). This observation (limited to the behaviour-critical invariants) was already made by Max Schäfer [36], and also by Jeffrey Overbye [31].

4 Why Building Refactoring Tools Is Hard: A Case Study

In his refactoring book [12], Fowler provides the following synopsis for the REPLACE INHERITANCE WITH DELEGATION refactoring:

A subclass uses only part of a superclasses interface
or does not want to inherit data.

*Create a field for the superclass, adjust methods to delegate to the superclass,
and remove the subclassing.*

The prototypical example of a class one might want to rid of its superclass using REPLACE INHERITANCE WITH DELEGATION is that of Stack extending Vector:

```
class Stack                          class Stack {
    extends Vector {                     Vector elems = new Vector();
    void push(Object o) {                void push(Object o) {
        add(o);              ⟹              elems.add(o);
    }                                    }
    ...                                  ...
}                                    }
```

Fowler prescribes the following mechanics for this refactoring [12]:

1. Create a field in the subclass that refers to an instance of the superclass. Initialize it to this.
2. Change each method defined in the subclass to use the delegate field. Compile and test after changing each method.
3. Remove the subclass declaration and replace the delegate assignment with an assignment to a new object.
4. For each superclass method used by a client, add a simple delegating method.
5. Compile and test.

What the prescription does not say is what to do if the program does not compile during step 2 or 5, or if any of the test cases fail. A yielding reaction would be to undo all changes and give up on the refactoring (assuming that the refactoring was not intended for the given case or, more formally, that the program did not meet the preconditions of the intended refactoring); a persisting reaction would be to find out the source of the problems, and work around them (suggesting that the mechanics failed to cover the special conditions — in the community often marginalized as "corner cases" — that led to the failure). Either way, a user of this refactoring, and even more so a tool builder, is left alone with learning its particulars.

(a)

```
package a;
class A {
  protected A(...) {...}
  protected void m() {...}
}
package b;
class B extends A {
  B(...) { super(...); }
  void n() { m(); }
}
```

(b)

```
class A implements I {}
class B extends A {}
I i = new B();
```

(c)

```
class B extends Throwable {...}
void m() throws B {...}
```

(d)

```
class A { int i; }
class B extends A {}
B b = new B(); b.i = 0;
```

(e)

```
class Thread() {
  void run() {}
  void start() {run();}
}
class B extends Thread {
  void run() {...}
}
B b = new B();
b.start();
```

(f)

```
class A {
  void m() {
    notify();
  }
}
class B extends A {
  synchronized void n() {
    wait();
  }
}
```

Fig. 1. Programs for which Fowler's Replace Inheritance with Delegation [12] does not work out-of-the box.

4.1   The Precondition Surprise

Although Fowler's treatise of Replace Inheritance with Delegation does not mention preconditions, it gives a few clues as to the refactoring's applicability. A trivial precondition that can be derived from Step 3 of its mechanics given above is that the inheriting class (the subclass to which the refactoring is to be applied) has a superclass other than Object, since in Java at least, every class implicitly inherits from Object. Other, slightly less obvious preconditions are that the superclass must be instantiable (i.e., not abstract) and that the superclass constructors (called from the subclass either implicitly or using super) must be accessible from the subclass even when it is no longer a subclass (Fig. 1(a)); also suggested by Step 3. Steps 2 and 3 together suggest a similar requirement: replacing this with the delegate field means that the members accessed via this field must still be accessible after the inheritance has been removed. This is not the case, for instance, if superclass and subclass reside in different packages and superclass members are declared protected (Fig. 1(a)). Not mentioned in Fowler's tractate is that the program must not require assignment compatibility between the subclass and the superclass; specifically, no instance of the (former) subclass must occur where an instance of the (former) superclass is expected.[3] While one could argue that removing subclassing, and with it subtyping, is the very purpose of the refactoring (which therefore cannot be applied when subtyping is required), the situation is actually less clear-cut for instance when the superclass implements interfaces (including marker interfaces) the subclass no longer implements (Fig. 1(b)). Also, subclassing cannot be removed without breaking the program if the subclass inherits from a class with special semantics, on which the program relies (Fig. 1(c)). Last but not least, the refactoring will fail if clients access fields (rather than methods as in Step 4) of the (former) superclass through the (former) subclass (Fig. 1(d)). This is so since in Java at least, field access cannot be delegated. For this, it would be necessary to introduce accessor methods for the fields first (the ENCAPSULATE FIELD refactoring), and to let the clients use them.

While violations of the above preconditions of the REPLACE INHERITANCE WITH DELEGATION refactoring are unveiled by the error reports of the compiler (if only after the fact; see Sect. 3.3 for how this relates to invariant preservation), the really nasty preconditions are discovered only by testing behaviour preservation. One is that the refactoring does not replace inheritance with *delegation* (as it claims), but with *forwarding*. For true delegation, it would be necessary that the use of this in a delegated method call refers back to this in the delegating method (the delegator), whereas with forwarding, this refers to the object being delegated to. This is a problem when the (fake) delegation calls a method on this that used to be overridden in the (former) subclass, as exemplified in Fig. 1(e) (using a home-brew implementation of Thread). This overriding, and with it the dynamic dispatching to the subclass, are however gone, usually resulting in changed behaviour.

Another hard to discover precondition arises in the context of multi-threading. In Java, synchronized method calls are guarded by a monitor associated with the receiver of the method call. After application of the REPLACE INHERITANCE WITH DELEGATION refactoring, however, invocations of methods formerly inherited are now "delegated" (actually: forwarded) to a different object, which has a different monitor. Synchronization may therefore fail, as in the case of Fig. 1(f).

One might argue that both of the above are corner cases that will rarely occur in practice, so that their neglect can be tolerated. However, it is somewhat assuming to claim that certain constructions are or will be rarely used[4]; at the same time, no one can predict the harm their neglect may cause.

---

[3] This includes instanceof tests, which will become ill-typed.

[4] In a study conducted by the author, dynamic dispatching affected 41%, and synchronization affected 3.5% of all attempted applications of REPLACE INHERITANCE WITH DELEGATION [24].

4.2   The Mechanics Adventure

While Fowler leaves the preconditions of REPLACE INHERITANCE WITH DEL-
EGATION mostly for the discovery by others, he leaves only little doubt as to
its mechanics, i.e., what needs to be done to perform the refactoring. The only
pitfall is hidden in Step 4, which requires that all method calls from clients
of the (formerly) inheriting class are identified (so that the required delegating
methods can be introduced). Precise identification of the calls is crucial to the
success of the refactoring: adding delegating methods that are never called by
clients counteracts the very purpose of the refactoring (the deflation of the class
interface), while missing out required delegating methods will lead to compile
errors. Unfortunately, an analysis of the class members required by the class's
clients is only seemingly simple; factually, it requires the type analysis underlying the EXTRACT INTERFACE refactoring [48], which is not trivial. Without
such an analysis at hand, performing the refactoring will be a trial and error
adventure (delegating methods are added until all type errors are resolved).

Generally, to keep the mechanics of a refactoring simple, the definition of
strong preconditions seems a good idea. However, as suggested by the preconditions of REPLACE INHERITANCE WITH DELEGATION derived from the examples
of Fig. 1, it may render the refactoring unusable in too many cases, making the
user perform preparatory refactorings required for doing the refactoring any-
how. Figuring out precisely which preparatory refactorings are required is an
adventure in its own right, in particular when considering that each preparatory
refactoring may suffer from the same problem recursively.

4.3   The Tool User's Dream: Relaxed Preconditions

Given the above, rather long list of preconditions for REPLACE INHERITANCE
WITH DELEGATION, it is indeed questionable whether a refactoring tool requiring
them all will be useful in practice, or will deny its service on too many occasions[5].
Also, given that at least some of the precondition violations seem easy to work
around (for instance, access modifiers can be adjusted, accessor methods can be
introduced), it is foreseeable that users will ask for a refactoring tool that can fix
these issues by itself, rather than suggest corresponding manual changes (see [50]
for some evidence of this). However, as other work has shown, changing access
modifiers consistently is not as easy as it may seem, and in Java can even lead to
changes of behaviour (by changing binding) [45]. Also, setter invocations cannot
generally replace for field assignments, so that both changes are rather complex
refactorings by themselves. As for the remaining preconditions: Even if there are
ways to do away with them, as we will see below this takes far more than can be
straightforwardly handled in an imperative (as opposed to declarative) fashion,
that is, through a sequence of steps ("mechanics"). *If building correct refactoring
tools is hard, relaxing their preconditions is harder.*

---

[5] In the same study [24], they prevented 84% of all naive refactoring applications in
four subject programs.

4.4   The Tool Builder's Nightmare: Evolving Languages

While creating correct refactoring tools for programming languages as complex as Java or C$^{\#}$ is already hard, evolving them to keep up with the further development of these languages is a nightmare. This is not only so because, after the compiler has been updated, the refactoring tools need to follow to accommodate the same set of new language features, but also because it raises expectations regarding tool support for migrating now legacy programs to the new language version. For instance, the introduction of generics to Java not only broke literally all type-related refactorings, it also led to the formulation of new refactorings introducing generics to legacy code [48]. Not surprisingly, developing these tools occupied some of the brightest minds in our field, and still left us with tools that are, strictly speaking, neither sound nor complete.[6]

5   Current Refactoring Practice and Research Challenge

Given the hardness of the refactoring problems exposed by the above case study, and given that most contemporary refactoring tools have not found good means of dealing with these problems, refactoring practice today often follows the pattern

1. Perform the refactoring as specified (using a tool, if available).
2. If the refactored program exhibits compile errors or changed behaviour,
   (a) either undo the refactoring or
   (b) perform corrective changes compensating for shortcomings in the mechanics of the refactoring.

In case 2(a), violation of the generic postconditions (Sect. 3.1) and assuming that the performed mechanics are correct suggest that the preconditions of the refactoring have not been met. In this case, the user can try to prepare the program manually for the refactoring. If the preconditions are not explicitly specified (as in Fowler's above specification of REPLACE INHERITANCE WITH DELEGATION), the reported compile errors or failed test cases may provide some hints for the necessary preparation; in any case, they are the sole instance deciding that the program is ready for the refactoring as implemented by its mechanics.

In case 2(b), the task of complementing the mechanically performed refactoring with the required additional changes is guided by the compiler and test suite, which serve as oracles of manual task completion. If the refactoring user is happy with this situation, one may indeed suggest that preconditions are relaxed as much as possible — as long as the resulting program can be easily fixed, it does not matter whether violations of the generic postconditions are due to violated preconditions or to shortcomings in the specification of the mechanics. From a tool builder's perspective, this is a pleasant prospect, since it makes the implementation of refactoring tools a much simpler task.

---

[6] I freely admit that I spent one summer trying to understand what it takes to cover Java's generics in every detail, and gave up highly frustrated.

No matter whether the tool user opts for (a) or (b): In either case, making a failing refactoring work relies on the knowledge encoded in the compiler and test suite. From an academic perspective, it is somewhat saddening that this knowledge is not exploited by the refactoring tools, for computing *all* changes required by a refactoring upfront. In fact, I find the prospect of being able to do so, so intriguing that it leads me to posing the following

---

Research challenge for the future of refactoring tools:

to evolve the decision procedure

"does this change constitute a refactoring?"

(as implemented, e.g., by the compiler and test suite) into a search procedure

"which additional changes are required to make this change a refactoring?"

Ideally, we can use the same implementation used for solving the decision problem for solving the search problem also. *This would not only greatly reduce the effort required to create new refactoring tools, it would also allow us to keep compiler and refactoring tools so closely coupled that changing (fixing or evolving) one suffices for both.*

In the next section, I will shed some light on systematic approaches to implementing refactoring tools known from the literature, with a special focus on how they exploit (program-independent) knowledge also encoded in the compiler. I will not address in the following how the knowledge captured in test cases (which is program-dependent) can be exploited; however, I do point out here that the Smalltalk Refactoring Browser can actually make some use of it [35].

6   Principled Approaches to Implementing Refactoring Tools

Considering the nature of refactoring tools as delineated in Sect. 3, it seems clear that any principled implementation of a refactoring tool must observe the generic pre- and postconditions of refactoring or, equivalently, preservation of its invariants. The research challenge phrased above additionally suggests that a refactoring tool should rely on the language expertise implemented in the compiler. The approaches presented in the following do both.

6.1   Dependency Preservation

In light of the problems with framing behaviour preservation (Sect. 2.2), it seems advisable to replace it with a notion that is better tractable. *Dependency preservation* as put forward by Schäfer [36] is such a notion.

Dependency preservation abstracts from behaviour preservation in that it promises to maintain all behaviour-critical relationships between program elements. For instance, it is perfectly plausible to require that, except for deliberate changes, after a refactoring

- all names in a program should bind to the same declarations,
- all method calls should be synchronized on the same monitors, and
- all methods should override the same methods

as before the refactoring. Indeed, any accidental change of binding, synchronization, or overriding (collectively referred to as a change of dependency by Schäfer) may lead to a change of behaviour and hence provides a reason for the rejection of the refactoring that causes it. Schäfer demonstrated the effectiveness of dependency preservation by implementing a large number of refactoring tools with correctness scores surpassing that of the Eclipse JDT's built-in refactoring tools, as measured by their own test suites [36].

Dependency preservation also solves some of the problems of the REPLACE INHERITANCE WITH DELEGATION refactoring presented in Sect. 4. For instance, in the code of Fig. 1(a), the method invocation m() in the body of B.n() is bound to the definition of m() in class A before the refactoring; since it cannot be bound after the refactoring (because m() has become inaccessible for n()), a dependency of the name on its declaration could not be preserved. Similarly, the binding of the field access b.i to A.i cannot be preserved, since after the refactoring, class B no longer offers such a field (Fig. 1d).

Going beyond name binding, the loss of synchronization arising from naively refactoring the code of Fig. 1(f) can be detected by the fact that wait() and notify() are now invoked on different objects (making synchronization depend on different monitors), whereas they were invoked on the same before. While such a change of dependency is hard to detect statically in the general case, in the case of REPLACE INHERITANCE WITH DELEGATION it is fairly simple, since this in the delegating class and this in the class being delegated to can never point to the same object. For the preservation of dynamic binding (Fig. 1e), the situation seems more complex, as it would require a static analysis of dynamic dispatching behaviour even for REPLACE INHERITANCE WITH DELEGATION; however, requiring that all overriding dependencies are preserved (independently of the fact whether or where overriding actually leads to dynamic binding) is sufficient for guaranteeing binding invariance (even though it may be too strong a condition in certain cases).

Thus, we have that dependency preservation can cover a broad spectrum of conditions that are otherwise difficult to express. However, as these examples also suggest, much of the art of implementing correct refactoring tools using dependency preservation relies on identifying and being able to extract the dependencies that guarantee behaviour preservation for arbitrary programs. Particularly for refactorings that change the control or data flow of a program, this may prove beyond reach.

6.1.1   Technical Enforcement

It is fairly obvious that dependency preservation is a special case of (generic) invariant preservation as delineated in Sect. 3.3. Technically, it is enforced by recording all dependencies before the refactoring (replacing for Step 2 in the procedure of Sect. 3.3), and by re-computing and comparing them after the refactoring (Step 5). If any dependency has changed as a result of the refactoring, it is rejected and all associated changes are undone. Since computing the dependencies can usually be trusted to the compiler, the refactoring tool implementation is spared from repeating some of the language specification in its own code. As noted by Schäfer, this is a huge advancement over traditional precondition checking, which often requires laborious reverse engineering of the language specification. On the downside, however, the fact that violated preconditions are now implicit makes it harder for the refactoring tool user to figure out what exactly led to a refusal.

For large programs, retrieving and storing all dependencies can be rather expensive. Therefore, in all practical applications of dependency preservation, only those dependencies that can be affected by a refactoring will actually be recorded. Unfortunately, deciding which these are is a problem in its own right; dependencies may stretch across several modules, and are not always obvious. Making mistakes here will make refactorings relying on dependency preservation unreliable.

6.1.2   Actively Preserving Dependencies

While being able to replace explicit precondition checking with attempting dependency preservation is certainly an advancement for the conscientious refactoring tool builder, it still leaves the tool user with the problem of "too strong preconditions", i.e., the rejection of a refactoring in cases in which some moderate additional changes would have made it possible. However, as has also been shown by Schäfer [36], in certain cases the compiler can be exploited to compute these additional changes also.

The original example of how this can work was given by Schäfer in his implementation of the RENAME refactoring [36]. The idea here is to let the refactoring tool compute the inverse of the binding function implemented by the compiler: rather than computing for a given name in a given location the declaration to which it binds (the binding function), a name is computed from a given declaration (the one originally bound to) and a given location (where the name is to be used; the same location as that of the original name) such that name, if it exists, is guaranteed to bind to the declaration. This not only propagates a change of the name of a declared entity to all references to (or accesses of) it, it also introduces name qualification where needed.

A simple example showcasing the power of active dependency preservation is given by the following code snippet (taken from [36]):

```
class A {
  int x;
  A(int newX) {
    x = newX;
  }
}
```

Supposing that the formal parameter newX is naively renamed to x, the declaration of the field of the same name, x, will be shadowed inside the constructor, so that the left-hand side of the assignment (now reading x = x) will also bind to the formal parameter, likely changing the behaviour of the program. However, computing the fully qualified name of field x referenced from the location of the assignment yields this.x; replacing the left-hand side of the assignment accordingly keeps the program intact. As Schäfer showed, this naming function can be constructed systematically with little effort and high accuracy, by reversing the name lookup function implemented by the compiler (see Sect. 6.3.2 for a constraint-based account). Whenever this lookup function needs to be adjusted (for instance, because the language evolves), its reverse can be adjusted in parallel, keeping all refactoring tools relying on it up-to-date (cf. Sect. 4.4).

It would seem that reversing name lookup can be extended to repair the broken binding introduced by applying REPLACE INHERITANCE WITH DELEGATION to the example of Fig. 1(a) also. Indeed, the compiler knows that for a non-inherited method to be accessed across package boundaries, the method must be declared public. It would therefore seem feasible to introduce a second function which computes, for a given location and declared entity to be accessed from that location, the set of access modifiers granting this access. *However, making a corresponding adjustment affects a declaration, rather than a reference (as above insertion of a qualified name did); it will therefore affect all other references to this declaration, too, and may interfere with other existing declarations.* While this may not seem problematic at first glance, as has been shown elsewhere [45], changing access modifiers in an ad-hoc fashion may not only lead to malformedness (for instance, in presence of overriding), but can also break binding dependencies. This will be picked up again in Sect. 6.3.

And yet, active dependency preservation is not limited to adjusting names at reference sites. For instance, as Schäfer demonstrated, synchronization dependencies can also be actively preserved, by making sure that method invocations remain synchronized on the same monitors as before a refactoring. Transferred to the synchronization problem of REPLACE INHERITANCE WITH DELEGATION (as exemplified by applying it to the code of Fig. 1e), dependency preservation requires that the delegating object is passed (as a parameter) to the method being delegated to. Following this advice, the naively refactored code below on the left (which exhibits the lost synchronization) is changed to that on the right (which preserves the original dependency):

```
class A {                          class A {
  void m() {                         void m(Object o) {
    notify();                          o.notify();
  }                                  }
}                                  }
class B {                ⟹        class B {
  A a = new A();                     A a = new A();
  void m() { a.m(); }                void m() { a.m(this); }
  synchronized void n() {            synchronized void n() {
    wait();                            wait();
  }                                  }
}                                  }
```

6.2   Language Extensions and Restrictions

While dependency preservation is a powerful concept, Schäfer also showed that it gets even more powerful when combined with language extensions and restrictions [36]. For instance, he observes that the `synchronized` method modifier in Java merely provides syntactic sugar for the more general `synchronized` block: a synchronized instance method is equivalent to a non-synchronized method whose body is wrapped by a block explicitly synchronizing on `this`. Java without synchronized methods, but with synchronized blocks, is thus a restricted language to which any Java program can be straightforwardly transformed. This restricted language is helpful, for instance, when performing the MOVE METHOD refactoring, as exemplified by moving method `m()` in the following code from class A to class B:

```
class A {
  synchronized void n() {}
  synchronized void m() {
    n();
  }
}

class B {}
```

```
class A {
  synchronized void n() {}
}

class B {
  void m(A a) {
    synchronized(a) {a.n();}
  }
}
```

$$\Downarrow \qquad\qquad\qquad \Uparrow$$

```
class A {
  void n() {
    synchronized(this) {}
  }
  void m() {
    synchronized(this) {
      this.n();
    }
  }
}

class B {}
```

$$\Rightarrow$$

```
class A {
  void n() {
    synchronized(this) {}
  }
}

class B {
  void m(A a) {
    synchronized(a) {a.n();}
  }
}
```

Here, the first step (indicated by the down arrow) is to convert the classes to Java without synchronized methods (and without assuming `this` as the default receiver). In the next step (right arrow), the method `m()` is moved as usual, making sure that `this` is converted to a formal parameter (Schäfer actually uses a *language extension* for this [37]). The last step (up arrow) converts the classes back to Java with synchronized methods; note that, since the body of `m(A)` is synchronized on a different object than `this`, conversion is possible only for `n()`. Were class B a subclass of A, `this` and `a` would always point to the same object, so that both methods could use the `synchronized` keyword.

As it turns out, name binding preservation can also be framed in terms of a restricted language [38]. For this, all names used in references and declarations of a program are replaced with unique names, or labels. Because each declaration now uses a different label, the binding rules of the language become extremely simple: Each reference binds to the sole declaration carrying the same label.[7] In particular, no hiding, shadowing, obscuring, or overloading may get in the way of a refactoring. After a refactoring, the declared entities can adopt their original names, and the inverted lookup function can be used to compute the names of the references.

However, as already noted in Sect. 6.1, there are refactoring problems that exceed the capabilities of dependency preservation and language extensions or restrictions. For instance, in the course of the REPLACE INHERITANCE WITH DELEGATION refactoring access modifiers may need to be adapted at the declaration site to keep a program well-formed (see Fig. 1a). In addition, if qualifiers (as part of the name computed by inverting the lookup function) must be introduced at the reference site, the names used for qualification may refer to inaccessible entities, requiring additional access modifier adjustments to avoid malformedness [38]. However, adjusting access modifiers can itself lead to a change of name binding, not only making binding preservation a recursive problem, but also intermingling well-formedness preservation with dependency preservation. The same applies to refactorings that may make a program ill-typed: For instance, when the subtype relationship is removed (again as with REPLACE INHERITANCE WITH DELEGATION), assignments (as in Fig. 1c) or member accesses (as in Fig. 1d) may become ill-typed. For dealing with these kinds of problems, another principled approach to implementing refactoring tools seems better suited: *constraint-based refactoring*.

6.3   Constraint-Based Refactoring

Constraint-based refactoring was pioneered by Frank Tip et al., who adopted Jens Palsberg and Michael Schwartzbach's constraint-based capture of object-oriented type systems [32] for the implementation of type generalization refactorings such as GENERALIZE DECLARED TYPE or USE SUPERTYPE WHERE POSSIBLE [48,49]. However, rather than following the historic trail of this seminal work, I present constraint-based refactoring as a way of *preserving refactoring invariants* in the spirit of Sect. 3.3 here.

6.3.1   Preserving Dependencies with Constraints

To show how refactoring invariants can be expressed in terms of constraints, I will start with preserving dependencies, as this allows me to draw some parallels to Schäfer's work. Below, I will address how well-formedness can be preserved, using the examples of accessibilities and types.

---

[7] Note the relationship to projectional editing, which uses references, or pointers, rather than names.

For the first part, we return to the name capture problem of Sect. 6.1:

```
class A {
  int x;
  A(int newX) {
    x = newX;
  }
}
```

A binding invariant of this snippet is expressed by the two simple constraints

$$ref_x.name = decl_x.name \tag{1}$$

$$ref_{newX}.name = decl_{newX}.name \tag{2}$$

Here, $decl_x$ and $decl_{newX}$ represent the *declared entities* of the program (currently named "x" and "newX", resp.), and $decl_x.name$ and $decl_{newX}.name$ represent *constraint variables* holding the names of these entities. Analogously, ref_x and ref_{newX} represent *references* to the declared entities, and $ref_x.name$ and $ref_{newX}.name$ their names.

As invariants, (1) and (2) enforce that the names of the references must always equal those of the declared entities they bind to, where the binding has been determined prior to the constraint generation (e.g., by querying the compiler; but see Sect. 6.3.2 for how binding can be computed using constraints). A RENAME refactoring is hence expressed as changing the value of one of the constraint variables; the violation of constraints that this immediately causes flags the loss of a dependency. For instance, if $decl_{newX}.name$ is changed to "x", (2) is immediately violated, since $ref_{newX}.name$ still holds the value "newX". However, the lost binding can easily be restored, simply by letting a constraint solver assign the other constraint variable ($ref_{newX}.name$ in the above example) the same name (representing a corresponding name change in the program), hence curing the violation. Thus, using a single set of constraints, we cannot only check dependency preservation, but also compute the corrective changes required to preserve dependencies actively (as in Sect. 6.1).

In constraint-based refactoring the name capture caused by renaming the formal parameter newX to "x" is avoided by adding a third constraint

$$decl_{newX}.name \neq decl_x.name \tag{3}$$

The generation of this constraint is justified by the fact that newX is declared in a scope in which it would shadow the declaration of x, if their names were the same. While not necessary for the program as is, it helps preserve the name binding under renaming either newX or x, by requiring that their names are always different. In fact, a constraint-based implementation of the RENAME refactoring would not need to reject the renaming of the formal parameter newX to "x"; rather, it would rename the field x to a different name and, observing (1), the reference to x with it. While this measure of actively achieving dependency preservation differs from Schäfer's (which worked by introducing qualifiers; see Sect. 6.1), it is equally successful. In fact, it works even in cases in which name qualification is impossible.

6.3.2 Aside: Implicit Specification of Name Lookup and Its Reversal Using Constraints

It is instructive to observe that, despite their technological differences, Schäfer's computation of the inverse of the binding function presented in Sect. 6.1 and the constraint-based capture of active dependency preservation presented above are closely related. This is revealed by the following slight modification of (1) and (2):

$$ref_x.name = ref_x.binding.name \qquad (4)$$

$$ref_{newX}.name = ref_{newX}.binding.name \qquad (5)$$

Here, the variable declarations to which the references ref_x and ref_{newX} bind have been replaced by the constraint variables $ref_x.binding$ and $ref_{newX}.binding$, resp. Assuming that all names in a program are fixated (so that the *name* variables do not change their values), a constraint solver will determine the bindings of ref_x and ref_{newX} by finding values for $ref_x.binding$ and $ref_{newX}.binding$ such that the constraints are satisfied. This corresponds to *computing the lookup function*.

Using the same constraints (4) and (5), that a binding must not change under refactoring (the binding invariance) is expressed by fixating the values of the constraint variables $ref_x.binding$ and $ref_{newX}.binding$ (the values just computed by the solver). Renaming declarations (by assigning $decl_x.name$ or $decl_{newX}.name$ new values) and making the values of the $ref_x.name$ and $ref_{newX}.name$ variable, then corresponds to *inverting the lookup function* as proposed by Schäfer, in that it propagates a changed name of a declared entity to its references. However, unlike for Schäfer's procedural approach, which needs to provide related, but still independent implementations for name lookup and name computation, constraint-based refactoring exploits that constraints are generally undirected ("*n*-way"), and makes do with a single specification. In fact, a single constraint-based specification can be used to

1. extract dependencies before the refactoring (corresponding to Step 2 in the generic procedure of Sect. 3.3),
2. check dependencies after the refactoring (Step 5), and
3. compute required corrective changes (part of Step 3).

As we will see next, constraints can also be used to

4. check well-formedness before and after a refactoring (Steps 1 and 4 in the generic procedure of Sect. 3.3), and to
5. compute corrective changes required to preserve well-formedness (again part of Step 3).

Note that Item 4 is also done by the compiler, which needs to check the same constraints. Elements of Item 1 must also be implemented by the compiler (for instance when resolving names or when creating tables for dynamic method dispatch), even though most compilers will not use constraints and constraint solving for this purpose.[8] Items 3 and 5 are actually part of the mechanics of a refactoring; I will return to this at the end of this section.

6.3.3 Accessibility Constraints

One of the refactoring problems classified in Sect. 6.1 as not being amenable to dependency preservation is that of adapting access modifiers. To get an impression of the problem, we adapt the code snippet of Fig. 1(a), adding C as a second subclass of A defining an overriding method m():

```
package a;
class A {
  protected void m() {...}
}
package b;
class B extends A {
  void n() { m(); }
}
class C extends A {
  @override protected void m() {...}
}
```

Recall that the problem of applying REPLACE INHERITANCE WITH DELEGATION on class B was that it makes A.m() inaccessible from the body of class B. This problem appears to be readily fixed by increasing the accessibility of A.m() to public; however, this makes the program malformed, since Java requires that overriding methods must be declared at least as accessible as the methods they override. In this particular case, this means that accessibility of C.m() needs to be adjusted to public as well; in other cases, other rules may apply.

A constraint-based solution to this problem is to express the well-formedness rules related to access modifiers in the same style as the name binding rules above. For instance, accessibility of A.m() from B can be expressed by the constraint

$$decl_{A.m()}.accessibility \geq (B <: A ? protected : public) \tag{6}$$

where $<:$ denotes the subtype relation and ? : is the ternary conditional operator (note that access modifiers are totally ordered in Java: $private < package < protected < public$). The constraint says that $protected$ accessibility for A.m() suffices as long as B is a subclass of A; otherwise, it must be $public$.[9] Note that this constraint is only justified if B (or any other class from a different package) requires access to A.m(); in the above example, it is required by the access through B.n().

---

[8] In fact, for efficiency reasons, it may not be advisable to use standard constraint solving for this purpose. However, efficient one-way computations may be synthesized from n-way constraints [22]. A conventionally implemented lookup function is a good use case for this. See also at the end of Sect. 9 in Part II of this briefing, where this issue is picked up again.

[9] This greatly oversimplifies matters — see [38] for a more thorough account of accessibility in Java.

The fact that accessibility of C.m() must be greater or equal than that of A.m() is expressed as the *conditional constraint*

$$C <: A \rightarrow (decl_{C.m()}.accessibility \geq decl_{A.m()}.accessibility) \qquad (7)$$

which says that if C is a subclass of A, accessibility of C.m() must be equal to or greater than accessibility of A.m(). Note that both constraints (6) and (7) use the subtype relation as a condition — this is important, since the REPLACE INHERITANCE WITH DELEGATION refactoring changes this relation, and access modifiers must adapt to the change.

Conditional constraints are commonplace in constraint-based refactoring (see, e.g., [2]); however, they also impact tractability and hence require special treatment. For instance, for refactorings that move program elements between scopes, constraint (3) of Sect. 6.3.1 would need to be conditioned on both declared entities residing in the same scope, so that the constraint is active when they do, and inactive otherwise. In general, it is not trivial to know which constraints will actually be needed in which form for a given refactoring, and generating all constraints, and each in its most general form, will be too expensive. Therefore, the constraint generation process must "foresee" all changes a refactoring may possibly make [43]. Note how this parallels the problem of extracting all and only the dependencies required for a specific refactoring in Schäfer's work (cf. Sect. 6.1.1).

6.3.4   Type Constraints

Some of the remaining problems of REPLACE INHERITANCE WITH DELEGATION discussed in Sect. 4 can be framed as typing problems, specifically as the loss of well-typedness. Similar to accessibility above, preserving well-typedness can be expressed as a constraint satisfaction problem.

To see how this works, we return to the example of Fig. 1, specifically the code snippet

```
class A implements I {}
class B extends A {}
I i = new B();
```

Recall that applying REPLACE INHERITANCE WITH DELEGATION to class B makes the assignment ill-typed, since B is no longer a subtype of I.

The corresponding typing invariant is expressed by the constraint

$$B <: decl_i.type$$

Clearly, this constraint, which is satisfied before the refactoring, is violated after it, since the current type of i, I, is no longer a supertype of B. However, a constraint solver can repair the broken constraint, either by changing the value of $delc_i.type$ to B (corresponding to a change of the declared type of i to B) or by changing the type hierarchy so that $B <: I$ (corresponding to letting class B implement interface I). However, in a program larger than the above, we must expect both changes to be subject to further constraints. For instance, class B must implement all methods declared in I. Conversely, if members are accessed on b, these members must be declared in interface I.

The latter constraint also plays a role in refactoring the code of Fig. 1(d), again repeated here for ease of access:

```
class A { int i; }
class B extends A {}
B b = new B(); b.i = 0;
```

Here, the access of i on receiver b requires that i is a field of b, expressed by the constraint

$$ref_b.type <: decl_i.host$$

Again, removing the subtype relationship between B and A violates this constraint. A constraint solver can compute a fix, however: by setting $decl_i.host$ to B, the constraint is satisfied again (and the declaration of field i is pushed down from class A to class B). In most real programs, however, this fix will be prevented by other constraints requiring that field i remains a member of class A.

A detailed presentation of the Java type constraints relevant for type-related refactorings is found in [48].

6.3.5   Generic Constraint-Based Refactoring Tool Implementation

It should be clear from the above that using constraints, we cannot only

– check well-formedness and dependency preservation of a program (and hence whether a refactoring was successful),

but also

– extract dependencies (as in the name binding example) to be preserved, and
– compute the corrective changes required to actively preserve well-formedness *and* dependencies.

What is missing from a completely constraint-based implementation of a refactoring tool is that the refactoring intent (see Sect. 3.1) is also expressed in terms of constraints. However, in as much as the changes constituting the refactoring intent can be expressed in terms of new values for constraint variables (as was the case for most examples presented in this section), this is easy: Simply add constraints forcing the new value (e.g., adding the constraint $decl_{newX}.name = \text{"x"}$ forces the renaming of newX). The constraint solver is then a generic refactoring engine capable of computing all changes required to realize a given refactoring intent.

7   Refactoring Résumé: Three Competing Camps

The previous sections suggest that three different perceptions of refactoring tools have emerged in the refactoring community:

– *Tool builders* maintain that to implement a refactoring correctly, it suffices
    1. to identify its preconditions and
    2. to specify the mechanics performing the changes that constitute the refactoring.

- *Tool users* suggest that for refactoring tools to be useful,
  1. an implementation of the mechanics and
  2. automated oracles checking the generic postconditions (compiler and test suite)

  are all that is required.
- *Tool researchers* hope that the necessary changes associated with a refactoring can be synthesized from
  1. the invariants of the refactoring and
  2. the specific changes to be seen in the program (the specific postconditions, or refactoring intent).

Reality catches up with:

- *tool builders* when the bug reports from users start coming in, and the struggle against the intricacies of the subject language leads to thoughts of resignation;
- *tool users* when they lose control over their code, because they are trapped in fixing bugs they did not introduce, in places they had not dreamt of; and
- *tool researchers*, when they apply their tools to real programs written in real programming languages and they learn how complex the semantics of these languages are.

Undoubtedly, building correct refactoring tools is hard. With the compiler specifying the semantics of a programming language, it seems that re-using as much of it as possible for the implementation of refactoring tools is *the* key to success.

Part II: Their Kin

Maybe the technical difficulties of producing correct refactoring tools and the expected benefit do not match well. Maybe the investment necessary to get refactoring right pays only if other programming tools profit from it, too. Maybe there is a common basis of a large variety of programming tools, of which refactoring tools are just one offspring.

Figure 2 depicts a bunch of such tools that all depend on a single software artefact, the specification of the static semantics of a programming language. In this bigger picture, it appears that refactoring merely plays a small, if not subordinate, role. However, we have seen that refactoring is also one of the harder problems in this bouquet, requiring some guarantees with respect to well-formedness *and* behaviour. For any specification sufficient for refactoring we may therefore expect that it is sufficient for the other problems as well.

8   Static Checking

Static checking is a central activity of compilers that comes straight after syntactic checking, or parsing. Depending on the language specification, it includes checks that all names are declared before they are used, that all expressions are

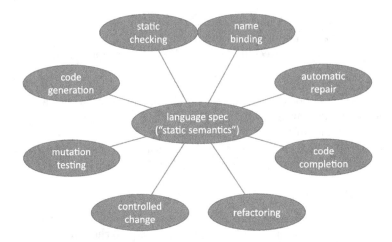

Fig. 2. Single investment, many pay-offs.

well-typed, etc. A program that passes all checks is considered well-formed, and ready for code generation or interpretation.

Static checkers can be implemented in a number of ways, with speed usually being a primary concern. However, there is a growing awareness of the fact that static checking is an option that can be traded for flexibility [6]. In addition, frameworks and even individual users of a programming language may define their own rules of well-formedness ("coding conventions"), which they want to see enforced by a compiler. JavaCOP [1] and the Checker framework [9] are two representatives of this movement in the Java field; for other, especially modelling, languages, the Object Constraint Language (OCL) is in use. Note that JavaCOP and OCL rely on constraints (but not constraint solving!) for static checking; since constraints are also the basis of constraint-based refactoring (Sect. 6.3), they are a hot candidate for our central capture of static semantics.

To see how rules of well-formedness can be expressed with constraints, we use a simple example. For any conventional programming language declaring names, we have a well-formedness condition stating that for all uses of (or references to) names there must exist a declaration introducing that name. More formally, we have that

$$\forall ref \; \exists decl : ref.name = decl.name \qquad (8)$$

Applied to the program

```
int i;
bool j;
i = 1;
j = true;
```

this rule gives us the two constraints

$$\exists decl : ref_i.name = decl.name \qquad (9)$$
$$\exists decl : ref_j.name = decl.name \qquad (10)$$

Note that this rule does not express to which declaration a name *does* bind — it just expresses that for a program to be well-formed, a declaration must exist to which the name *can* bind.

Another well-formedness rule that is straightforwardly expressed using constraints is usually found in statically type-checked programming languages. It requires that the types on both sides of an assignment must equal. Expressing this rule with constraints and applying it to the above program will give us something like

$$ref_i.binding.type = lit_1.type \qquad (11)$$
$$ref_j.binding.type = lit_{true}.type \qquad (12)$$

As in Sect. 6.3, the constraint variables $ref_i.binding$ and $ref_j.binding$ represent the declarations (declared entities) the references bind to. The above well-formedness constraints (9) and (10) guarantee that a value can be found for these variables (because a declaration carrying the same name as the reference must exist), but for the type checking to be effective, the variables need to have values assigned. While one could argue that since constraints are generally undirected, the type constraints (11) and (12) can be used to compute the bindings of i and j (taking (11) and (12) as implicit specifications of the binding function; cf. Sect. 6.3.2), generally, type information does not suffice to determine binding unambiguously (what if i and j had the same type?) — this is what the names are for.

9 Name Binding

In contemporary programming languages like Java, name binding is the Siamese twin of static checking: One cannot live without the other. While a more thorough treatment of the interrelationship can be found in a companion briefing on "Name Binding" by Guido Wachsmuth (in this Volume), I want to emphasize here that name binding can in principle be expressed as a constraint satisfaction problem, and thus thrive on the same (constraint-based) specification of static semantics as all other tools discussed in this part of my briefing. In particular, expressing both static checking and name binding as one constraint satisfaction problem, the two tasks are automatically intertwined by the constraint solver.

Section 6.3, specifically constraints (4) and (5), already provided a brief glimpse of how names can be bound using constraints. Here, we note that for name binding, we need to complement the well-formedness constraints (9) and (10) guaranteeing that the names *can* be bound with a set of rules expressing *how* they are bound. Just like the constraints (4) and (5), the constraints

$$ref_i.binding.name = ref_i.name \tag{13}$$

$$ref_j.binding.name = ref_j.name \tag{14}$$

provide an *implicit specification* of the binding function applied to ref_i and ref_j. Interestingly, the well-formedness constraints (9) and (10) and the binding constraints (13) and (14) are related by Skolemization, with *binding* being the Skolem function.[10] Given that Skolemization makes (9) and (13), as well as (10) and (14), equisatisfiable, and given that (13) and (14) are more useful (they can be used for well-formedness checking and to compute name binding), the well-formedness constraints (9) and (10) appear dispensable. This is the more so since (13) and (14) can be used to detect ambiguity: if the constraint solver finds more than one value for a *binding* variable, binding cannot be uniquely determined. (Note how this amounts to replacing $\exists$ in (9) and (10) with $\exists_1$.)

10   Automatic Repair

If constraints can be used to check the well-formedness of a program, it seems natural that using constraint solving instead of constraint checking, the same constraints can also be used to correct a malformed program, simply by replacing fixated values in the failing constraints with constraint variables for which a constraint solver can compute new values. These new values then represent the fixes that mend the program.[11] However, contemporary IDEs implement auto-fixes (also called quick fixes) imperatively.

The auto-fixing implementations offered by contemporary IDEs are often short-sighted in that they offer fixes that break the program in other places. As for refactoring tools, there is a discussion whether this presents a bug or a feature: While a fix introducing a bug may not be a fix to some users, others may argue that it is still helpful if it saves manual edits. Without delving into this discussion, we note here that the same erratic behaviour can be obtained by solving violated constraints locally; if undesired, this behaviour can be cured by submitting all derivable constraints constraining the variables to the solver [42]. As for constraint-based refactoring (Sect. 6.3), this may turn out to be too expensive; again, as noted at the end of Sect. 6.3.4, much of the art of using constraints lies in deciding precisely which constraints to generate.

To give the reader an impression of how constraint-based auto-fixing works, we look at the following piece of malformed code written in our sample language:

```
int i;
bool j;
i = 1;
k = true;
```

---

[10] See [41] for some more details on how Skolemization relates well-formedness checking and binding.

[11] Note that we do not consider syntax errors here.

Most programmers would agree that the obvious way to fix the name binding problem is to replace k in the program text with j, but not knowing what the intention of the programmer was, all fixes

```
int i;          int i;          int k;          int i;
bool j;         bool j;         bool j;         bool k;
i = 1;          i = 1;          i = 1;          i = 1;
j = true;       i = true;       k = true;       k = true;
```

are equally conceivable. In fact, all these fixes can be derived from solving the (combined well-formedness and binding) constraint

$$ref_k.name = ref_k.binding.name \tag{15}$$

with $ref_k.name$, $ref_k.binding$, $decl_i.name$, and $decl_j.name$ all being variable. If a tool user has a preference for changing the names of references rather than declarations, this can be expressed by fixating the values of the constraint variables $decl_i.name$ and $decl_j.name$ to their current values; if the preference is on changing the names of declarations, the value of $ref_k.name$ can be fixated. Note that tying all variables to their current values makes the constraint unsolvable; it reflects the malformedness of the program in its present form.

As the alert reader will have noticed, two of the above fixes are short-sighted, in that they produce malformed programs. However, the resulting programs do not suffer from name binding problems — they are ill-typed. The problematic fixes can thus be prevented by adding the relevant type constraints to the constraints to be solved, in the above example

$$ref_k.type = ref_k.binding.type$$
$$ref_k.type = lit_{true}.type$$
$$decl_i.type = type_{int}.val$$
$$decl_j.type = type_{bool}.val$$

The constraint variable connecting the name constraint (15) with the above type constraints is $ref_k.binding$; if its value is changed in the course of solving the name constraint, this change propagates to the type constraints, where it leads to the computation of the (new) type of the reference ref_k. With all constraint variables representing types having fixated values, the only solution of the joint constraint system is setting $ref_k.name$ to "j"; accepting new values for type variables also results in alternative fixes adjusting types in declarations or literals. Whether these additional fixes make sense and should be offered to the user is a different discussion; here it is important to note that (a) all fixes have been computed from the very same constraints used for detecting malformedness and (b) no fix computed by these constraints leaves the program malformed. As can easily be imagined, obtaining the same guarantee from an imperatively implemented auto-fix tool is hard.

A first delineation of constraint-based repair (together with constraint-based code completion) appeared in [46]; a more comprehensive treatise (based on constraint attribute grammars) has only recently been published [42].

11   Code Completion

Using constraints and constraint solving, auto-completion corresponds to computing values for constraint variables that do not have initial values that could be derived from a program as is. For instance, when the current program reads

```
int i;
bool j;
i = ∧
```

and the user is about to enter a name at the caret position which represents a new reference, ref_{new}, the constraints

$$ref_{new}.name = ref_{new}.binding.name$$
$$ref_{new}.type = ref_{new}.binding.type$$
$$ref_i.type = ref_{new}.type$$

known from Sects. 8 and 9, and given that the current value of $ref_i.type$, int, is fixated, suffice to compute $ref_{new}.name := $ "i" as the only valid completion of the program. Note that, analogously to auto-fixing, not generating all constraints would give us alternative completions (such as $ref_{new}.name := $ "j"), which would however give us a malformed program.

Auto-completion is the dual to auto-fixing: most, if not all, incomplete programs can be thought of as being malformed (if only by introducing a random program element that renders the program so), so that the repairs represent the completions; and most, if not all, malformed programs can be thought of as being incomplete, so that eliminating the parts that are thought to cause the malformedness, and completing the resulting program, presents a fix. Therefore, it is highly advisable that auto-completion and auto-fixing are based on the same implementation; in current IDEs, however, this does not seem to be the case.

12   Controlled Change

It is safe to claim that programming is an alternating sequence of behaviour-altering change and refactoring. With refactoring being increasingly supported by corresponding tools, the next challenge is to support behaviour-altering changes also. At the very least, such support should guarantee that behaviour-altering changes leave a program well-formed; at a more advanced level, such support would ensure preservation of arbitrary, selected properties the program had before the change. We call a change that is guaranteed to preserve selected properties a *controlled change*. Refactoring is a controlled change in which the selected property is behaviour.

Arguably, the same discussion that is currently being led with regard to refactoring can also be led with regard to controlled change: Given some decision procedure ("oracle") for the desired properties, a tool or the programmer can go ahead and change a program in any way they deem appropriate, and the oracle can report the accidentally introduced errors later. In particular, any property that can be cast into a static check can be preserved this way. For Java programs this includes non-nullness, object confinement [20], etc. (see [1,9] for many more examples).

However, for academics at least, this would seem too modest a solution to be satisfactory. In fact, given how far we got in Part I of this briefing by computing from the same specification used for checking the very changes required to pass a check, why could the same not be achieved for other controlled changes? And indeed, the principle is the same: Identify the relevant invariants and make sure that they are preserved.

There is however a major difference between (arbitrary) controlled changes and refactoring: While refactorings usually follow patterns (refactorings are catalogued!), other controlled changes may not. Indeed, unless we go down to atomic changes (such as the changes used in mutation testing; see below), it is not clear whether we will ever see a compilation of controlled changes that receives the same recognition as Fowler's refactoring catalogue [12]. The source manipulation menus of contemporary IDEs such as Eclipse (containing entries like "surround with try-catch") may provide a starting point for implementing more complex controlled changes, however.

On the other hand, not all refactorings are catalogued: Firstly, a programmer is free to make any changes she pleases manually, and still demand tool support making sure that these changes constitute a refactoring. Secondly, tools can be devised for non-catalogued, ad-hoc refactorings (or "refactorings without names" [44]) also. If these can be made to work, other non-catalogued controlled changes should work also.

13 Mutation Testing

Mutation testing or, as it is sometimes also referred to, mutation analysis, is the technique of changing a program in such a way that it still compiles, but exhibits changed behaviour. Mutation testing is useful for testing the adequacy of test suites: for each behaviourally changed program — called *mutant* — that does not get caught, an additional test case should be added which catches it.

Traditional mutation testing works by applying mutation operators to programs. This suffers from two major problems: (1) The mutation operators may make the mutant malformed, and (2) the mutant may exhibit equivalent behaviour. While the former can be avoided by applying only mutation operators that cannot make a program malformed, or (somewhat expensively) by rejecting generated mutants that do not compile, the latter is a hard problem (undecidable in general) and in any case requires human inspection.

The attentive reader will have noticed that mutation testing (or, more specifically, the generation of non-equivalent mutants) is a special case of controlled change (Sect. 12). In fact, it is a complement of refactoring, one in which well-formedness is to be preserved, but behaviour is to be changed. The great advantages of implementing mutation testing as a controlled change activity are that (a) it does not limit mutations to the application of (single) mutation operators that cannot introduce malformedness, without having to pay the price of time-consuming compiler checks rejecting malformed mutants; and that (b) mutants are more likely to exhibit changed behaviour, namely when behaviour-critical dependencies (Sect. 6.1) have been changed by the mutation.

To give a concrete example of how this may work, we use our simple language again and start with the program

```
int i;
int j;
bool k;
i = 1;
j = 0;
k = true;
i = j;
```

A traditional mutation operator would replace the literal 1 with 0 (or vice versa), or true with false, which cannot make the program malformed. However, replacing names (identifiers) in the same shallow manner risks making the program ill-typed, as evidenced by replacing i with k in an assignment. By separating the set of constraints generated for the above program into ones that preserve well-formedness and ones that preserve behaviour-critical dependencies (see Sect. 6.1 for examples of these), and by negating one constraint of the latter kind, we can let the constraint solver compute a change that leaves the program well-formed, but (likely) exhibiting changed behaviour. For instance, for the last line of the above program we get the constraint

$$ref_j.binding.name = ref_j.name$$

which is solved by the assignment $ref_j.binding := decl_j$ (an extracted invariant in the case of refactoring; cf. Sect. 6.3.2). By adding a constraint

$$ref_j.binding \neq decl_j$$

(which negates the extracted invariant) and solving all constraints we get a new program in which j in the last line has been replaced with i (assuming that the names of declarations have been fixated; however, this is not required for the approach to work). Note that the well-formedness constraints (which have not been touched) prevent that i is replaced with k, since this would make the program ill-typed. Standard mutation operators do not have this language intimacy, and always apply their changes indiscriminately.

14   Code Generation

Code generation is the big brother of code completion (Sect. 11): it can be seen as the iterative completion of a program, starting with no (or the empty) program. A trivial approach to generating (arbitrary) well-formed code follows

Listing 1. Definite clause grammar generating (and accepting) only well-formed programs of a given length.

```
program(LOCs) -->
  decls([], Tab, LOCs, LOCsR),
  assigns(Tab, LOCsR, 0).
decls(Tab, Tab, LOCs, LOCs) --> [].
decls(In, Out, LOCs, LOCsR) -->
  {LOCs > 0},
  decl(In, Tmp),
  {LOCsD is LOCs - 1},
  decls(Tmp, Out, LOCsD, LOCsR).
decl(Tab, [var(Name, Type)|Tab]) -->
  type(Type),
  var(Name),
  {nonmember(var(Name, _), Tab)}.
type(int) --> [int].
type(bool) --> [bool].
var(i) --> [i].
var(j) --> [j].
assigns(Tab, LOCs, LOCs) --> [].
assigns(Tab, LOCs, LOCsR) -->
  {LOCs > 0},
  assign(Tab),
  {LOCsD is LOCs - 1},
  assigns(Tab, LOCsD, LOCsR).
assign(Tab) -->
  var(Name),
  {member(var(Name, Type), Tab)},
  [=],
  lit(Type).
assign(Tab) -->
  var(Name1),
  {member(var(Name1, Type), Tab)},
  [=],
  var(Name2),
  {member(var(Name2, Type), Tab)}.
lit(int) --> [0] | [1].
lit(bool) --> [true] | [false].
```

the *generate-and-test* paradigm: Syntactically well-formed programs, generated using the language's grammar or constructor invocations on an object-oriented capture of the language's abstract syntax, are subjected to static checking, dismissing all (semantically) malformed programs. However, while straightforward, this approach is usually too expensive for practical use.

A more practical approach to generating (arbitrary) well-formed code is to use attribute grammars enhancing the syntax rules of a target language with the rules of (static) semantics [25]. By replacing the computation of the attribute values of such a grammar with constraint solving, we can make sure that all programs generated by this grammar are well-formed [42]. For instance, the definite clause grammar (DCG) of Listing 1 can be used to generate all well-formed programs of our little sample language having a given number of lines of code (LOCs). Note that it uses unification and backtracking for constraint solving, which are also the main mechanisms of parsing in Prolog.

However, the use cases for generating *arbitrary* well-formed programs are fairly limited (but note that they include model checking language specifications [17] and testing programming tools [8], which both are highly relevant in the context of this briefing). What is needed more often is the generation of programs devised to fulfil some given purpose. In the most general case, a program generator would be an arbitrary program (written in a generator, or meta, language) that produces, from some given input, an output program in a target, or object, language that is well-formed according to the rules of that language.

The problems of and solutions for safe program generation are the topic of the companion briefing on "Structured Code Generation Techniques" provided by Yannis Smaragdakis et al. in this Volume, to which I would like to refer interested readers at this point. However, I will not leave them without noting that any proof of correctness of such program-generating programs via their compiler (the meta-language compiler), i.e., the proof of the fact that a given program-generating program can produce, for any input, only output programs that are well-formed in the target language, requires a full and formal capture of the well-formedness rules of the host language, for instance in first-order logic [23]. The constraints presented throughout this briefing are first order; hence, it seems justified to add structured code generators to the circle of programming tools profiting from the same single specification of a language's static semantics.

Acknowledgements. The work presented in this briefing has been supported by Deutsche Forschungsgemeinschaft (DFG) under grants STE 906/4-1&2 and STE 906/5-1. I thank Andreas Thies, Jens von Pilgrim, Frank Tip, Max Schäfer, and Bastian Ulke for their collaboration.

References

1. Andreae, C., Noble, J., Markstrum, S., Millstein, T.D.: A framework for implementing pluggable type systems. In: Tarr, P.L., Cook, W.R. (eds.) Proceedings of the 21th Annual ACM SIGPLAN Conference on Object-Oriented Programming, Systems, Languages, and Applications, OOPSLA 2006, 22–26 October 2006, Portland, Oregon, USA, pp. 57–74. ACM (2006). http://doi.acm.org/10.1145/1167473.1167479

2. Balaban, I., Tip, F., Fuhrer, R.M.: Refactoring support for class library migration. In: Johnson, R.E., Gabriel, R.P. (eds.) Proceedings of the 20th Annual ACM SIGPLAN Conference on Object-Oriented Programming, Systems, Languages, and Applications, OOPSLA 2005, 16–20 October 2005, San Diego, CA, USA, pp. 265–279. ACM (2005). http://doi.acm.org/10.1145/1094811.1094832

3. Bannwart, F., Müller, P.: Changing programs correctly: refactoring with specifications. In: Misra, J., Nipkow, T., Sekerinski, E. (eds.) FM 2006. LNCS, vol. 4085, pp. 492–507. Springer, Heidelberg (2006). doi:10.1007/11813040_33

4. Beck, K.: Extreme Programming Explained: Embrace Change. Addison-Wesley Longman Publishing Co. Inc., Boston (2000)

5. Borba, P., Sampaio, A., Cavalcanti, A., Cornélio, M.: Algebraic reasoning for object-oriented programming. Sci. Comput. Program. **52**, 53–100 (2004). http://dx.doi.org/10.1016/j.scico.2004.03.003

6. Bracha, G.: Pluggable type systems. In: OOPSLA Workshop on Revival of Dynamic Languages, vol. 1. Citeseer (2004)

7. Brant, J., Steimann, F.: Refactoring tools are trustworthy enough and trust must be earned. IEEE Softw. **32**(6), 80–83 (2015). http://dx.doi.org/10.1109/MS.2015.145

8. Daniel, B., Dig, D., Garcia, K., Marinov, D.: Automated testing of refactoring engines. In: Crnkovic, I., Bertolino, A. (eds.) Proceedings of the 6th Joint Meeting of the European Software Engineering Conference and the ACM SIGSOFT International Symposium on Foundations of Software Engineering, 2007, Dubrovnik, Croatia, 3–7 September 2007, pp. 185–194. ACM (2007). http://doi.acm.org/10.1145/1287624.1287651

9. Dietl, W., Dietzel, S., Ernst, M.D., Muslu, K., Schiller, T.W.: Building and using pluggable type-checkers. In: Taylor, R.N., Gall, H.C., Medvidovic, N. (eds.) Proceedings of the 33rd International Conference on Software Engineering, ICSE 2011, Waikiki, Honolulu, HI, USA, 21–28 May 2011, pp. 681–690. ACM (2011). http://doi.acm.org/10.1145/1985793.1985889

10. Dig, D., Marrero, J., Ernst, M.D.: Refactoring sequential Java code for concurrency via concurrent libraries. In: 31st International Conference on Software Engineering, ICSE 2009, 16–24 May 2009, Vancouver, Canada, Proceedings, pp. 397–407. IEEE (2009). http://dx.doi.org/10.1109/ICSE.2009.5070539

11. Foster, S.R., Griswold, W.G., Lerner, S.: Witchdoctor: IDE support for real-time auto-completion of refactorings. In: Glinz et al. [16], pp. 222–232. http://dx.doi.org/10.1109/ICSE.2012.6227191

12. Fowler, M.: Refactoring - Improving the Design of Existing Code. Addison Wesley Object Technology Series. Addison-Wesley, Boston (1999)

13. Garrido, A., Meseguer, J.: Formal specification and verification of Java refactorings. In: Proceedings of the Sixth IEEE International Workshop on Source Code Analysis and Manipulation, SCAM 2006, pp. 165–174 (2006). http://dx.doi.org/10.1109/SCAM.2006.16

14. Ge, X., DuBose, Q.L., Murphy-Hill, E.R.: Reconciling manual and automatic refactoring. In: Glinz et al. [16], pp. 211–221. http://dx.doi.org/10.1109/ICSE.2012.6227192

15. Gligoric, M., Behrang, F., Li, Y., Overbey, J., Hafiz, M., Marinov, D.: Systematic testing of refactoring engines on real software projects. In: Castagna, G. (ed.) ECOOP 2013. LNCS, vol. 7920, pp. 629–653. Springer, Heidelberg (2013). doi:10.1007/978-3-642-39038-8_26

16. Glinz, M., Murphy, G.C., Pezzè, M. (eds.): 34th International Conference on Software Engineering, ICSE 2012, 2–9 June 2012, Zurich, Switzerland. IEEE (2012)

17. González, C.A., Büttner, F., Clarisó, R., Cabot, J.: EMFtoCSP: a tool for the lightweight verification of EMF models. In: Gnesi, S., Gruner, S., Plat, N., Rumpe, B. (eds.) Proceedings of the First International Workshop on Formal Methods in Software Engineering - Rigorous and Agile Approaches, FormSERA 2012, Zurich, Switzerland, 2 June 2012, pp. 44–50. IEEE (2012). http://dx.doi.org/10.1109/FormSERA.2012.6229788

18. Griswold, W.G.: Program restructuring as an aid to software maintenance. Ph.D. thesis, University of Washington (1991)

19. Griswold, W.G., Notkin, D.: Automated assistance for program restructuring. ACM Trans. Softw. Eng. Methodol. **2**(3), 228–269 (1993). http://doi.acm.org/10.1145/152388.152389

20. Grothoff, C., Palsberg, J., Vitek, J.: Encapsulating objects with confined types. ACM Trans. Program. Lang. Syst. **29**(6) (2007). http://doi.acm.org/10.1145/1286821.1286823

21. Heuzeroth, D., Aßmann, U., Trifu, M., Kuttruff, V.: The COMPOST, COMPASS, Inject/J and RECODER tool suite for invasive software composition: invasive composition with compass aspect-oriented connectors. In: Lämmel, R., Saraiva, J., Visser, J. (eds.) GTTSE 2005. LNCS, vol. 4143, pp. 357–377. Springer, Heidelberg (2006). doi:10.1007/11877028_14

22. Hottelier, T., Bodík, R.: Synthesis of layout engines from relational constraints. In: Aldrich, J., Eugster, P. (eds.) Proceedings of the 2015 ACM SIGPLAN International Conference on Object-Oriented Programming, Systems, Languages, and Applications, OOPSLA 2015, part of SPLASH 2015, Pittsburgh, PA, USA, 25–30 October 2015, pp. 74–88. ACM (2015). http://doi.acm.org/10.1145/2814270.2814291

23. Huang, S.S., Zook, D., Smaragdakis, Y.: Statically safe program generation with safegen. Sci. Comput. Program. **76**(5), 376–391 (2011). http://dx.doi.org/10.1016/j.scico.2008.09.007

24. Kegel, H., Steimann, F.: Systematically refactoring inheritance to delegation in Java. In: Schäfer, W., Dwyer, M.B., Gruhn, V. (eds.) 30th International Conference on Software Engineering (ICSE 2008), Leipzig, Germany, 10–18 May 2008, pp. 431–440. ACM (2008). http://doi.acm.org/10.1145/1368088.1368147

25. Knuth, D.E.: Semantics of context-free languages. Math. Syst. Theory **2**(2), 127–145 (1968). http://dx.doi.org/10.1007/BF01692511

26. Lämmel, R.: Towards generic refactoring. In: Fischer, B., Visser, E. (eds.) Proceedings of the 2002 ACM SIGPLAN Workshop on Rule-Based Programming, Pittsburgh, Pennsylvania, USA, 2002, pp. 15–28. ACM (2002). http://doi.acm.org/10.1145/570186.570188

27. Ludwig, A., Heuzeroth, D.: Metaprogramming in the large. In: Butler, G., Jarzabek, S. (eds.) GCSE 2000. LNCS, vol. 2177, pp. 179–188. Springer, Heidelberg (2001). doi:10.1007/3-540-44815-2_13

28. Murphy-Hill, E.R., Parnin, C., Black, A.P.: How we refactor, and how we know it. IEEE Trans. Softw. Eng. **38**(1), 5–18 (2012). http://doi.ieeecomputersociety.org/10.1109/TSE.2011.41

29. Opdyke, W.F.: Refactoring object-oriented frameworks. Ph.D. thesis, University of Illinois at Urbana-Champaign (1992)

30. Opdyke, W.F., Johnson, R.E.: Creating abstract superclasses by refactoring. In: Kwasny, S.C., Buck, J.F. (eds.) Proceedings of the ACM 21th Conference on Computer Science, CSC 1993, Indianapolis, IN, USA, 16–18 February 1993, pp. 66–73. ACM (1993). http://doi.acm.org/10.1145/170791.170804

31. Overbye, J.L.: A toolkit for constructing refactoring engines. Ph.D. thesis, University of Illinois at Urbana-Champaign (2011)
32. Palsberg, J., Schwartzbach, M.I.: Object-Oriented Type Systems. Wiley Professional Computing. Wiley, Chichester (1994)
33. Raychev, V., Schäfer, M., Sridharan, M., Vechev, M.T.: Refactoring with synthesis. In: Hosking, A.L., Eugster, P.T., Lopes, C.V. (eds.) Proceedings of the 2013 ACM SIGPLAN International Conference on Object Oriented Programming Systems Languages & Applications, OOPSLA 2013, part of SPLASH 2013, Indianapolis, IN, USA, 26–31 October 2013, pp. 339–354. ACM (2013). http://doi.acm.org/10.1145/2509136.2509544
34. Roberts, D., Brant, J., Johnson, R.E.: A refactoring tool for Smalltalk. TAPOS 3(4), 253–263 (1997)
35. Roberts, D.B.: Practical analysis for refactoring. Ph.D. thesis, University of Illinois at Urbana-Champaign (1999)
36. Schäfer, M.: Specification, implementation and verification of refactorings. Ph.D. thesis, Oxford University Computing Laboratory (2010)
37. Schäfer, M., de Moor, O.: Of gnats and dragons: sources of complexity in implementing refactorings. In: Workshop on Refactoring Tools (WRT) (2009)
38. Schäfer, M., Thies, A., Steimann, F., Tip, F.: A comprehensive approach to naming and accessibility in refactoring Java programs. IEEE Trans. Softw. Eng. 38(6), 1233–1257 (2012). http://doi.ieeecomputersociety.org/10.1109/TSE.2012.13
39. Soares, G., Gheyi, R., Massoni, T.: Automated behavioral testing of refactoring engines. IEEE Trans. Softw. Eng. 39(2), 147–162 (2013). http://dx.doi.org/10.1109/TSE.2012.19
40. Soares, G., Mongiovi, M., Gheyi, R.: Identifying overly strong conditions in refactoring implementations. In: IEEE 27th International Conference on Software Maintenance, ICSM 2011, Williamsburg, VA, USA, 25–30 September 2011, pp. 173–182. IEEE Computer Society (2011). http://dx.doi.org/10.1109/ICSM.2011.6080784
41. Steimann, F.: From well-formedness to meaning preservation: model refactoring for almost free. Softw. Syst. Model. 14(1), 307–320 (2015). http://dx.doi.org/10.1007/s10270-013-0314-z
42. Steimann, F., Hagemann, J., Ulke, B.: Computing repair alternatives for malformed programs using constraint attribute grammars. In: Visser, E., Smaragdakis, Y. (eds.) Proceedings of the 2016 ACM SIGPLAN International Conference on Object-Oriented Programming, Systems, Languages, and Applications, OOPSLA 2016, part of SPLASH 2016, Amsterdam, The Netherlands, 30 October – 4 November 2016, pp. 711–730. ACM (2016). http://doi.acm.org/10.1145/2983990.2984007
43. Steimann, F., von Pilgrim, J.: Constraint-based refactoring with foresight. In: Noble, J. (ed.) ECOOP 2012. LNCS, vol. 7313, pp. 535–559. Springer, Heidelberg (2012). doi:10.1007/978-3-642-31057-7_24
44. Steimann, F., von Pilgrim, J.: Refactorings without names. In: Goedicke, M., Menzies, T., Saeki, M. (eds.) IEEE/ACM International Conference on Automated Software Engineering, ASE 2012, Essen, Germany, 3–7 September 2012, pp. 290–293. ACM (2012). http://doi.acm.org/10.1145/2351676.2351726
45. Steimann, F., Thies, A.: From public to private to absent: refactoring JAVA programs under constrained accessibility. In: Drossopoulou, S. (ed.) ECOOP 2009. LNCS, vol. 5653, pp. 419–443. Springer, Heidelberg (2009). doi:10.1007/978-3-642-03013-0_19

46. Steimann, F., Ulke, B.: Generic model assist. In: Moreira, A., Schätz, B., Gray, J., Vallecillo, A., Clarke, P. (eds.) MODELS 2013. LNCS, vol. 8107, pp. 18–34. Springer, Heidelberg (2013). doi:10.1007/978-3-642-41533-3_2

47. Sultana, N., Thompson, S.J.: Mechanical verification of refactorings. In: Glück, R., de Moor, O. (eds.) Proceedings of the 2008 ACM SIGPLAN Symposium on Partial Evaluation and Semantics-based Program Manipulation, PEPM 2008, San Francisco, California, USA, 7–8 January 2008, pp. 51–60. ACM (2008). http://doi.acm.org/10.1145/1328408.1328417

48. Tip, F., Fuhrer, R.M., Kiezun, A., Ernst, M.D., Balaban, I., Sutter, B.D.: Refactoring using type constraints. ACM Trans. Program. Lang. Syst. **33**(3), 9 (2011). http://doi.acm.org/10.1145/1961204.1961205

49. Tip, F., Kiezun, A., Bäumer, D.: Refactoring for generalization using type constraints. In: Crocker, R., Jr., G.L.S. (eds.) Proceedings of the 2003 ACM SIGPLAN Conference on Object-Oriented Programming Systems, Languages and Applications, OOPSLA 2003, 26–30 October 2003, Anaheim, CA, USA, pp. 13–26. ACM (2003). http://doi.acm.org/10.1145/949305.949308

50. Vakilian, M., Chen, N., Negara, S., Rajkumar, B.A., Bailey, B.P., Johnson, R.E.: Use, disuse, and misuse of automated refactorings. In: Glinz et al. [16], pp. 233–243. http://dx.doi.org/10.1109/ICSE.2012.6227190

Implementing a Linear Algebra Approach to Data Processing

Rogério Pontes[1]([✉]), Miguel Matos[1,2], José Nuno Oliveira[1], and José Orlando Pereira[1]

[1] HASLab, INESC TEC, University of Minho, Braga, Portugal
rapontes@inesctec.pt
[2] IST/INESC-ID, Lisbon, Portugal

Abstract. Data analysis is among the main strategies of our time for enterprises to take advantage of the vast amounts of data their systems generate and store everyday. Thus the standard relational database model is challenged everyday to cope with quantitative operations over a traditionally qualitative, relational model.

A novel approach to the semantics of data is based on (typed) *linear algebra* (LA), rather than relational algebra, bridging the gap between data dimensions and data measures in a unified way. Also, this bears the promise of increased parallelism, as most operations in LA admit a 'divide & conquer' implementation.

This paper presents a first experiment in implementing such a typed linear algebra approach and testing its performance on a data distributed system. It presents solutions to some theoretical limitations and evaluates the overall performance.

Keywords: Formal methods · Linear algebra · Big data · Map reduce · Hive

1 Introduction

In a world where data are generated faster than humans can analyze and comprehend, only decision support systems are capable of keeping up and providing analytics on time. Among these, Online Analytical Processing databases (OLAP) are used by data analysts to navigate across vast amounts of data and find business advantages or new opportunities.

Databases have long used *relational algebra* (RA) to model data storage, the operations that are carried out on data and the language used to interact with them. The so-called *relational model* is the formal underpinning of both OLTP[1] applications and OLAP[2] systems, in spite of serving two very distinct purposes and requirements. OLTP applications target small transactions and focus on the

---

[1] OLTP stands for "Online Transaction Processing".

[2] OLAP stands for "Online Analytical Processing".

© Springer International Publishing AG 2017
J. Cunha et al. (Eds.): GTTSE 2015, LNCS 10223, pp. 215–222, 2017.
DOI: 10.1007/978-3-319-60074-1_9

business frontend. OLAP systems focus on aggregating data to create information that is used by data analysts, so that these can decide which action might be best for their purposes. Harrah's Entertainment improved their customer practices and increased its revenue due to insights obtained from their customer center warehouses [1]. Another well-known example is Google's prediction of the influenza outbreaks in 2009. The prediction was made much quicker than the center of disease control (CDC) [2].

Similar results are achieved through *analytical queries* which, however, take a long time to complete, some taking hours or even days [3]. As data grow, this has a twofold impact. If, on one hand, queries take longer to complete, on the other hand more information can be extracted from the increased amount of data. As business success relies more and more on this kind of technology, it becomes increasingly important to have a fast and correct solution.

Macedo et al. [4] argue that relational algebra is adequate for giving semantics to the *qualitative* side of data, falling short where *quantitative* information is handled. They provide a novel approach based on *linear algebra* (LA) capable of not only expressing the semantics of OLAP system constructions such as data cube, roll up and cross tab, but also providing formal semantics for both the quantitative and the qualitative side of data. Their approach is columnar in the sense of representing columns in data relations by typed matrices, and is algebraic in the sense of relying only on matrix operations to encode queries.

One of the core promises of the typed linear algebra approach is the amount of parallel computation that can be performed, since matrix multiplication is a well-known 'divide & conquer' operation. On the negative side, the matrices involved are very large and sparse. If a proper storage format is not leveraged or if the data structure used does not take into account the operations required by a query, problems of performance and memory arise. Moreover, the theory requires an additional matrix product, named the *Khatri-Rao* product. This operation is essential to the algebra, capturing data joins in a simple and algebraic way.

Contribution. The main aim of this paper is to provide a distributed implementation of LA-based data processing. One of the challenges is that information needs to be consistent over a set of independent nodes. As such, the paper contributes to the LA-based approach to data analytics in several ways:

- Selection and improvement of an adequate sparse matrix format to handle the data and computation.
- Proposal of a *Khatri-Rao* product algorithm that can work on dense and sparse matrices.
- Proposal of a matrix encoding to keep the data consistent on a distributed setting.
- Evaluating the performance of query analysis tasks on a distributed setting with a typed linear algebra computation.

2   Background

Let T be a relational data table in a relational database. Looking at T we find two kinds of attributes (columns of the table): either they are numeric, and their values can be subject to numeric operations, or they are symbolic. Attributes of the first kind are *quantitative* in nature — they are referred to as data *measures*; those of the second kind are *qualitative* and are known as *dimensions*.

This dimension/measure binomial leads to two kinds of matrices in the LA approach: *dimension* matrices, also called *projection functions*, and *measure* matrices. The latter are diagonal matrices with as many rows/columns as the number of data in the corresponding data column. The former are Boolean matrices whose cells addressed by (d, n) hold 1 iff the data value d can be found in record n of the table and 0 otherwise. These two kinds of matrix are exemplified by the middle and bottom tables of Fig. 1, respectively.

As can be seen from these examples, both matrices tend to be sparse; a projection matrix with n lines and m rows will have $m(n-1)$ zeros; if n and m are the same, then there are $n^2 - n$ zeros (quadratic growth), which is what happens in every measure matrix.

To work with matrices of this kind one needs special matrix formats that minimize memory usage. Fortunately, this topic has been heavily studied in the literature [5]. From the many formats available, one seems to the best suited: *Compressed Sparse Column* (CSC). It uses three arrays to store the information of a matrix: (a) an array "Values" holding all non-zero values, sorted by columns; (b) another array "Rows" keeping track of the original row position of values; (c) a final array "Pointer" indicating where every column starts and ends.

Many algorithms have been proposed for matrix product, from the naive $O(n^3)$ algorithm to the Strassen algorithm, which is $O(n^{2.81})$ operations, or the one proposed by Coppersmith and Winograd which is $O(n^{2.38})$ [6]. By contrast, the Khatri-Rao product which is central to the typed linear algebra [4] approach has not driven much attention in the literature. To the best of our knowledge, Sect. 3 presents the first version of the algorithm tuned for sparse matrices.

Seasons	Quantity
Spring	20
Summer	35
Spring	10
Autumn	50

$[\![T]\!]_{Quantity}$	0	1	2	3
1	20	0	0	0
2	0	35	0	0
3	0	0	10	0
4	0	0	0	50

$t_{Seasons}$	1 2 3 4
Spring	1 0 1 0
Summer	0 1 0 0
Autumn	0 0 0 1

Fig. 1. Example of source data (top table), measure matrix (middle table) and dimension matrix (bottom table).

3   Matrix Generation and Computation

Improving the CSC format. Dimension and measure matrices, illustrated in the middle and bottom table of Fig. 1, have a special property: each matrix column contains one non-zero element only. This makes it possible to improve the CSC format even further. On the measure matrices the improvement is to use a single array containing only the values, instead of using the standard three-array version of CSC format. By storing the values sequentially and by storing the initial column position of the matrix when divided in multiples parts, it is possible to know the correct position of each value.

We want to store and process the matrix data in a distributed system, where each independent node stores an horizontal partition of each table. As a single node of the system only has a partial view of the whole table and it is going to generate part of the global matrices, it must be able to generate unique identifiers for every attribute. To solve this issue without relying on a global entity that keeps track of the id of every attribute, we apply a 64base encoding[3] that creates a unique *id* for each attribute and can be directly mapped to the attribute. The application of 64base encoding with the proposed matrix storage format is a novel matrix encoding that can be used to generate, store and process typed matrices in a data-distributed setting.

Implementing the Khatri Rao matrix product. Given two matrices A and B, with dimensions $n \times m$ and $p \times m$, respectively, the result of the Khatri Rao product of A by B, denoted by $A \triangledown B$, is a matrix with dimensions $np \times m$. The computation of $A \triangledown B$ can be seen as an iteration over the columns of the argument matrices (this is why A and B must have the same number of columns), by multiplying every element of each column of matrix A by every element of the corresponding column of B. Essential to understanding the algorithm being presented is to know how to calculate the position of the results on the output matrix. If M is the current matrix A row, N is the current matrix B row then the resulting position is given by $p \times M + N$.

Algorithm 1. KhatriRao product

Require: Marix $A(n \times m)$, Matrix $B(p \times m)$
Ensure: Matrix $C(n * p \times m)$
  $C \leftarrow [n * p][m]$
  for $i = 0$ to $m - 1$ **do**
    for $j = 0$ to $n - 1$ **do**
      for $k = 0$ to $p - 1$ **do**
        $value \leftarrow A[j][i] * B[k][i]$
        $destLine \leftarrow p \times j + k$
        $C[destLine][i] \leftarrow value$
      end for
    end for
  end for
  return C

---

[3] Cf. 64 base encoding.

This algorithm has been added to the standard Linear Algebra library matrix-toolkits-java. This is an open source, high performance numerical library for matrix computation in Java. The algorithm has been adapted to work with the compressed matrix format presented in the previous section. In this format, when two projection functions are multiplied by a Khatri Rao product and since there is only one element per column the operation can be carried out in a lazy manner without having to create a dense matrix.

4   Evaluation

TPC-H[4] is an industry accepted OLAP benchmark. This section describes the experiments carried out to evaluate the implementation of our matrix encodings and operations using a modified version of TPC-H query 1. This evaluation was carried out with an Hadoop cluster with five servers, each with Ubuntu 14.04 64 bit, running on Intel Core i3-3240 @ 3.40 GHz, 3K cache and 8 GB of RAM. Data are generated from the TPC-H benchmark in the standard way. In this section we will introduce the derived query, its translation to a LA encoding and the overall set up of the tests carried out.

The query and its LA encoding. TPC-H query 1 was selected as first benchmark because it matches with several aspects of [4], namely: data are taken from a single raw data set (table), grouping involves two attributes only and the operation to be computed is a slice of a data cube. Thus data can be encoded as a vector filtered by the "where" clause.

Listing 1. Adapated TPC-H query1

```
SELECT Returnflag, Linestatus, Sum(Quantity)
FROM Lineitem
WHERE  Shipdate <= date ``1998-12-01'' - interval ``95'' day
GROUP BY Returnflag, Linestatus
```

Query 1 calls for three projection functions, one per attribute ($Returnflag$, $Linestatus$, $Shipdate$) and for a measure matrix for attribute $Quantity$. The 'group by' aggregation corresponds to the Khatri-Rao product of projection functions $Returnflag$ and $Linestatus$. The result of this operation returns a matrix recording all possible combinations of values of such attributes:

$$(t_{Returnflag} \triangledown t_{Linestatus}) \cdot [T]_{Quantity} \cdot filter \tag{1}$$

Second in the pipeline is the measure matrix which, composed with the Khatri-Rao outcome, yields the corresponding values for each combination. The final step,

$$filter = (!_{Shipdate \geqslant 1998-08-28 \wedge Shipdate \geqslant 1998-12-01})^{\circ}$$

[4] URL: http://www.tpc.org/tpch/default.asp.

is the multiplication by a column vector, which encodes the filtering of the data, which is denoted using the "!" notation of [4]. Altogether, this pipeline aggregates the values in the matrix rows and filters the results by a predicate on the *Shipdate* attribute.

Results. Pipeline (1) relies mostly on matrix multiplication, an operation which can be performed in a "divide and conquer" fashion, making the script a candidate for distributed data processing. This section gives the results of benchmarking this script on top of the Hadoop framework. This framework provides a fault tolerant distributed file system (HDFS) and a "Map-Reduce" application that allow us to run our query on top of it. Upon failures, the framework automatically resubmits failed jobs, hiding such complexity from the implementation. Additionally, resource scheduling in the cluster is of no interest in this experiment as it is a controlled environment that runs only the tasks that we assign them. The tasks are executed in batch mode and as such we don't seek to assess the execution of the experiments with concurrent users.

We measure the job latency and resource usage. We compare our results with Hive [7], a Hadoop application that translates SQL to Map-Reduce jobs. Both applications divide a database table horizontally through the nodes and require an initial loading phase where the files containing the raw data are loaded and converted to the internal formats. In the experiments, Hive will be assessed with text file and optimized row format (ORC) without compression. Our approach does not use any compression either.

One machine hosts the HDFS name-node, the YARN resource manager and the Hive server. The remaining machines contain the HDFS data node and the YARN node manager. Each resource is given a 1 GB JVM. In each machine 4 GB are made available to YARN, which makes a cluster with a total amount of 16 GB of RAM with 32 virtual cores. Each HDFS block has size 64 MB.

The experiment was executed over data generated by the TPC-H *LineItem* data table with the different scale factors that generate tables of increasing size. Scale factor 2 generates a table with an approximate size of 1.5 GB while the scale factor 32 a table with size 23.5 GB. The presented results are the average of a 10 run experiment. Figure 2 presents the average time it took to complete a job in the cluster. As can be observed, our approach has a significant improvement on the time it takes to compute the results. The improved latency comes mainly from the matrix encoding

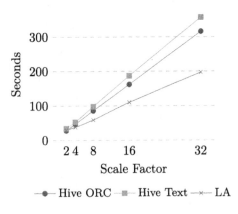

Fig. 2. Job latency

that not only allows to read the necessary dataset but also can be efficiently processed by the Khatri-Rao product. While relational algebra approaches

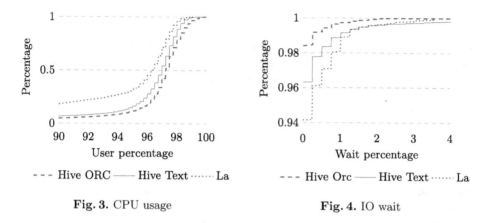

Fig. 3. CPU usage

Fig. 4. IO wait

require the processing to read every column of a dataset, our approach, similar to column oriented solutions, just processes the subset of the data crucial for the query [8].

The results presented in Figs. 3 and 4 are a CDF (Cumulative Distribution Function) from all the experiments of the CPU usage using the *dstat* tool on the nodes that carry out the computation. From these plots we gather that the ORC format does a much better job at using the CPU as its usage percentage is between 96 and 100 while spending less time waiting for I/O operations. On the other hand, our approach has the CPU usage more distributed between 90 and 100%, which means that it spends more time waiting on I/O operations as can be seen in Fig. 4. Even though not perceived in Fig. 4, the ORC formats spends considerable less time in I/O.

Hadoop reads a block of a file locally if available or reads it through the network otherwise. So we decided to aggregate the values from both channels to see which approach needs to read the least amount of bytes. From Fig. 4 it becomes clear that the textual format used in Hive is the least efficient while a distinct pattern can not be found in the other approaches. Nonetheless, the Hive ORC on average seems to use less data on smaller sizes while our approach seems to use less data as scale factor increases. These results relate

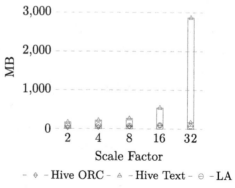

Fig. 5. Data read from disk and over the network.

nicely with the latency time, explaining why our approach terminates much faster (it needs to read less information).

5 Conclusions and Future Work

This paper presents a first implementation and test of a typed linear algebra (LA) approach to data processing in a distributed environment. These preliminary results indicate that, compared to a standard Hive implementation, we have an interesting solution to further explore and test, as we witness an increase of 60% at most in the latency of the jobs and use about 45% less data on the best case. On the other hand Hive has a relative better CPU usage.

Recent developments [9] show similar advantages of the typed LA approach to data processing in parallel environments, while a strategy for translating SQL analytical queries to LA scripts is defined. We plan to automate this process, which will make our experiments much easier to carry out for the other TPC-H queries. This could also be applied to translating MDX queries [10]. Last but not least, and as anticipated in [9], linear algebra enables formally correct transformation of LA scripts, making it possible to compare different LA implementations of the same query for performance.

In spite of such positive results, definite conclusions can only be drawn once a comprehensive set of TPC-H queries is benchmarked. The main contribution of this short paper is to give a preliminary evaluation of the performance of LA scripts generated from SQL analytical queries running on a data distributed environment. This is a promising area of research that we intend to develop further in the future.

References

1. Watson, H.J., Wixom, B.: The current state of business intelligence. IEEE Comput. **40**, 96–99 (2007)
2. Ginsberg, J., Mohebbi, M.H., Patel, R.S., Brammer, L., Smolinski, M.S., Brilliant, L.: Detecting influenza epidemics using search engine query data. Nature **457**, 1012–1014 (2009)
3. Codd, E.F., Codd, S.B., Salley, C.T.: Providing OLAP to user-analysts: an IT mandate. In: Ann ArborMichigan, p. 24 (1993)
4. Macedo, H., Oliveira, J.N.: A linear algebra approach to OLAP. Formal Aspects Comput., 1–25 (2014)
5. Silva, M.: Sparse matrix storage revisited, pp. 230–235 (2005)
6. Coppersmith, D.: Rectangular matrix multiplication revisited. J. Complex. **13**, 42–49 (1997)
7. Hive
8. Floratou, A., Patel, J.M., Shekita, E.J., Tata, S.: Column-oriented storage techniques for MapReduce. In: PVLDB, pp. 419–429 (2011)
9. Oliveira, J.: Towards a linear algebra semantics for query languages, June 2016
10. Bergamaschi, S., Interlandidi, M., Longo, M., Po, L., Vincini, M.: A meta-language for MDX queries in elog business solution. In: 2012 IEEE 28th International Conference on Data Engineering, pp. 1417–1428 (2012)

STRAF: A Scala Framework for Experiments in Trace-Based JIT Compilation

Maarten Vandercammen[(✉)], Quentin Stiévenart, Wolfgang De Meuter, and Coen De Roover

Software Languages Lab, Vrije Universiteit Brussel, Brussel, Belgium
{mvdcamme,qstieven,wdmeuter,cderoove}@vub.ac.be

Abstract. We introduce STRAF , a Scala framework for recording and optimizing execution traces of an interpreter it is composed with. For interpreters that satisfy the requirements detailed in this paper, this composition requires but a small effort from the implementer to result in a trace-based JIT compiler. We describe the framework, and illustrate its composition with a Scheme interpreter that satisfies the aforementioned requirements. We benchmark the resulting trace-based JIT compiler on a set of Scheme programs. Finally, we implement an optimization to demonstrate that STRAF enables further experimentation in the domain.

Keywords: Tracing compilation · JIT compilation · Execution traces · Scala

1 Introduction

Trace-based just-in-time (JIT) compilers do not compile an entire program upfront, but rather start by interpreting the program and identifying its frequently executed loops at run-time. Instructions of these loops are recorded into a *trace*. Once one iteration of such a loop has been traced, the compiler compiles and optimizes the resulting trace. Subsequent iterations will execute the optimized trace rather than interpret the original loop, resulting in speed-ups.

Most trace-based JIT compilers are constructed specifically for one particular programming language. As a result, few efforts are shared between implementations. The RPython framework for implementing trace-based JIT compilers [1] addresses this problem. Its runtime is capable of tracing various interpreters. However, while RPython enables constructing performant language runtimes, its focus on maximizing performance may hinder its comprehensibility and adaptability. In contrast to RPython our framework does not focus on performance. Instead, it aims at being minimalistic, comprehensible, and extensible. This way, our framework should facilitate further experimentation in the domain of trace recording and optimization.

This paper reports on the integration of our earlier ideas [12] in SCALA-AM [10], a framework for implementing interpreters from abstract machine formalizations and using these abstract machines as static program analyzers.

© Springer International Publishing AG 2017
J. Cunha et al. (Eds.): GTTSE 2015, LNCS 10223, pp. 223–234, 2017.
DOI: 10.1007/978-3-319-60074-1_10

We call the resulting Scala framework for developing trace-based JIT compilers STRAF . Its integration into the SCALA-AM static analysis framework specifically, though not uniquely, enables experimenting with employing static analysis to improve optimization of traces. The complete implementation of STRAF is available at https://github.com/mvdcamme/scala-am.

2   Trace-Based JIT Compilation

Trace-based JIT compilers build on two assumptions: most of a program's execution time is spent in loops, and several iterations of the same loop are likely to take the same path through the program [1]. They therefore optimize frequently executed loops, whereas method-based JIT compilers optimize methods only.

Trace-based JIT compilers are generally conceived as a mixed-mode execution involving an interpreter and a compiler. The interpreter executes the program and simultaneously profiles loops to identify the frequently executed ones. When a "hot" loop is detected, the interpreter starts *tracing* its execution: every operation performed by the interpreter is recorded. Tracing continues until a full loop iteration is complete. The compiler optimizes the recorded trace next. Subsequent iterations of the loop then execute the compiled trace directly. Conditions that held when a trace was recorded might no longer hold when the trace is executed. Trace-based JIT compilers therefore add *guards* to the trace to verify these conditions. When a guard fails, trace execution is aborted and regular interpretation of the program is resumed.

Figure 1 depicts a Scheme function `fact` that computes the factorial of 5. The recursive calls implement a loop that, when recorded, results in the trace of operations depicted on the right. If the condition `(= n 0)` evaluated to `false` while recording, the trace will feature a guard `ActionGuardFalse` verifying that this condition still evaluates to `false` when the trace is executed. As such, the trace corresponds to the operations performed by the interpreter in the `false`-branch of the if-expression. Should this guard fail at run-time, trace execution is aborted and interpretation will resume from the other branch.

```
                                              ...
                                   ActionEvalPush("=", FrameFunCallFunction(List("n", 0)))
                                   ActionLookupVar("=")
                                   ActionPushValue
                                   ActionPopKont
(letrec ((fact (lambda (n)         ActionEvalPush("n", FrameFunCallFunction(List(0)))
             (if (= n 0)           ActionLookupVar("n")
                 1                 ActionPushValue
                 (* n (fact (- n 1))))))))   ActionPopKont
    (fact 5))                      ActionEvalPush(0, FrameFunCallArgs(List()))
                                   ActionLiteralValue(0)
                                              ...
                                   ActionGuardFalse(...)
                                   ActionEvalTraced((* n (fact (- n 1))))
                                              ...
```

Fig. 1. A Scheme program containing a loop and part of the corresponding trace.

3   The STRAF Framework for Building JIT Compilers

STRAF decouples tracing mechanisms from language semantics through a fixed *tracing machine* (or tracer) that can be composed with a developer-provided *abstract machine* (or interpreter) [5]. The abstract machine handles regular program execution while the tracing machine is responsible for trace recording and execution. Any abstract machine can be used, on the condition that it satisfies the requirements outlined in Sect. 3.1. Section 3.2 describes an example of such an abstract machine for the Scheme programming language. The tracing machine of our framework is detailed in Sect. 3.3.

3.1   Requirements on the Abstract Machine

Program State. The interpreter must be conceived as an abstract machine that transitions between program states. This way, the tracing machine can easily resume program evaluation from a particular state. Instructions recorded into a trace then correspond to state transitions. Interpreters modeled after the ubiquitous CESK machine [6] trivially satisfy this requirement. However, we do not impose any constraints on the actual state representation used by the abstract machine.

Tracing Signals. The tracing machine is to record "hot" loops, but their form is language-specific. For instance, loops are typically implemented using recursive functions in Scheme. For STRAF to remain language-agnostic, the abstract machine it is composed with must signal when it has started one loop iteration by using a `SignalStart` instance. It must also label each loop-expression in the program. This enables the tracing machine to associate traces with loops.

Guards. Traces include guard instructions verifying that their control flow remains valid for a later execution. These too have to be provided by the abstract machine STRAF is composed with. Guards need to provide a *restart point* from which the abstract machine can resume interpretation when the guard fails during trace execution. No other constraints are imposed on their implementation.

Hooks. Finally, the abstract machine must provide the following functions to the tracing machine:

- A function `step` which, given a program state, returns a `Step` instance encapsulating the actions to be applied on this state. A `Step` can also include a `SignalStart`.
- An `applyActions` function which consecutively applies the actions from a `Step` to a given program state, and returns the new resulting program state.
- A `restart` function which takes a program state and the *restart point* of a failed guard as input and returns a new program state.

– An `optimize` function which, given a previously recorded trace and the program state observed at the start of the recording of this trace, returns an optimized version of this trace. Implementing this function in the abstract machine ensures that STRAF itself remains language-agnostic.

3.2   A CESK-based Interpreter for Scheme

Section 4 will compose STRAF with a Scheme interpreter to evaluate the resulting trace-based JIT compiler. Being modeled after a CESK-machine [6], this interpreter trivially satisfies the requirements of Sect. 3.1. Listing 1 defines its representation of program states. Their first component `control` is either an expression to be evaluated or a continuation frame to be followed. In addition, their environment component `env` maps variables to addresses and their store component `sto` maps these addresses to Scheme values. The remaining components are a continuation stack `kstack`, a value register `v` containing the value of the last expression that was evaluated, and a value stack `vstack` which is used to save lexical environments and argument values while evaluating a function call.

```
type Storable = Either[Value, Environment]
case class Step(actions: List[Action], signal: Signal])
case class ProgramState(control: Control, env: Environment, sto: Store,
                        kstack: Stack[Frame], v: Value, vStack: Stack[Storable])
```

Listing 1. Representation of program states.

To evaluate a composite expression, the interpreter pushes a specific *continuation frame* onto the continuation stack before evaluating its subexpressions. This frame is later popped and continued with when the interpreter has finished evaluating the subexpressions. States corresponding to the latter case feature the popped continuation frame as their `control` component instead of an expression. For those states, the interpreter's `step` function (cf. the hooks defined above) applies a function `stepKont` on the continuation frame and the contents of the value register `v`.

```
def stepEval(exp: SchemeExp): Step = exp match {
    case SchemeVarRef(varName) =>
        Step(List(ActionLookupVar(varName), ActionPopKont),
            SignalFalse)
    case SchemeFuncall(function, args) =>
        Step(List(..., ActionEvalPush(function, FrameFunCallFunction(args)))),
            SignalFalse)
    ...
}
```

Listing 2. Handling function application and variable lookup in `stepEval`.

StepEval. Listing 2 illustrates how function `stepEval` evaluates atomic expressions such as variable references and composite expressions such as function calls. For variable references, the interpreter returns a list of actions `ActionLookupVar` and `ActionPopKont` which respectively perform the variable lookup, placing the resulting value in v, and pop the topmost continuation from the stack. For a function call, stepEval returns an ActionEvalPush among its actions which pushes a FrameFunCallFunction onto the continuation stack before proceeding to evaluate the function subexpression. The pushed continuation encapsulates the function arguments that need to be evaluated next. For neither expression a loop is entered. This is communicated to the tracer using the SignalFalse argument to Step.

StepKont. Listing 3 details how stepKont handles the remainder of function call evaluation. stepKont takes as input the value v that was just computed and the frame that was popped from the continuation stack. The former either corresponds to the invoked procedure (i.e., for FrameFunCallFunction frames) or to one of the argument values (i.e., for FrameFunCallArg frames). Function evalFunctionCall is delegated to in either case. If no more arguments remain to be evaluated, evaluation proceeds to the body of the called procedure (ActionStepIn). Otherwise, the newly computed value is saved on the value stack (ActionPushVal) and evaluation proceeds to a new argument by pushing FrameFunCallArgs onto the continuation stack. As loops are typically implemented through recursion in Scheme, any call can potentially start a loop. The interpreter therefore sends a SignalStart whenever a procedure is stepped into. The body of the invoked procedure functions as loop label.

```
def evalFunctionCall(functionValue: FunctionValue, args: List[SchemeExp]): Step = args match {
    case Nil =>
        Step(List(... , ActionStepIn),
            SignalStart(functionValue.body))
    case e :: rest =>
        Step(List(... , ActionPushVal, ActionPushTraced(e, FrameFunCallArgs(functionValue, rest))),
            SignalFalse))
}

def stepKont(v: Value, frame: Frame): Step = frame match {
    case FrameFunCallFunction(args) =>
        evalFunctionCall(v, args)
    case FrameFunCallArg(functionValue, args) =>
        evalFunctionCall(functionValue, args)
    ...
}
```

Listing 3. Continuation of function call evaluation in stepKont.

Applying Actions. Listing 4 illustrates how the applyActions hook applies a single action to a given program state. In the case of an ActionEvalPush, the interpreter retrieves the expression exp to be evaluated and places a corresponding ControlExp in the control component of the program state. The given frame is also pushed onto the continuation stack.

Guards. Listing 5 illustrates how the interpreter communicates guard instruction to the tracer for (if **pred cons alt**) expressions. An ActionGuardTrue with a restart point that refers to the alt-expression is emitted when pred evaluates to **true**. Like other actions, this guard will be executed by the applyAction function. Should it then find that the expression last evaluated (i.e., `pred`) did *not* evaluate to `true`, the function calls `restart` with the current program state and the restart point encapsulated in the guard. As depicted in the same listing, `restart` only has to replace the old control component of the state by this restart point.

```
def applyAction(state: ProgramState, action: Action): ProgramState = action match {
    case ActionEvalPush(exp, frame) =>
        state.copy(control = ControlExp(e), kstack = state.kstack.push(frame))
    ...
}
```

Listing 4. Applying a single `ActionPush` action to a given program state.

```
case class ActionGuardTrue(restart: RestartPoint) extends Action
case class RestartGuardIfFailed(exp: SchemeExp) extends RestartPoint

def stepKont(v: Value, frame: Frame, sto: Store): Step = frame match {
    case FrameIf(cons, alt) =>
        if (v.isTrue()) {
            Step(List(ActionGuardTrue(RestartGuardIfFailed(alt)) ...),
                SignalFalse) }
        else { ... }
    ...
}

def restart(state: ProgramState, restart: RestartPoint): ProgramState = restart match {
    case RestartGuardIfFailed(exp) =>
        state.copy(control = ControlExp(exp))
    ...
}
```

Listing 5. Emitting guards for an `if`-expression.

3.3   Tracing Machine

The tracing machine controls the mixed-mode execution of the program. Figure 2 depicts the transitions between its three modes: (1) *normal interpretation*, in which the interpreter executes the program without interference from the tracing machine; (2) *trace recording*, in which the tracer records all actions undertaken by the interpreter; and (3) *trace execution* in which the tracing machine executes a previously recorded trace.

Normal Interpretation. In this mode, the tracer repeatedly asks the abstract machine to perform a single interpretation step. The tracer updates the current program state by applying the actions returned by the interpreter. If these actions do not include a tracing signal, the tracer continues running in normal interpretation mode. Upon encountering a `SignalStart`, the tracing machine either starts recording a new trace for unseen loops or starts executing a previously recorded trace for seen loops. Note that, in contrast to the basic scheme described here, STRAF does wait for a loop to become hot before tracing it, by counting how many times a `SignalStart` was sent for a particular procedure, and tracing it once a threshold has been reached.

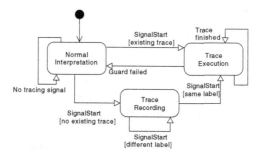

Fig. 2. Transitions between execution modes of the tracing machine.

Trace Recording. This mode is similar to the previous one, but the tracing machine records all actions communicated by the interpreter into a trace. The tracer keeps recording these actions until the interpreter sends a new `SignalStart` *for the loop currently being recorded*, as this indicates that one full iteration of the loop has been completed. The recorded trace is then optimized via the `optimize` hook of the interpreter and subsequently stored. Note that if the interpreter executes an inner loop in the loop being traced, and therefore sends another `SignalStart` for that inner loop, this entire loop will be unrolled in the trace.

Trace Execution. A previously recorded trace is executed by consecutively applying the actions it is composed of. When the end of the trace has been reached, the tracer loops back to its beginning. At some point, a guard will fail and execution of the trace will be aborted. The interpreter's `restart` hook is then called with the restart point of the guard that failed and the current program state. Execution of the program is resumed under the normal interpretation mode with the program state that is returned.

4   Evaluation

STRAF does not aim for top performance, but strives to facilitate experimentation in the domain through the qualities of minimalism, comprehensibility and extensibility. Our evaluation therefore focuses on whether it is possible to easily extend the framework, e.g., with new trace optimizations or tracing mechanisms. To this end, we compose STRAF with the Scheme interpreter described in Sect. 3.2 and implement several optimizations as well as extensions to the previously described tracing mechanism. Section 4.1 gives a high-level overview of some trace optimizations and extensions to STRAF 's tracing mechanism. Section 4.2 describes and evaluates one of these optimizations in detail.

4.1   Extensions to STRAF

We have designed and implemented several trace optimizations, including a constant folding [4], a type specialization [2] and a variable folding optimization.

These optimizations together span around 400 lines of code[1]. Additionally, we have also extended STRAF with a hot loop detection and a guard tracing mechanism. The former enables STRAF to detect hot loops by counting the number of SignalStarts sent for each procedure and only tracing procedures for which the number of SignalStarts that were sent has crossed some threshold. The latter makes it possible to not only trace procedures, but also to start tracing from the point of a guard failure. When the guard fails again at some later point in the execution, execution jumps to the trace that was recorded for this guard, instead of resuming normal interpretation. This reduces the performance penalty incurred for a guard failure, as execution can jump from one optimized trace to another instead of returning to normal interpretation. These two additional mechanisms were completed in only 100 lines of code[2].

4.2   Continuation Stack Optimization

We now describe and evaluate an additional trace optimization, the *continuation stack optimization*, which eliminates all pairs of actions from a trace that push and pop a continuation frame. This is sound because continuation frames only affect the control flow, which is fixed for a particular trace. Care must be taken, however, that no guard instruction is located between these actions. The continuation stack *must* be kept up-to-date if normal interpretation might be resumed after a guard failure. In practice, applying this continuation stack optimization often reduces the length of a trace by up to 25%. The implementation of this optimization spans about 50 lines of code, and was completed in about an hour's effort. We evaluate this optimization on a set of several programs ranging from just two lines of code to around 240. These stem from the benchmark suite included with the SCALA-AM framework on top of which STRAF is implemented.

Evaluation. Figure 3 depicts the effectiveness of the continuation stack optimization. It shows the number of continuation stack operations that are applied throughout the execution of a benchmark as a fraction of the number of continuation stack operations that are applied when the optimization is not applied on the collected traces. This optimization drastically reduces the number of such applications, by up to 95% in some cases.

   We also evaluate the optimization in terms of the performance improvement it brings to the compiler. We conducted this evaluation on an Intel I7–4870HQ CPU at 2.50 GHz with 6 MB cache and 16 GB of RAM. The machine ran 64 bit OS X 10.11.6 and Scala 2.11.7. Each program was executed thirty times, with each run on a separate JVM; measurements only started after JVM warm-up was completed. Figure 4 shows the median execution times, along with its 95% confidence interval, of the programs when traces were collected and executed,

---

[1] https://github.com/mvdcamme/scala-am/blob/master/src/main/scala/tracing/SchemeTraceOptimizer.scala.

[2] https://github.com/mvdcamme/scala-am/blob/master/src/main/scala/tracing/SchemeTracer.scala.

Normalised Number of Continuation Stack Operations Applied

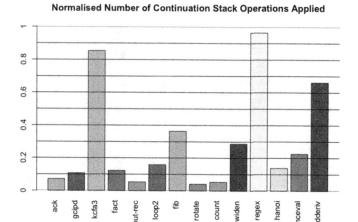

Fig. 3. Number of continuation stack operations executed, normalized with respect to the unoptimized execution.

Baseline Execution Time

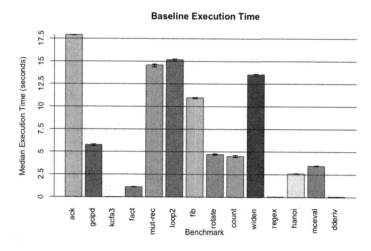

Fig. 4. Median execution time of the benchmarks when traces are not optimized.

but not optimized. These numbers serve as the baseline with respect to which the effectiveness of the continuation stack optimization is compared. Figure 5 shows the execution time of these same benchmarks, normalized to the baseline execution time and with the 95% confidence interval included.

When the continuation stack optimization is applied, performance conclusively improves in 5 out of 14 cases. In the remaining cases, it is likely that the traces are either too short or the hot loop detection mechanism prioritized tracing a loop which was afterwards not executed often enough. In both cases, the overhead of tracing and optimizing negates any improvement made by the optimization.

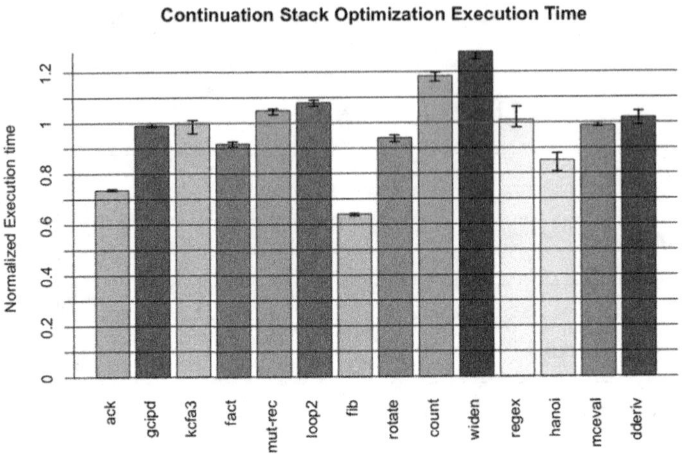

Continuation Stack Optimization Execution Time

Fig. 5. Median execution time of the benchmarks with just the continuation stack optimization enabled, normalized with respect to the baseline results.

5   Related Work

We reported an earlier version of the core principles behind the separation of the tracer and the interpreter in prior work [12]. That work relied on a formalization and a Scheme implementation of the framework. This paper extends that work by transposing the described ideas to the SCALA-AM framework [10], by specifying its implementation instead of offering a formal model, by describing optimization strategies for traces and by evaluating STRAF via a set of benchmarks detailing its performance.

Several widely-used trace-based JIT compilers have been deployed, such as HotPath [8], TraceMonkey [7], Tamarin-Tracing [3]. However, these compilers all execute one particular language and cannot be composed with a variety of different interpreters.

The RPython framework is a meta-compilation framework that applies the technique of *meta-tracing* [1]: instead of tracing the execution of a program directly, a meta-tracer traces the execution of an interpreter *while this interpreter executes the program*. Similarly to STRAF, RPython thus enables language implementers to provide a regular interpreter, annotated with certain hints to guide tracing and optimization, to benefit from the advantages of trace-based compilation without having to construct a dedicated JIT compiler for the language. RPython greatly reduces the engineering effort required by language implementers and is also successful in lifting the performance of the meta-traced interpreter to the same order of magnitude than a dedicated JIT compiler [9]. However, the complexity of RPython and its focus on performance makes it less suited for experimenting with novel trace recording or trace optimization strategies. In contrast, STRAF focuses exclusively on providing a minimalistic yet extensible framework that facilitates studying of and experimenting with trace-based compilation strategies.

6   Conclusion and Future Work

We have introduced the STRAF framework for recording and optimizing execution traces of an interpreter it is composed with. For interpreters that satisfy a limited set of requirements, this composition results in a trace-based JIT compiler. STRAF does not aim to generate trace-based JIT compilers that outperform existing ones, but to facilitate further experimentation with trace recording and trace optimization. To this end, it achieves low coupling between tracing mechanisms and language semantics.

STRAF is the embodiment of our earlier ideas on JIT compilation [12] into the SCALA-AM framework [10] for implementing interpreters as abstract machines and for deriving static analyses from these interpreters. We are currently investigating whether trace-based JIT compilation can benefit from whole-program static analysis, by providing information about the program that lies beyond the boundaries of the trace. We have recently described an approach [11] for using a whole-program static analysis to find constant variables in a program and using this information to improve trace optimization: if the compiler knows that a variable will remain constant throughout the program's execution, it can replace a lookup of the variable in the trace by its value as it was observed during trace recording. Our approach enables detecting more constants than would be found by other trace-based compilers because these compilers only consider the local part of the program that is actually traced and do not look beyond the boundaries of this trace. By integrating STRAF into the SCALA-AM framework, we can construct an abstract machine based interpreter for a language, derive a static analysis from it by using the SCALA-AM framework and couple the interpreter to the tracing machine. Using the same abstract machine for both functions makes it possible to easily alternate between these functions, enabling us to perform static analysis over parts of the program *at run time*. This in turn increases precision of the static analysis, as we can include observed runtime values in the program analysis instead of having to predict these statically. The minimalistic but extensible implementation of STRAF facilitates these kinds of experiments in hybrid trace optimizations.

References

1. Bolz, C.F., Cuni, A., Fijalkowski, M., Rigo, A.: Tracing the meta-level: Pypy's tracing JIT compiler. In: Proceedings of the 4th ICOOOLPS Workshop (2009)
2. Chang, M., Bebenita, M., Yermolovich, A., Gal, A., Franz, M.: Efficient just-in-time execution of dynamically typed languages via code specialization using precise runtime type inference. Technical report ICS-TR-07-10, University of Irvine, Department of Computer Science (2007)
3. Chang, M., Smith, E., Reitmaier, R., Bebenita, M., Gal, A., Wimmer, C., Eich, B., Franz, M.: Tracing for web 3.0: trace compilation for the next generation web applications. In: Proceedings of the 2009 ACM SIGPLAN/SIGOPS International VEE Conference (2009)
4. Corporation, N.: Constant folding. http://www.compileroptimizations.com/category/constant_folding.htm. Accessed 24 May 2016

5. Felleisen, M., Friedman, D.P.: Control Operators, the SECD-machine, and the λ-calculus. Indiana University, Computer Science Department (1986)
6. Felleisen, M., Friedman, D.P.: A calculus for assignments in higher-order languages. In: Proceedings of the 14th ACM SIGACT-SIGPLAN POPL Symposium (1987)
7. Gal, A., Eich, B., Shaver, M., Anderson, D., Mandelin, D., Haghighat, M.R., Kaplan, B., Hoare, G., Zbarsky, B., Orendorff, J., Ruderman, J., Smith, E.W., Reitmaier, R., Bebenita, M., Chang, M., Franz, M.: Trace-based just-in-time type specialization for dynamic languages. In: Proceedings of the 30th ACM SIGPLAN PLDI Conference (2009)
8. Gal, A., Probst, C.W., Franz, M.: Hotpathvm: an effective JIT compiler for resource-constrained devices. In: Proceedings of the 2nd International VEE Conference (2006)
9. Marr, S., Ducasse, S.: Tracing vs. partial evaluation: comparing meta-compilation approaches for self-optimizing interpreters. In: Proceedings of the 2015 ACM International OOPSLA Conference (2015)
10. Stiévenart, Q., Nicolay, J., De Meuter, W., De Roover, C.: Building a modular static analysis framework in scala (tool paper). In: Proceedings of the 2016 7th ACM SIGPLAN Symposium on Scala, SCALA 2016, NY, USA, pp. 105–109 (2016). http://doi.acm.org/10.1145/2998392.3001579
11. Vandercammen, M., De Roover, C.: Improving trace-based JIT optimisation using whole-program information. In: Proceedings of the 8th International Workshop on Virtual Machines and Intermediate Languages, VMIL 2016, NY, USA, pp. 16–23 (2016). http://doi.acm.org/10.1145/2998415.2998418
12. Vandercammen, M., Nicolay, J., Marr, S., De Koster, J., D'Hondt, T., De Roover, C.: A formal foundation for trace-based JIT compilers. In: Proceedings of the 13th WODA (2015)

Author Index

Biboudis, Aggelos 154
Bordignon, Mirko 98

De Meuter, Wolfgang 223
De Roover, Coen 223
Dwyer, Matthew B. 1

Figueira Filho, Fernando 124
Filieri, Antonio 1
Fourtounis, George 154

Geldenhuys, Jaco 1
German, Daniel M. 124
Gerrard, Mitchell 1
Gonzalez-Perez, Cesar 26

Hanenberg, Stefan 45
Hochgeschwender, Nico 98

Matos, Miguel 215

Nordmann, Arne 98

Oliveira, José Nuno 215

Pǎsǎreanu, Corina S. 1
Pereira, José Orlando 215
Pontes, Rogério 215

Rubin, Julia 73

Schultz, Ulrik Pagh 98
Singer, Leif 124
Smaragdakis, Yannis 154
Steimann, Friedrich 179
Stiévenart, Quentin 223
Storey, Margaret-Anne 124
Stoy, Kasper 98

Vandercammen, Maarten 223
Visser, Willem 1

Wrede, Sebastian 98

Zagalsky, Alexey 124

Printed in the United States
By Bookmasters